英语国际人

英语畅谈
中国文化50主题

50 Topics On
Chinese Culture

李霞 著　董玉国 译

外文出版社
FOREIGN LANGUAGES PRESS

Foreword

Many students of English are often bothered by more or less the same problem. They find it difficult to express themselves properly when talking about complex topics. The reason is actually very simple. There is a lack of sufficient understanding of the cultural context. This book aims to address this problem. Readers will learn to discuss topics about China in effective English.

Cultural topics as a good vehicle for communications.

There is a popular item called "break the iceberg" on the agenda of campus gatherings at US universities. Students from different countries will break the ice by talking about subjects of their own culture. In such a situation, a person's cultural background is probably his or her most recognizable identity. Similarly, it will be very desirable for a Chinese student to discuss interesting Chinese cultural topics in fluent English.

Chinese cultural topics most relevant to foreigners.

This book covers a range of topics, from traditional Chinese culture to current social phenomena. Most of these topics have been reported in the Western media in recent years. Hopefully this will allow the readers not only to understand what are making headlines in the West, it also helps to expose them to these topics, enabling them to think and communicate in everyday English.

A diverse and open state of mind.

Every culture has its value. No culture is superior to the other. It takes a diverse and open mindset, as well as a sense of humor, to look at each of them. Discussions of the Chinese cultural elements in this book are based on a multi-dimensional, rather than self-centered, perspective. Both Chinese and Western cultures are viewed in their own right.

Simple and practical language.

As much as possible, English expressions in this book tend to be simple, basic and practical to enable the readers to engage in simple and unpretentious conversations. The writer wishes to thank Mr. Dong Yuguo. His English proficiency and his exposure to different cultures have helped achieve this goal.

My special thanks go to Ms. Cai Qing at the Foreign Languages Press. Without her outstanding work, this book would not have become a reality. Mr. Graham Paterson, the language consultant, has made this book more readable as far as language is concerned. I am indebted to Mr. Huo Jianying of the *China Today* magazine. His knowledge of traditional culture has been a valuable source of help. Lastly, my son Dong Xiaoxia has made constructive comments which, in turn, have made the dialogues more relevant.

I also want to thank every reader who buys this book. I hope you will find it worthwhile.

Li Xia

前　言

∷∷

　　不少英语学习者在对外交往中有一个共同的困惑：涉及到较深层次的话题时，言词便捉襟见肘。为什么？答案很简单：不熟悉文化交往中特定的表达方式。这本书试图帮助你突破语言障碍，学会用得体的英语介绍中国国情、表达独立的观点。

文化是相互沟通的最佳介质

　　在美国大学校园国际学生组织举办的聚会上，常常有这样一个节目："打破坚冰"，学生们就各自国家的文化展开交谈。在类似的国际交流场合中，个人所代表的民族文化是最显著的身份标识。用流利的英文谈论一些中国文化中有意思的话题，是一名中国人展示个性魅力的最佳选择。

外国人关心的中国文化话题

　　本书的主题涉及中国传统文化，以及当下中国的社会现象，题材多来自近年英美媒体对中国的报道。从这个途径选取谈资，既是为了让读者了解外国人对中国文化的兴趣点，也是为了帮助读者关注现实问题，学会用英文去思考、表达你对世界的认识。

多元的视角和包容的心态

　　每一种文化都有其存在的理由和价值，无所谓优劣和高下。对于自己和别人的文化都需要有多元的视角、包容的心态和幽默感。因此，本书在介绍中国文化时，不以老大自居，而是从跨文化的角度，客观地评价中西文化的异同。

简洁有效的语言

　　本书的英文表达秉承简洁、平和、有效的原则，让谈话者看上去有修养、不做作。达到这个目的，得益于本书的翻译者董玉国先生。他深厚的英文功底以及对中西文化的透彻了解，使得本书的英文表达得体且不失格调。

　　感谢外文出版社的蔡箐女士，她的工作使想法成为现实；感谢本书的语言教练帕特森先生，他的校订使本书增色不少；感谢《今日中国》杂志的霍建瀛先生，他以深厚的传统文化学养给予了本书极大的帮助；还要感谢我的儿子董晓夏，他所贡献的新奇而有价值的观点，使本书内容更开放、更时尚。

　　最后，我要特别感谢购买并阅读本书的读者。幸运的是，它值得您的关注。

作者　李霞

学习指南

....

巧学活用本书能达到以一当十的效果，你至少可以做以下练习：

语音练习：选取你最感兴趣的课文，尽力模仿录音中的语音语调，把自己的朗读录下来和录音比较，找出差距反复模仿，直到乱真。

口语练习：利用书中对话做两人对练，或者和录音对练。就书中的主题换一个论点或谈话思路进行开放式对话创作。

听力练习：利用随书的 MP3 录音做精听和泛听练习。常用的内容精听，即反复听直到听懂每一个字并能流利跟读为止；其他内容泛听，能听懂大意并基本能跟读即可。

听写练习：听写能力表现在做课堂笔记和讲座笔记、会议记录等。利用本书的 MP3 可以做听写练习，反复听写直到没有错误为止。

语汇练习：利用书中的词汇表，并摘录课文中精彩实用的句型或用法，建立自己的主题词汇库。

翻译练习：利用书中句型和对话做汉译英或英译汉练习，口译或笔译均可。

你可以根据自己的英语水平、工作需要和学习习惯将各种方法融会贯通，形成最适合自己的学习方法。当然，如果仅限于书本，再多的练习也只是纸上谈兵。如果你有找人开练的强烈愿望并付诸行动，离你的学习目标也就不远了。

Contents
目　录

Folk Customs 新老民俗

Fashion 时尚生活

Pop Culture 流行文化

Culture Conflicts 文化碰撞

英语畅谈
中国文化50主题

50 Topics On
Chinese Culture

1. The Art of Calligraphy

奇妙的书法

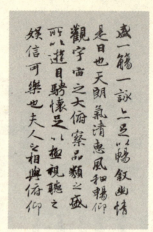

Dialogue

A: Some critics **suggest** that different genres of Chinese calligraphy have different political implications. Take Wang Xizhi for example. His calligraphy was repudiated as unorthodox during his lifetime but, only a few decades after his death, was established as an orthodox genre.

B: That's for sure! Historically, Chinese calligraphy and politics were closely intertwined. Over 2,000 years ago, Emperor Qin Shihuang, the first Emperor in Chinese history, established the official Chinese writing characters. The new, simplified characters made writing calligraphy less complicated. It **allowed** people to use characters with more straight strokes, thus making it easier to write with brushes. This created the Li genre. **Over time**, other variations were also developed, which eventually lead to the formation of the five genres in Chinese calligraphy. These were the Zhuan, Li, Kai, Xing and Cao genres.

A: I've heard that most emperors were **good at** calligraphy. The Tang Dynasty Emperor Li Shimin was an avid collector of Wang Xizhi's writings.

B: That's right. Qing Dynasty Emperor Qian Long **played a key role** in compiling an authoritative collection of calligraphy. **To some extent**, preferences of the Emperors had an influence on the **rise and fall** of certain calligraphy genres.

A: Ordinary Chinese people also seemed to like calligraphy a lot.

B: Part of the reason was the sponsorship by the Emperors. Another reason was the Imperial Civil Service examinations that started in the 7th century. Those examinations were focused on writing and provided a way for ordinary people to achieve a better life. As a result, calligraphy became widely accepted. Calligraphy also had its practical values because it was a good way to **make friends** and was more presentable as a gift rather than jewelry or money.

A： Does calligraphy still have these practical functions now?

B： Yes. Many people practice calligraphy as a way to raise their cultural accomplishment. Older people use calligraphic writing as a method to **keep fit**. They believe that when a person concentrates on writing calligraphy, his inner wellbeing is stimulated.

A： I had thought computers would lead to the disappearance of Chinese calligraphy. Now I understand that's not likely to happen. How can you give your boss computer-printed calligraphy as a gift?

B： You don't, unless you want him to fire you!

对 话

A： 有评论家认为中国书法的不同流派都有其政治含义。比如王羲之，他的书法曾经被视为对正统文化的攻击而遭诟病，但在他死后几十年，却被朝廷封为书法的正宗。

B： 是这样。历史上，中国书法与权力密不可分。两千多年前，中国的第一个皇帝秦始皇统一了中国的文字。新的简化汉字使书写变得简单。人们使用适合毛笔书写的直线笔画写字，由此产生了隶书。随着时间的推移，其他字体也产生了，最后形成中国书法的五种字体：篆、隶、楷、行、草。

A： 我听说中国的皇帝大多擅长书法，唐代皇帝李世民就热中于收集王羲之的作品。

B： 对。清朝皇帝乾隆还编纂了一套字帖，把他认为正宗的书体收录其中。从某种程度上说，皇帝的好恶决定了不同书法流派的兴衰。

A： 普通中国人似乎也热爱书法。

B： 这一方面是因为历代皇帝的提倡，另一方面是因为朝廷从 7 世纪开始实行的科举考试。这种考试借文章选拔人才，成为平民百姓的晋身之阶。书法因此受到重视。此外，书法还有着实际的效用，比如结交朋友。比起珠宝或金钱，送人一幅书法作品就来得高雅、体面。

A： 现在书法还有这样的功效吗？

B： 还有。很多人研习书法的目的是提升文化素养；老年人学习书法是为了保健强身。人们认为，在凝神定气地思考布局运笔的过程中，体内的气会随之运动，对健康颇有益处。

A： 我一直认为电脑的出现会导致中国书法的衰落。现在看来，这不太可能。你怎么能拿着一幅从电脑中打印出来的书法作品送给上司呢？

B： 除非你想让他炒掉你。

Brush 毛笔

The brush is the traditional Chinese writing tool. Its tip is made of soft hairs from a sheep, weasel or rabbit. The carefully selected hairs are tied together, trimmed into a tapering shape and fixed onto one end of a bamboo or wooden holder. The hair is both soft and elastic. The outer layers of the brush are shorter, making it easier to absorb ink. The tip end has longer hairs which come to a tiny point, so that both wrinkle dotting and line drawing can be done easily.

毛笔是中国的传统书写工具。笔尖由羊毛、黄鼬毛或兔毛制成。先要精心选择毫毛，将一端修剪成尖的形状，然后将另一端固定在竹子或木制的笔管上。毛笔的毫毛既软又有弹性。笔头外部的毫毛稍短，使它更易吸收墨汁。尖端用较长的毛，以形成笔尖，这样可以轻易地写出点或线的形状。

Chinese Ink 墨

Chinese ink is made by mixing soot from burning tung oil and pine tar with gelatin, Chinese herbs and spices. Ink is produced by grinding the solid ink with water against an inkstone. There is a saying that "(black) ink has five colors," because Chinese painters use ink meticulously to produce a number of subtle shades.

墨是由桐油燃烧后的煤烟与松木炭加上明胶和一些草药及香料混合而成。墨汁是将坚固的墨块与水一道在砚台上反复研磨而成的。中国有"（黑）墨有五色"之说，因为中国的画家们精心地用墨调和出各种层次的阴影。

Xuan Paper 宣纸

Xuan paper was originally produced in Xuanzhou in Anhui Province in the Tang Dynasty. Xuan paper has a close texture, making it pliable yet tough, and resistant to moth damage. In addition, this kind can be achieved with heavier or lighter strokes, or when the stroke is quickened or slowed down. With so many advantages, Xuan paper largely replaced the silk fabric which had been used for painting before. Silk is not absorbent, but is suitable for meticulous line drawing and applying heavy colors.

宣纸最初是唐代时产自安徽省的宣州。宣纸的质地紧密、具有韧性，可以防虫咬。此外，在这样质地的纸上书写，笔划轻重缓急皆可。由于有这么多的长处，宣纸取代了曾经常用作绘画材料的丝绸。丝绸的吸附力低，但是它更适合于细致的线描和重彩。

suggest 认为	allow 可以，允许	over time 一段时间之后，斗转星移
good at 善于	play a key role 起关键作用	to some extent 在某种程度上
rise and fall 兴衰	make friends 交朋友	keep fit 保持健康

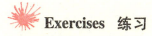 **Exercises** 练习

Answer these questions.
1. What did Emperor Qing Shihuang do?
2. Why did calligraphy become popular in the past?
3. Why do people like calligraphy now?

Translate these sentences into Chinese.
1. Different genres of Chinese calligraphy have different political implications.
2. Historically, Chinese calligraphy and politics were closely intertwined.
3. The new, simplified characters made writing calligraphy less complicated.
4. Over time, other variations were also developed.
5. Different writing styles were used for different official documents.
6. Most Emperors were good at calligraphy.
7. Emperor Qian Long played a key role in compiling a collection of calligraphy.
8. Examinations provided a way for ordinary people to achieve a better life.
9. Calligraphy was a good way to make friends.
10. Many people practice calligraphy as a way to keep fit.

Complete this paragraph with suitable words.
Historically, Chinese calligraphy, and politics, were __1__ intertwined. __2__ 2000 years ago, Emperor Qin Shihuang, the __3__ Emperor in the Chinese history, established the __4__ Chinese writing characters. The new __5__ characters made writing calligraphy __6__ complicated. It __7__ people to use characters with more straight strokes, thus making it easier to write __8__ brushes. This created the Li genre.

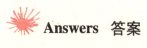 **Answers** 答案

Translate these sentences into Chinese.
1. 中国书法的不同流派都有其政治含义。
2. 历史上，中国书法与权力密不可分。
3. 新的简化汉字使书写变得简单。
4. 随着时间的推移，其他字体也产生了。
5. 不同的字体用于不同的律令。
6. 中国的皇帝大多擅长书法。
7. 乾隆皇帝在书法集的编纂中起到了关键作用。
8. 考试成为平民百姓的晋身之阶。
9. 书法是结交朋友的一种好方法。
10. 许多人练习书法是为了保健强身。

Complete this paragraph with suitable words.
1. closely 2. Over 3. first 4. official 5. simplified 6. less 7. allowed 8. with

2. The Significance of Chinese Paintings

中国画的含意

Dialogue

A: It's interesting that Chinese paintings can be created on the spot, even though most of them have similar subjects. Peony, plum blossoms, mountains, creeks or cottages are very popular. There are often painters at significant celebratory and commemorative events.

B: Their educational function is, in fact, a unique feature of Chinese paintings. Human profiles were used as a method to either glorify heroes or condemn traitors 2,000 years ago. Tang Dynasty officials even tried to bring painting into Confucian ideology. The Court of the Song Dynasty published an official guide to paintings. This raised **criteria** not only for human profiles but also for landscape and object paintings.

A: Oh, what was that?

B: It **classified** paintings into ten categories covering religious beliefs, Confucianism and state power. This classification gave an official definition of the value and significance of the paintings. The purpose of landscape paintings was to portray the five mountains, while fruit and birds were used to exemplify or eulogize the Gods. In this case, the subjects were used as references to people in order to **deliver** moral messages. For example, peony and peacocks represented wealth and fortune; pine trees, bamboo, plum blossoms and orchids represented elegance and accomplishment; and pine trees and cypresses symbolized loyalty.

A: **As far as** I know, painters who did not have to **make a living** by painting used different skills to those specified in the guide, even though they painted the same subjects.

B: Artists are usually against pragmatism. They like to give meaning to the subjects they paint. Bamboo symbolizes integrity and simplicity; the orchid symbolizes modesty and misfortune; and pine trees symbolize never giving up. Artists also like landscapes. It doesn't take a lot of training to paint landscapes. It all **depends on** the painter's personality and ability, as well as his unique touch. Most of today's non-professional painters follow the landscape style. The objective of these painters is purely entertainment and self-satisfaction. The more successful artists have the opportunity to exhibit at public functions. That is probably the climax of their painting careers.

A: What are professional painters doing?

B: Some of them make a great effort to improve their painting skills. They want to develop new and innovative painting methods by borrowing from other genres. Others are busy making money. They have found ways to produce commercially attractive paintings. Some people say they are no longer artists. Instead they have become manufacturers of paintings.

对 话

A: 这真有意思：中国画是可以现场表演的。在一些庆典或纪念性的场合，你可以看到画家们挥毫泼墨。画的题材大致相同：牡丹、梅花、山水、林中小屋等。

B: 其实，这是中国画的一个特点：强调绘画的宣传功能。早在两千年前，人物画就被政府机构广泛用作宣传工具，表彰忠臣烈士，批判乱臣贼子。唐代的士大夫们甚至试图把绘画创作纳入儒家的思想体系。到了宋代，政府专门出版了官方画谱，不但对人物画的功能提出要求，对山水画和花鸟画也如此。

A: 都是些什么要求？

B: 这个画谱将绘画分为十类，涵盖宗教思想、儒家理论和政权统治，论述了各类绘画存在的价值与意义。山水画的存在价值是能描绘"五岳"；瓜果、花鸟有敬神的作用。绘画因此起到以物比人的教化作用。比如，牡丹、孔雀表现富贵；松、竹、梅、兰比喻高人雅士；松、柏象征忠贞。

A: 不过，据我所知，古代那些不靠绘画谋生的文人，虽然也画同样的题材，但他们的技法与官方画谱规定的不同。

B: 文人反对实用主义，他们的画有不同的象征意义：竹子代表正直、质朴；兰花代表谦虚和怀才不遇；松树代表自强不息。文人也喜画山水，这不需要进行长期的技巧训练，完全取决于画家的个性和修养，还有独特的笔触。今天，一些非职业画家依然沿袭古代文人的路子，为自娱自乐、修身养性而画。他们当中知名度较高的能参加各种活动，现场作画。这大概是他们艺术价值的最高体现了。

A: 职业画家在干什么？

B: 一些人在苦心研习技巧，试图多方借鉴，开发出不同凡响的画法；另一些人忙于赚钱，他们绘制具有商业价值的作品。有人说他们其实已经不算画家，只是画匠而已。

Background Reading 背景阅读

Traditional Chinese Paintings 传统中国绘画

Traditional Chinese paintings constitute a unique school of fine art, a school that, in style and techniques is vastly different from any other fine art school in the world. Traditional Japanese fine art may be the only exception, but it has to be remembered that it has been heavily influenced by Chinese culture.

The Chinese do paintings with brushes, dipping their brushes in ink or paint and then skillfully wielding them. Painters produce on the paper pictures with lines and dots—some heavy, and some light, and some deep, and some pale. In the hands of a good painter, brushes and ink can be highly expressive. Because of this, they are seemed not only as tools for drawing pictures, but also as a collective symbol of artistic pursuit.

In comparison to ink and wash painting, fine brushwork, minute attention to details and rich, elaborate coloring characterize traditional Chinese paintings of a style known as *gong bi zhong cai* that originate from palace paintings. Palace paintings thrived in the Song Dynasty. The country's best painters were grouped in the imperial academy of paintings, where they were ranked the same way as officials according to their artistic accomplishments. For a time in the dynasty, there were schools of calligraphy and paintings to bring up painters and calligraphers qualified for work in service of the imperial family and ranking officials.

传统中国绘画是一门独特的艺术，无论是风格还是技巧都与世界其它艺术门类迥然不同。传统的日本画可能算是例外，但不要忘了，它是深受中国文化影响的。

中国人绘画采用毛笔蘸墨汁或颜色，灵巧地挥洒纸上。画家用深、浅、浓、淡的点和线构成一幅图画。在优秀画家的手里，毛笔和墨汁非常具有表现力，它们不仅是绘画的工具，也是画家艺术追求的象征。

与水墨画相比，源于宫廷的工笔重彩的特点是其细腻的画法、对细节的描绘，以及丰富的色彩。宫廷画盛行于宋代，当时全国的优秀画家都云集宫廷画院，并采用与朝廷命官同样的方法，按照其各自在绘画方面的成就排序。曾几何时，有一些机构专门培养在宫廷中和一些高官显贵府内工作的书法家和画家。

---

criteria 标准	classify 分类	deliver 传达，传递
as far as 就…而言	make a living 谋生	depend on 取决于

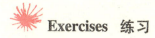 **Exercises 练习**

Answer these questions.

1. What is an unique feature of Chinese painting?
2. What is the Song Dynasty, guide to painting, about?
3. What are the professional painters doing now?

Translate these sentences into Chinese.

1. It's interesting that Chinese paintings can be created on the spot.
2. This in fact is an unique feature of Chinese paintings.
3. It classified paintings into ten categories.
4. Painters who did not have to make a living by painting used different skills.
5. They like to give meaning to the objects they paint.
6. It doesn't take a lot of training to paint landscapes.
7. It all depends on the painter's personality and ability.
8. The more successful artists have the opportunity to exhibit at public functions.
9. Some of them make a great effort to improve their painting skills.
10. They want to develop new and innovative painting methods.

Complete this paragraph with suitable words.

It doesn't __1__ a lot of training to paint landscapes. It all depends __2__ the painter's personality and ability, as __3__ as his unique touch. Most of today's, non-professional, painters __4__ this style. The __5__ of these painters is purely entertainment and self-satisfaction. The __6__ successful artists have the opportunity to __7__ at public functions. This is, __8__, the climax of their painting careers.

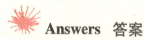 **Answers 答案**

Translate these sentences into Chinese.

1. 这真有意思：中国画是可以现场表演的。
2. 其实，这是中国绘画的一个特点。
3. 它将绘画分为十类。
4. 不靠绘画谋生的画家采用不同的技法。
5. 他们喜欢在画的题材里加入不同的象征意义。
6. 画山水不需要进行长期的技巧训练。
7. 这完全取决于画家的个性和修养。
8. 知名画家能参加各种活动。
9. 一些人在苦心研习技巧。
10. 他们想开发出不同凡响的画法。

Complete this paragraph with suitable words.

1. take 2. on 3. well 4. follow 5. objective 6. more 7. exhibit 8. probably

3. Rediscover Confucius

重新发现孔子

Dialogue

A： Did you see the statue of Confucius launched by the China Confucius Fund?

B： Yes, I did. It doesn't quite **match** the Confucius image in my mind though. I heard there are many **different opinions** about this so-called official statue. But, to be fair, it's an impossible job to create an official statue of someone who lived more than 2,500 years ago. No one knows what he looked like, just like no one in the West knows what Plato looked like. Nevertheless, Confucius was a great philosopher, an educator, a politician, as well as the founder of Confucianism, which still has a **tremendous** influence over people today.

A： Confucianism seems to be back in fashion again. As far as I know, about five to six million Chinese students are currently studying *The Analects of Confucius*. Some companies are using Confucianism as **a management tool**. The government is also promoting the Confucian values of ethics, fairness, and honesty. They see it as a way to address the social problems that have emerged as a result of the accelerated economic growth.

B： Confucianism is the **backbone** of Chinese culture. Confucius developed his philosophy around the concept of benevolence. *The Analects of Confucius* is a record of his political views. Confucianism represents a set of moral principles because it stresses fairness and harmony in **human relationships**, as well as the individual's social responsibility for their country. For Confucius, political honesty is based on individual ethical integrity.

A： Some American scholars did a **comparative study** of Confucius with Greek and Roman philosophers. Their conclusion was that there is more practical value in Confucianism. Why it that?

B： Well it has extensive application in Chinese society. Confucius was also an **accomplished** educator. He treated his students as his equal by teaching them democratic and open-minded ideas. In the words of the American scholars, Confucius wanted to train his students to become more unrestrained and adaptable to external

10

influences.

A： There is also an increasing awareness of Confucianism in other parts of the world. This may be a result of various political, cultural, and environmental challenges due to China's growing economic importance. As a result, the rise of individualism in the community has become a serious threat to social harmony and progress. A different set of values are needed as a **counterbalance**. Confucianism emphasizes "courtesy" and "respect" when dealing with people or nature so it should be very beneficial for building harmony in any society.

B： You are right. A scholar once said that answers concerning our survival can be found in the wisdom of Confucius, even though he lived more than 25 centuries ago.

对 话

A： 你看到中国孔子基金会发布的孔子标准像了吗？

B： 看到了，但它不完全是我心目中的孔子形象。据说有很多人对这个标准像持不同意见。这也难怪，孔子毕竟生活在2 500多年前，没有谁能够想像他真实的长相，就像你们西方人不知道柏拉图的面孔一样。但是，孔子对今天中国人的生活和思想依然有着重大的影响。他是中国古代的思想家、教育家、政治家，也是儒学的创始人。

A： 儒家思想似乎又风行起来了。就我所知，中国有五六百万的孩子在学习《论语》；不少企业家把儒家思想引进到企业管理中；中国政府也试图通过倡导道德、公正和廉洁的儒家思想，来解决经济高速发展带来的社会问题。

B： 儒家思想是中国传统文化的主干。孔子的哲学体系以"仁"为核心，《论语》记载着他的政治学说。儒学是一套伦理道德，强调的是为人处事的正派、人际关系的和谐以及个人对国家的责任感。在孔子看来，政治的廉洁是以人品的正直为基础的。

A： 有的美国学者将孔子与古希腊罗马哲人相比较，认为他的思想更具有实用价值。为什么？

B： 因为它被广泛运用于中国社会。孔子还是个了不起的教育家，他平等对待学生，教给他们民主、开放的观念。用美国学者的话说就是：培养能够自然从容并适应环境的君子。

A： 据我所知，儒家学说也在世界其他地方逐渐引起了重视。这也许与中国经济的高速发展所带来的各种政治、文化，以及环境等问题的巨大挑战有关。个人主义在商品社会中的极端发展，对社会的和谐与进步构成威胁，必须寻求另一种价值观来取得平衡。而孔子的学说恰好提倡以"礼"来处理人际关系及与自然的关系，对于和谐社会的构建大有益处。

B： 有道理。正如一位学者所说：21世纪的生存问题，必须回到25个世纪之前孔子的智慧中去寻求解决的答案。

Background Reading 背景阅读

To learn and at due times to repeat what one has learnt, is that not after all a pleasure? That friends should come to one from afar, is this not after all delightful? To remain unsoured even though one's merits are unrecognised by others, is that not after all what is expected of a gentleman?

学而时习之，不亦说乎？有朋自远方来，不亦乐乎？人不知而不愠，不亦君子乎？

Tzu-chang asked Master K'ung about Goodness. Master K'ung said, "He who could put the Five into practice everywhere under Heaven would be Good." Tzu-chang begged to hear what these were. The Master said, "Courtesy, breadth, good faith, diligence and clemency. He who is courteous is not scorned, he who is broad wins the multitude, he who is of good faith is trusted by the people, he who is diligent succeeds in all he undertakes, he who is clement can get service from the people."

子张问仁于孔子。孔子曰："能行五者于天下，为仁矣。""请问之。"曰："恭、宽、信、敏、惠。恭则不侮，宽则得众，信则人任焉，敏则有功，惠则足以使人。"

At fifteen I set my heart upon learning. At thirty, I had planted my feet firm upon the ground. At forty, I no longer suffered from perplexities. At fifty, I knew what were the biddings of Heaven. At sixty, I heard them with docile ear. At seventy, I could follow the dictates of my own heart; for what I desired no longer overstepped the boundaries of right.

吾十有五而志乎学，三十而立，四十而不惑，五十而知天命，六十而耳顺，七十而从心所欲，不逾矩。

Respect the young. How do you know that they will not one day be all that you are now? But if a man has reached forty or fifty and nothing has been heard of him, then I grant there is no need to respect him.

后生可畏，焉知来者之不如今也？四十、五十而无闻焉，斯亦不足畏也已。

He who learns but does not think, is lost. He who thinks but does not learn is in great danger.

学而不思则罔，思而不学则殆。

Yu, shall I teach you what knowledge is? When you know a thing, to recognize that you know it, and when you do not know a thing, to recognize that you do not know it. That is knowledge.

由，诲女知之乎？知之为知之，不知为不知，是知也。

---

match 符合，匹配	different opinions 不同意见	tremendous 巨大的
a management tool 管理手段	backbone 主心骨，中坚	human relationship 人际关系
comparative study 比较研究	accomplished 学识渊博的，事业有成的	
counterbalance 抗衡，弥补		

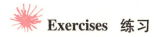 **Exercises 练习**

Answer these questions.

1. Why is the government promoting Confucian values, now?
2. What does Confucianism stress?
3. Why is there an increasing awareness of Confucianism in other parts of the world?

Translate these sentences into Chinese.

1. It doesn't quite match the Confucius image in my mind though.
2. There are many different opinions about this so-called official statue.
3. Confucianism still has a tremendous influence over people today.
4. Confucianism seems to be back in fashion again.
5. The government is also promoting the Confucian values of ethics, fairness and honesty.
6. Confucius developed his philosophy around the concept of benevolence.
7. It stresses fairness and harmony in human relationship.
8. Confucius was also an accomplished educator.
9. There is an increasing awareness of Confucianism in other parts of the world.
10. Confucianism emphasizes "courtesy" and "respect" when dealing with people or nature.

Complete this paragraph with suitable words.

It doesn't quite match the Confucius ___1___ in my mind though. I heard there are many different ___2___ about this, so-called, official statue. But, to be ___3___, it's an impossible job to create an official statue of someone who lived more than 2,500 years ago. No one knows what he ___4___ like, just like no one in the West knows ___5___ Plato looked like. Nevertheless, Confucius was a ___6___ philosopher, an educator, a politician, as ___7___ as the founder of Confucianism, which still has a tremendous influence ___8___ people today.

 Answers 答案

Translate these sentences into Chinese.

1. 它与我心目中的孔子形象不太一样。
2. 据说有很多人对这个标准像持不同意见。
3. 儒家思想对今天的中国人依然有着重大的影响。
4. 儒家思想似乎又在成为时尚。
5. 政府也在倡导道德、公正和廉洁的儒家思想。
6. 孔子的思想体系以"仁"为核心。
7. 它强调人际关系的公正和谐。
8. 孔子还是个了不起的教育家。
9. 儒家学说在世界其它地方逐渐引起了重视。
10. 孔子的学说提倡以"礼"来处理人际关系及与自然的关系。

Complete this paragraph with suitable words.

1. image 2. opinions 3. fair 4. looked 5. what 6. great 7. well 8. over

4. Differences between Chinese and Western Medicines

中西医的差异

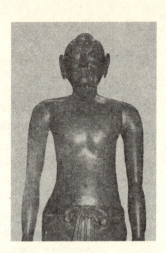

Dialogue

A: For many years, there have been **repeated** discussions to give up Chinese medicine. It's recently become a hot topic once again. Advocates believe that Chinese medicine is not scientifically based in comparison to Western medicine.

B: Although it is debatable whether Chinese medicine is scientifically sound, you can not deny that it has rich philosophical significance. This is very different from Western medicine. Usually a Chinese medicine practitioner **approaches** the illness from a broader perspective, emphasizing its entirety and dialectical implications. This is why some people view it as holistic medicine. In contrast, a Western doctor deals directly with the symptoms. For instance, if someone has a **sore throat**, a Western doctor will treat it as a throat problem, while a Chinese doctor may link it to the **disorder** of the patient's stomach.

A: What's the difference between Chinese and Western medicines?

B: A Chinese doctor examines his patient by using methods like observing, smelling, asking and feeling. His Western **counterpart** relies on symptoms or evidence like body temperature and lab tests. The Chinese doctor determines the problems of the patient's internal organs by inference through observing various exterior signs, such as complexion or the tongue. A Western doctor, on the other hand, makes his judgment based on the results of a lab test on the internal organs. He then **reinforces** his judgment by examining exterior symptoms. A Western doctor uses chemical-based medicines and surgery, while a Chinese doctor relies on herbal medicines and acupuncture.

A: For a patient, which is preferable?

14

B: It depends. Usually a Chinese doctor will recommend Western medicine for **intensive treatment**, and Chinese medicine for the recovery. In fact, Chinese medicine is probably more effective in treating some functional diseases where the cause is difficult to discover.

A: What will happen if Chinese medicine is indeed abandoned?

B: No idea. But for people with **terminal diseases**, Chinese medicine may be their **last resort**. Chinese medicine can not only alleviate pain, but also offers the option of a different treatment.

对 话

A: 据说，近几十年来出现过多次要求取消中医的呼吁，最近还闹得厉害。倡导者认为，与西医相比，中医没有科学依据。

B: 中医是不是科学有待论证，但中医有着深厚的哲学内涵却毋庸置疑。从这点上说，它与西医迥然不同。中医通常从宏观角度认识问题，强调整体性和辩证施治，有人称其为整体医学。西医则从微观入手。比如一个人咽喉痛，西医诊断为咽炎，中医则有可能判断为脾胃失衡的症状。

A: 中西医的疗法有什么不同？

B: 中医通过望、闻、问、切来诊病；西医注重症状，重"证据"，如体温和化验结果。中医通过看人的气色、舌质等外部症状来分析内部病变；西医则是通过化验手段判断脏器的病变，然后检查病人的外在症状证明他的判断。西医多用化学合成药物或手术；中医多用天然药物或针灸等疗法。

A: 对病人来说，中医和西医哪个是最好的选择？

B: 这要依情况而定。中国医生通常建议在治疗阶段选择西医，在恢复阶段选择中医。一些难以查出问题的功能性疾病，用中医的方法调理也许更有效。

A: 如果取消中医，结果会怎么样？

B: 我无法预料。对于那些身患绝症的人来说，中医也许是他们最后的希望。它可以缓解病痛，为患者提供另一种治疗方案。

Background Reading 背景阅读

Chinese Medicines 中医药

Chinese herbs are usually combined in formulae to enhance their properties and functions. Symptoms and signs are matched with therapeutic effects, reflecting the particular conditions and needs of each patient. Age-old medical wisdom has it that tonic formulae restore eroded body resources; regulating formulae decongest the qi (the animating force that gives us our capacity to move, think, feel, and work); moisture and blood formulae relieve discomfort; and purging formulae eliminate adverse internal climates, inviting clear weather. A summary of medical knowledge in the *Hunagdi Nei Jing* (*Yellow Emperor's Classic of Medicine*), compiled some time between 475 and 221BC, describes the use of acupuncture and moxibustion, the pathology of the meridians and viscera, acupuncture points, indications, contraindications and the application of nine kinds of needles.

The famous Chinese surgeon Hua Tuo was an expert in acupuncture in the Han Dynasty, and through him the "tsun", a measurement system using the width of a joint of the patient's own finger, was developed to locate the acupoints more accurately. A book appeared around 400AD called *Zhen Jiu Jia Yi Jing* (*A Classic of Acupuncture and Moxibustion*), which described the names and number of points for each channel, their exact locations, indications, and methods of manipulation; these are still used in modern acupuncture and acupressure. The Qing Dynasty once issued a decree banning acupuncture practice because it was thought to be inferior medicines being introduced by invading Western cultures. But, the people were convinced that acupuncture worked and it remained in widespread use. In fact, acupuncture and herbal medicine were exported to Europe in the 17th century.

中草药通常以各味药配方来发挥其药效。症状和表征与疗效相配合，反应的是每个病人不同的状况和需求。老中医用滋补的药方来恢复虚弱的身体；调理性的药方有理气之效（所谓气是指赋予我们行动、思考、感情以及劳作等能力的一种驱动力量）；补气的药方可以缓解身体的不适；清热解毒的药方能够排除体内不良的征候，增加有益的因素。有关中医药理论的概括性内容可见于《黄帝内经》，它于公元前 475 至公元前 221 年间编撰而成，对针灸、经络、脏器、穴位、针法，禁忌以及九种不同的针型进行了描述。

中国著名的外科医生华佗是汉代针刺疗法的专家，他发明了一种用病人自己手指关节的长度来衡量穴位距离的方法，以"寸"为单位，使得穴位的确定更加准确。一本出现于约公元 400 年的书《针灸家易经》描述了每一个穴位的名称、准确位置、适应症，以及操作方法。这些在现代的针灸及指压治疗中仍在使用。清代时曾颁布一个法令，禁止使用针灸，因为这被认为是由西方入侵者传入的劣等疗法。但是，人们相信针灸的疗效，所以它一直被广泛应用。事实上，针灸和中药疗法在 17 世纪时已传入欧洲。

---

repeated 反复的	approach 接近，入手	sore throat 嗓子疼
disorder 紊乱，失调	counterpart 对应的人，对手	reinforce 加强，强化
intensive treatment 强化治疗	terminal disease 不治之症	last resort 最后的办法

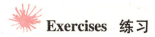 **Exercises** 练习

Answer these questions.

1. What are some typical differences between Chinese and Western medicines?
2. Do you think Chinese medicine should be abandoned?
3. Which is preferable, Chinese or Western medicine?

Translate these sentences into Chinese.

1. There have been repeated discussions to give up Chinese medicine.
2. Chinese medicine is very different from Western medicine.
3. A Chinese medicine practitioner approaches the illness from a broader perspective.
4. A Western medicine practitioner deals directly with the symptoms.
5. The Chinese doctor may link it to the disorder of the patient's stomach.
6. A Western doctor makes his judgment on the basis of lab test results.
7. A Chinese doctor relies on herbal medicines and acupuncture.
8. The Chinese doctor may recommend Western medicine for intensive treatment.
9. For people with terminal diseases, Chinese medicine may be their last resort.
10. Chinese medicine offers the option of a different treatment.

Complete this paragraph with suitable words.

Usually, a Chinese medicine practitioner approaches the illness from a __1__ perspective, with __2__ on its entirety and dialectical implications. This is __3__ some people view it as __4__ medicine. In contrast, a Western, medicine practitioner, __5__ directly with the symptoms. For instance, if someone has a __6__ throat, a Western doctor will __7__ it as a throat problem, while a Chinese doctor may __8__ it to the disorder of the patient's stomach.

 Answers 答案

Translate these sentences into Chinese.

1. 已经出现过多次要求取消中医的呼吁。
2. 中医与西医的差异非常大。
3. 中医从宏观角度看待疾病。
4. 西医直接从症状入手。
5. 中医可能联系到患者的脾胃紊乱。
6. 西医根据化验结果诊断。
7. 中医多用天然药物或针灸等疗法。
8. 中医可能会建议采用西医进行强化治疗。
9. 对于绝症患者来说，中医也许是他们的最后希望。
10. 中医提供了另外一个治疗方案。

Complete this paragraph with suitable words.

1. broader 2. emphasis 3. why 4. holistic 5. deals 6. sore 7. treat 8. link

5. The Role of Operas
戏曲的作用

Dialogue

A: In his book *Chinese Characteristics*, which was written more than 100 years ago, A. H. Smith said that Chinese people liked opera. To them, opera was the only entertainment, like sports for the British and bullfighting for the Spaniards.

B: In a traditional Chinese society, opera was used as a vehicle to spread knowledge and ethical teachings. Most operas were based on historical events, folklore, or classical novels. They promoted traditional values and moral principles, such as punishing evil and **eulogizing** the good; loyalty and kindness; and the denunciation of the ungrateful. Operas were able to **fill the gaps** in education and teaching, especially in an agricultural society.

A: Opera fans were like today's popular music fans. They enjoyed singing the arias.

B: The Dowager Empress Cixi of the Qing Dynasty was a super opera fan. She often had opera troupes perform for her in the Court. This is why Peking Opera overtook all other folk operas and became a national entertainment. It was said that the Empress was deeply influenced by the teachings of the operas, especially those relating to gratitude.

A: I know she would **pardon** anyone to whom she felt **indebted**, **regardless of** their mistakes.

B: That's right. Some historians even suggest that when she engaged the Boxers to fight against the Westerners, she was **under the illusion** they were invincible. She got the notion from the operas that they could not be hurt by bullets. Of course, she was wrong and the Boxers were quickly defeated by the Westerners.

A: Well, if operas had so much influence on the Dowager Empress, I think it would be **even more so** on ordinary people. Since Peking Opera is no longer as popular as it was, does it still have an influence on people?

B: Now it is TV. Since every household has a TV, its influence should not be

underestimated. There was a popular Korean TV drama not long ago, which captivated the audience by its costumes and food. As a result, some studios in Beijing began taking photo portraits in Korean costumes and some restaurants introduced similar Korean food.

A: Now I understand why the government **discourages** TV hosts from imitating Hong Kong and Taiwan accents. It also explains why TV stations are forbidden from airing programs about adultery and other unethical topics.

B: That's correct. China has been experiencing an increasingly high divorce rate where adultery is cited as a main reason.

对 话

A: 亚瑟·史密斯在他一百多年前写的《中国人的德行》一书中说：中国人喜好戏曲，就像英国人喜好体育，西班牙人喜好斗牛一样。戏曲成为中国人唯一的娱乐。

B: 是这样。在传统中国社会，戏曲还有着普及文化知识和教化社会的作用。戏曲的题材多取自历史典故、民间传说或古代小说。它宣扬传统的价值观和伦理道德，比如惩恶扬善、忠孝仁义，以及贬斥忘恩负义。戏曲填补了文化教育的不足，特别是在农村地区。

A: 戏迷就像现在的歌迷一样，喜欢学着唱戏。

B: 对。清朝的慈禧太后就是一个超级戏迷，她常请戏班子进宫演出。京剧因此在众多地方剧种中脱颖而出，成为中国主要的剧种。据说，京剧所宣扬的传统伦常，比如知恩图报的思想，也给了西太后很大的影响。

A: 我知道凡是有恩于她的人，不论犯了什么过失，她都会宽恕。

B: 是这样。甚至有历史学家认为，她利用义和团打洋人的举动，也是出于相信京剧神怪戏宣扬的神力，以为义和团的人刀枪不入。结果她当然错了，义和团被洋人打得一败涂地。

A: 戏曲对这样的大人物影响尚且如此，对老百姓就不用说了。现在京剧不像过去那么流行，它还有影响力吗？

B: 现在是电视当道。在几乎家家有电视机的今天，电视的影响不可低估。前些时候播出了一部韩国的古装电视剧，其中的服装和饮食受到观众的追捧。北京的照相馆开始提供韩服拍照，餐馆也推出这部电视中的食谱。

A: 这下我就理解了为什么政府部门要求电视节目主持人不可模仿港台腔，也不让播出宣扬"第三者"等有悖社会伦理的电视剧了。

B: 对。据说中国的离婚率增高，"第三者"是离婚的主要原因之一。

Background Reading 背景阅读

Peking Opera 京剧

Peking opera is a theatrical art that incorporates singing, dancing, acting and acrobatics. But what we see on the Peking opera stage does not imitate real life. For example, Peking opera uses special imagery in the creation of characters. All roles are classified according to sex, personality, age, profession and social status. Hangdang is the general term for role types in Peking opera. There are four types of role in Peking opera today, namely, the sheng (male role), dan (female role), jing (painted face) and chou (clown). The sheng is the male protagonist, the dan the female protagonist, the jing a male supporting figure with distinct characteristics. And chou a comic or negative figure or foil for the protagonist. The four role types are a result of the large variety of roles from earlier stages in the history of Peking opera being combined and reduced.

The four basic role types have their subdivisions, each with its own specialties and techniques. For example, the sheng role is divided into elderly (laosheng), young (xiaosheng), military (wusheng), red-faced (hongsheng) and young boy (wawasheng) roles, and the elderly male role can be further divided into singing, acting and martial laosheng roles, and so on. The role types cover all the characters on stage, and every actor or actress specializes in a particular role type.

Based on the role types, a complete set of standards has been formed for aspects such as costumes and facial makeup. These aspects and the classification of role types supplement each other, both being very important in the creation of characters and demonstrating the full beauty of Peking opera.

京剧是融合了歌唱、舞蹈、表演和杂技的舞台艺术。但我们在京剧舞台上看到的并不是对真实生活的摹仿。比如，京剧在人物形象的塑造上使用特殊的表现手法。所有的角色都按其性别、个性、年龄、职业和社会地位类型化。"行当"就是对京剧中角色类型的说法。京剧中的角色有四种类型——生、旦、净、丑。"生"指男主角，"旦"是女主角，"净"是有着独特个性的男配角，"丑"是喜剧或反面角色。这四种类型的角色都是从早期京剧中大量的角色中合并或缩减而来。

这四种类型的角色还可细分，每一个都有其特点和技能。比如，"生"角分为老生、小生、武生、红生和娃娃生。老生这一角色还可以进一步分为唱、做和打等。这些角色类型涵盖了所有舞台上的人物形象，每一个男女演员都专攻不同角色。

在角色类型的基础上，形成了一整套程式化的表现方法，诸如服装和脸谱。这些表现方法相互补充，在人物形象的塑造以及京剧的整体美等方面十分重要。

---

eulogize 称赞，歌颂	fill the gaps 弥补不足，填补空缺	pardon 原谅，宽恕
indebted 感激，有恩于别人	regardless of 不管，不顾	under the illusion 以为
even more so 乃至，更有甚者	underestimate 低估	discourage 不鼓励

 **Exercises** 练习

Answer these questions.

1. What was the role of opera in a traditional Chinese society?
2. How deeply was Dowager Empress, Cixi, influenced by opera?
3. Why does the government forbid TV programs about unethical topics?

Translate these sentences into Chinese.

1. Most operas are based on historical events.
2. They promote traditional values.
3. Operas are able to fill the gaps in education.
4. The Dowager Empress was deeply influenced by the teachings of the operas.
5. She was under the illusion they were invincible.
6. Beijing Opera is no longer as popular as it was.
7. The influence of TV should not be underestimated.
8. People were captivated by its costumes and food.
9. The government discourages TV hosts from imitating Hong Kong and Taiwan accents.
10. China has been experiencing an increasingly high divorce rate.

Complete this paragraph with suitable words.

It was ___1___ that, the Dowager Empress, Cixi, was ___2___ influenced by the teachings of the operas. She would pardon ___3___ to whom she felt ___4___, regardless of their mistakes. Some historians even ___5___ that when she engaged the Boxers to fight against the Westerners, she was under the illusion they were ___6___. She got the ___7___ from the operas that they could not be hurt by bullets. Of course, she was wrong and the Boxers were ___8___ defeated by the Westerners.

 Answers 答案

Translate these sentences into Chinese.

1. 戏曲的题材多取自历史典故。
2. 它们宣扬传统价值观。
3. 戏曲填补了教育的不足。
4. 慈禧太后深受京剧所宣扬的传统伦常的影响。
5. 她以为他们是战无不胜的。
6. 现在京剧不像过去那么流行了。
7. 电视剧的影响不可低估。
8. 人们被其中的服装和饮食深深地迷住了。
9. 政府不鼓励电视节目主持人模仿港台腔。
10. 中国的离婚率正在不断增高。

Complete this paragraph with suitable words.

1. said   2. deeply   3. anyone   4. indebted   5. suggest   6. invincible   7. notion
8. quickly

6. Gardens and Bonsais

园林和盆景

Dialogue

A: Have you ever been to Suzhou? You can find over 100 private gardens from the old times in this city.

B: Suzhou is one of my favorite cities. Gardens in that area are known for their **skillful** combination of landscapes. They use man-made structures, such as creeks, rocks, trees, plants, pavilions, platforms, terraces, and bridges. Together they create a **poetic** atmosphere, just like a painting that combines poems, **calligraphy** and scenery all in one. The rocks in the garden don't have to be huge to look meaningful as long as they are arranged in order. The same is true with the creeks. It is not the length of the creeks but the turns and curves which give the garden a feeling of liveliness. This is a manifestation of the Confucian belief of harmony between man and nature and the Taoist worship of nature.

A: I don't see a lot of harmony between man and nature in those particular gardens. There is too much human **interference**. You never find vast expanses of grass and trees. Most objects are symbolic and artificial and they are separated from the outside world by a wall.

B: This has something to do with Chinese philosophy. The imitation of nature reflects both a worship of nature and a pursuit of a poetic state of mind. The walls around the gardens are in effect a way to show modesty and **unpretentiousness**. Also, it separates people with different backgrounds.

A: Human interference is at its utmost with Chinese **bonsais**. Instead of allowing them to grow freely, the plants are restricted and distorted in a cramped space.

B: Indeed, bonsais have forced a different environment upon the plants. However, people like them for their philosophical implications, representing an interaction with the world through a potted landscape. There used to be a saying that goes, "Three leaves and two flowers represent the world." In other words, the few pieces of leaves and the flowers are enough to make you feel the change in the weather, the earth, and the universe. That's the beauty of bonsais. The **miniature** gives people a feeling of closeness to nature.

A: Frankly, I still think it's a bizarre way to enjoy nature by distorting it **in the first place**. But thanks for your explanation it helps me understand that this is an unique view through an unique culture.

B: This is a diversified world. We need to learn to **accommodate** each other. Maybe this is what traditional Chinese gardens and bonsais are all about.

对 话

A: 你去过苏州吗？这个城市有一百多处古代的私家园林。

B: 苏州是我最喜欢的城市之一。那里的园林以自然景观与人造建筑融为一体而著称。园林中有溪流、假山、树木，以及亭、台、阁、桥，造成一种集诗、书、画于一体的诗意环境。山不在高，贵在层次；水不在深，妙在曲折。它既体现了儒家文化中人与自然和谐相处的观念，也表达着道家崇尚自然的理念。

A: 但是我并不认为江南园林是人与自然的和谐之作。这种园林似乎有太多人为的痕迹，里面很少大片的草地和森林，多是象征性的、人为的景观。而且它们被围墙围起来，与外界隔绝。

B: 这与中国传统哲学有关。仿造自然，是内心对自然的膜拜，也是对诗意境界的追求。用围墙将小环境圈起来，也是出于古人对内敛、谦逊品性的推崇。从另一个角度说，这也能够把与他们生活不相关的不同层次的人隔开。

A: 中国的盆景也有过于人工化的问题。各种植物不是在自然环境中生长，而是被圈在一个有限的空间里畸形生长。

B: 的确，盆景扼杀了植物生长的本性。但为什么那么多人欣赏盆景呢？因为它渗透着传统哲学的理念：以小见大，见微知著。古人说"三叶两花一世界"，就是说花叶虽小，但透过它们的变化可以体悟到四季、风土甚至宇宙的变迁。盆景之美就在于此，让人在方寸之间体味到与自然景物的亲近。

A: 坦率地说，我感到这种抑制自然本性的艺术有些变态。不过经你这么解释，我也就理解了在特有文化中形成的特有的审美观。

B: 世界是多样的，我们要学会相互包容。这也许是中国古典园林和盆景给当代人的启示。

Background Reading 背景阅读

Tranquil Interior Surrounded by Solid Walls 高墙中的宁静

Unlike Greek architecture, which is an organic combination of blocks, Chinese traditional architecture emphasized unobstructedness and tone, and displays the rich variance and connotation of the tone with innumerable flowing lines.

Large, solid walls not only function as a protective surrounding defense, they also embody tranquility. Secluding the residence from the outside world, the thick, solid walls block noise from outside and keep the inside quiet.

Partitions such as railings, pierced stonework or brickwork, and window lattices act as frames and agents of distancing. Connection between the exterior and the interior is one of the artistic methods used in Chinese architecture. The combination of partition and connection can be achieved with a bamboo curtain, a door or a window. The lattices in partitions, doors and windows make ideal frames, separating the outside scenery into several sections.

Simple and elegant beauty is a major feature of the traditional Chinese residence. Most dwellings have no ceilings, and the beams and rafters are exposed. The railing structure shows even the ground floor, accompanied only with some decoration in certain corners. The exterior usually consists of plain brick walls. Wooden eaves are seldom painted, but only coated with tung oil as a damp-proof treatment.

与古希腊建筑街区间有机的结合不同，中国传统建筑强调的是通透和情调，展现的是丰富的变化，并用无数流畅的线条表达出含蓄的情调。

高大、坚固的围墙不仅有保护宅院的功能，也营造了宁静的氛围。院墙挡住了外部的喧嚣，保持了家宅的安静，从而为居住者创造了安宁。

隔离物，诸如栏杆、通透的石雕或砖雕，以及花窗都起着疏离的作用。内部与外部的连接是中国传统建筑所采用的艺术手法之一。可以借助竹帘、门窗来达到疏离与连接相结合的效果。花窗、门和窗户在疏离的效果中有着理想的结构，可以将外部景致分隔成不同的部分。

简约与典雅之美是中国传统民居的主要特点。多数的居所没有天花板，横梁与椽都暴露在外。栏杆的结构配之以某些角落的装饰，在第一层展示出来。房舍的外部通常是朴素的砖墙。木制的屋檐也很少粉饰，只是涂上桐油起到防潮的作用而已。

---

skillful 巧妙的	poetic 诗情画意的	calligraphy 书法
interference 干预	unpretentiousness 不张扬	bonsais 盆景
miniature 微缩，微型	in the first place 首先	accommodate 包容，容纳

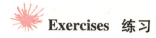 **Exercises 练习**

Answer these questions.
1. What are the gardens in Suzhou known for?
2. Do you see a lot of harmony in Suzhou gardens?
3. Is there any human interference in Chinese bonsais?

Translate these sentences into Chinese.
1. In Suzhou you can find over 100 private gardens from the old times.
2. Suzhou gardens are known for their combination of landscape and man-made structures.
3. The rocks don't have to be huge to look meaningful.
4. There is too much human interference.
5. This has something to do with the Chinese philosophy.
6. The plants are restricted and distorted in a cramped space.
7. The miniature gives people a feeling of closeness to nature.
8. It's a bizarre way to enjoy nature.
9. This is a diversified world.
10. We need to learn to accommodate each other.

Complete this paragraph with suitable words.
Gardens in Suzhou are known for their __1__ combination of landscapes and man-made structures. The rocks in the garden don't __2__ to be huge to look meaningful, as __3__ as, they are arranged in __4__. The same is __5__ with the creeks. It is not the length of the creeks __6__, the turns, and the curves, that give the garden a __7__ of liveliness. This is a manifestation of the Confucian belief of harmony __8__ man and nature and the Taoist worship of nature.

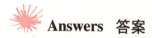 **Answers 答案**

Translate these sentences into Chinese.
1. 苏州有一百多处古代的私家园林。
2. 苏州园林以将自然景观与人造建筑融于一体而著称。
3. 山不在高。
4. 那里有太多的人工痕迹。
5. 这与中国哲学有关。
6. 植物被圈在一个有限的空间里畸形生长。
7. 方寸之间使人感到与自然的亲近。
8. 这样欣赏自然有些变态。
9. 世界是多样的。
10. 我们应该学会相互包容。

Complete this paragraph with suitable words.
1. skillful 2. have 3. long 4. order 5. true 6. but 7. feeling 8. between

7. Glazed Tiles and Imperial Architecture
琉璃瓦与宫廷建筑

Dialogue

A: I went to the Forbidden City on Sunday. It was a beautiful day with a blue sky and white clouds. The yellow tiles looked **gorgeous**.

B: Glazed tiles are unique to Chinese architecture. They were used **exclusively** on Imperial Palaces and buildings. Junior officials or ordinary people were not allowed to use them. That's why you can only see them in the Forbidden Palace, the Summer Palace or other Imperial architecture. There is a place in Beijing called *Liu Li Chang*, which means "glazed tile factory." It is where glazed tiles were made during the Ming Dynasty.

A: Is yellow the only color for those tiles?

B: No, there are other colors such as green, blue, purple and black. There were strict rules for the use of the tiles: yellow tiles for Imperial Palaces and green tiles for the homes of the Emperor's brothers.

A: Sounds special! Could you tell me more about the colors?

B: The colors are related to the five elements that make up our world. Those elements are metal, wood, water, fire and earth, and they are represented by the colors of white, green, black, red and yellow. Each element is also influenced by the four seasons. The five regions on earth are ruled, **respectively**, by five different Emperors. The Yellow Emperor is in the center and is assisted by the God of Earth. In the east is the Green Emperor, who is assisted by the God of Wood and is responsible for spring. The Red Emperor in the south is assisted by the God of Fire and is responsible for summer. The White Emperor is in the west. He is assisted by the God of Metal and is responsible for autumn. The Black Emperor is in the north, being assisted by the God of Water and responsible for winter. So, the colors used in traditional architecture **correspond** to the theory of the Five Elements and the Five Regions.

A：Are those theories used in any of the **contemporary** buildings?

B：Not much. The Ten **Milestone** buildings, built in the 1950s, followed the traditional style but not today's **landmark** buildings in Beijing. Those buildings were designed together with Western architects. They seldom use any of the traditional colors.

A：If Beijing uses the five Olympic colors to **dress up** the city it will definitely look very impressive. It will also be in tune with the Five Color theory.

B：That's an interesting thought. Unfortunately there is no white in the Olympic colors, otherwise it would be a perfect match to the Five Colors.

对 话

A：星期天我去了故宫。在蓝天白云下，故宫的黄色琉璃瓦显得壮美极了。

B：琉璃制品是中国古建筑中特有的材料，但只限于在皇家建筑中使用。一般官宦以及平民百姓是不准用的。所以你只能在故宫、颐和园等皇家建筑中看到琉璃。北京有个地方叫琉璃厂，在明代这里是烧制琉璃瓦的地方。

A：琉璃瓦都是黄色的吗？

B：不，还有绿色、蓝色、紫色和黑色。对于各色琉璃瓦的使用有着严格的等级规定：皇宫用黄色；亲王府用绿色。

A：真奇特！你能多讲讲那些颜色吗？

B：说到颜色，不得不提五行学说。传统上，五色（白、青、黑、红、黄）象征五行（金、木、水、火、土），并与春夏秋冬四季变化相联系。天下五方由五帝统治——黄帝居中，由土神相助，其色属黄；东方为青帝，以木神相佐，其色属青，掌管春季；南方为炎帝，以火神相助，其色属红，掌管夏季；西方称白帝，由金神相助，掌管秋季；北方称黑帝，由水神相佐，掌管冬季。中国古代建筑所用的颜色就与传统五行、五方说相关。

A：现代建筑依然按照这些学说来设计吗？

B：不完全是。20 世纪 50 年代，北京标志性的十大建筑特别强调传统建筑风格。这几年，外国建筑师成为京城标志性建筑的参与者，他们很少采用传统的颜色。

A：如果北京按照奥运五环的色彩来装饰，效果一定惊人。这也符合五色之说。

B：这个主意挺有意思。遗憾的是奥运五环里没有白色，否则就与中国的五色说相符合了。

Background Reading 背景阅读

Palace Architecture 宫廷建筑

In the long history of Chinese feudal society, the emperors, as the wielders of supreme power, had palaces and other structures built which exalted them far above the rest of the populace. Thus, palace architecture represents the quintessence of the architectural techniques and esthetic aspirations of that epoch.

Ancient records describe the now vanished Epang Palace of the Qin Dynasty, Weiyang Palace of the Han Dynasty and Daming Palace of the Tang Dynasty as being huge constructions with broad courtyards, and magnificent halls, pavilions, terraces and tower. The only imperial palaces extant nowadays are the Forbidden City in Beijing and the Imperial Palace in Shenyang, which were built during the Ming and Qing dynasties, respectively. The Forbidden City in Beijing was completed in 1420 during the reign of Yongle. It was constructed totally in accordance with the traditional regulations of ancient Chinese palaces, and reflects the traditional features of Chinese palace architecture from the general layout to the specific appearance of structures and decorations. The Forbidden City concentrates the highest technical and artistic achievements of ancient palace architecture.

在中国漫长的封建历史过程中，拥有至高无上权力的帝王们为自己建造了普通大众可望而不可即的宫廷楼宇，这些建筑代表了当时建筑技术的精髓和审美追求。

据史料记载，秦代的阿房宫、汉代的未央宫，以及唐代的大明宫都是宏大的建筑群，有宽阔的庭院、宏伟的殿堂，以及亭台楼榭等。目前仅存下来的帝王宫殿是分别建于明清两代的北京紫禁城和沈阳故宫。紫禁城完工于明永乐年间的1420年，从整体布局到具体结构和细节装饰，完全按照中国传统宫殿的要求建造，代表了古代宫廷建筑技术和艺术的顶峰。

---

gorgeous 漂亮，华丽	exclusively 专属的，独有的	respectively 各自
correspond 一致，相对应	contemporary 当代	milestone 里程碑
landmark 标志性	dress up 装扮	

 **Exercises** 练习

Answer these questions.
1. Is yellow the only color used for the glazed tiles?
2. What are the five elements?
3. What are the rules for the use of glazed tiles?

Translate these sentences into Chinese.
1. It was a beautiful day, with a blue sky and white clouds.
2. The yellow tiles looked gorgeous.
3. Junior officials or ordinary people were not allowed to use them.
4. It is where glazed tiles were made during the Ming Dynasty.
5. The five regions on earth are ruled, respectively, by five Emperors.
6. The Red Emperor in the south is responsible for summer.
7. There were also strict rules for the use of the tiles.
8. The Ten Milestone buildings built in the 1950s followed the traditional style.
9. They seldom use any of the traditional colors.
10. It will also be in tune with the Five Color theory.

Complete this paragraph with suitable words.
There are also other colors, ___1___ as, green, blue, purple and black. The colors are ___2___ to the five elements ___3___ metal, wood, water, fire and earth, which are ___4___ by white, green, black, red and yellow. Each element is also ___5___ by the four seasons. To be ___6___, the five regions on earth are ___7___, respectively, by five Emperors. The Yellow Emperor is in the ___8___ and is assisted by the God of Earth.

 **Answers** 答案

Translate these sentences into Chinese.
1. 那天天气晴朗，蓝天白云。
2. 黄色的琉璃瓦显得壮美极了。
3. 一般官宦以及平民是不准使用的。
4. 在明代这里是烧制琉璃瓦的地方。
5. 天下五方分别由五帝统治。
6. 南方为炎帝，负责掌管夏季。
7. 琉璃瓦的使用也有严格的等级规定。
8. 上世纪 50 年代，北京标志性的十大建筑强调传统建筑风格。
9. 他们很少使用传统颜色。
10. 这也符合五色说。

Complete this paragraph with suitable words.
1. such   2. related   3. of   4. represented   5. influenced   6. specific   7. ruled   8. center

8. Two Boats in the Yangtze River

长江里的两条船

Dialogue

A: A Norwegian was told by his Chinese friend that, **figuratively**, the Yangtze River has two boats, one called "fame" and the other, "wealth." He said that Chinese students are **in a** busy **pursuit of** fame and wealth, while their Western counterparts are more interested in "an ordinary life."

B: Although many Westerners **are critical of** the **obsession** with fame and wealth by young Chinese people, few Westerners understand the reason behind it. In traditional Chinese culture, fame and wealth were two indicators of a family's glory. Every man had an obligation to both their immediate and extended families, as well as to the entire village. His actions would either glorify or defame his family.

A: Why is that?

B: Well China is a developing country with scarce resources and opportunities, which means that one has to be very successful in order to live a quality life. For example, in the rural areas in order for someone in the family to go to university, his brothers and sisters may have to drop out of school to save costs. After graduation, this student will do everything he can to gain fame and wealth, in the hope of **lifting** his family **out of poverty**. Such is a popular story line of a number of movies, but Gao Jialin in a 1980s movie called "Life" is probably the most well-known. He has to do everything he can in order to live in a city, even though it is achieved **at the expense of** giving up his hometown sweetheart.

A: To be fair though, there are also many young Chinese people who are less interested in fame and wealth and are more focused on a lifestyle they can enjoy.

B: Correct. China's economic progress has made it possible for these young people to choose that sort of lifestyle. Young people of different time periods have different pursuits. In the 1950s and 1960s, shortly after the People's Republic was founded, people truly believed there wouldn't be any personal wealth without building a prosperous country **in the first place**. So, they devoted themselves to the construction of a new China. The economic reforms in the 1980s and 1990s gave people an opportunity to focus on their **personal pursuits**. Today, thanks to increased **disposable income**, people are able to constantly upgrade their lifestyle. However, many people have begun to worry about China's future, because they see a diminishing sense of family and social responsibility among the younger generation.

A: I'm not too worried though. As people become more affluent, their sense of responsibility will become stronger and they will make decisions which best reflect their values. Many young people in the West have chosen to do voluntary work in Asia, Africa and other underdeveloped areas. As a matter of fact, more and more young Chinese people have also signed up as volunteers.

对 话

A: 曾经有一个中国人告诉他的挪威朋友说：长江里有两条船，一条为名，一条为利。他说中国的大学生们热衷于追求功名，而西方的青年更在意"平凡着，生活着。"

B: 不少西方人对中国青年追逐名利持批评态度，但是他们并不了解这种情况产生的原因。中国文化中的确有这种成就功名、光宗耀祖的传统。在宗法制度下，每一个人对家庭、家族、村落都有着自己的责任。一个人无论做了什么，对他的家庭来说是一损俱损、一荣俱荣。

A: 为什么会这样？

B: 中国是一个发展中国家，经济不发达，导致资源和机会的不平等。只有出人头地，才能有高质量的生活。比如，一个农民的孩子上了大学，也许他的弟弟或妹妹就不得不辍学。大学毕业后，谋得功名和财富使家人过上好日子就成为他的生活目标。在一些影视作品中常可以看到这种故事。最典型的形象要算创作于20世纪80年代的电影《人生》中的主人公高加林，他为了摆脱低下的社会地位而努力，甚至抛弃爱情，最终过上了城里人的生活。

A: 现在，也有一些中国的年轻人看淡功名和财富，按自己的意愿生活。

B: 对。中国经济的发展，为年轻人提供了这样生活的可能。说到年轻人的追求，不同年代并不相同。二十世纪五六十年代，新中国建立之初，人们认为只有国家富裕了人民才能过上好日子，所以当时的年轻人有为国奋斗的责任感；八九十年代，改革开放给人们带来了个人奋斗的机会；今天，中国人有了较富足的生活，开始追求舒适感。但是不少人担心，年轻人只图个人安逸而失去了对家庭和社会的责任感，未来的中国何以为继？

A: 这不必担心。当人们富裕起来，有了一定的社会责任感，他们就可能做出有益的选择，以实现自己的价值。你看不少的西方青年就热衷于去亚洲、非洲和不发达地区做志愿者。其实，现在中国的年轻志愿者越来越多，就证明了这一点。

Background Reading 背景阅读

Youth Live with Anxiety 年轻人的生存压力

A recent online survey by the social research center of China Youth Daily found that 55 per cent of young people thought they lacked enthusiasm for life, and 71 per cent considered themselves under heavy pressure.

It is hard to judge whether the whole social group is so pessimistic just based on the result of a survey of about 4,000 people. But anxiety is surely a common phenomenon among young Chinese today. According to psychologists, a healthy mental status should be one of optimism and confidence. Anxiety is a mental problem, whose roots are in inner fear over the uncertainties in life. Or, say, it is a feeling of insecurity. The prospering market economy reflected in conspicuous consumption is the reason for some people's anxiety. Brand-name cars, luxurious houses and elitist lives are within sight of common people with high profiles. But as they are hardly achievable for many, some people feel frustrated.

Such anxiety over the worship of money, however, is not representative. The major reasons causing anxiety for most people are high housing prices, education expenses and medical costs. People are living under high pressure, but they see little hope for escape as their incomes are low and their increases are slow. At a time that seems to be full of opportunities, people live with many anxieties.

据《中国青年报》最近的网上调查显示，55% 的中国青年认为自己对生活缺乏热情，71% 的人认为他们承受着巨大的压力。

仅仅依据这项调查所问及的 4000 名受访者，很难判断是否整个社会的这一群体都对生活如此悲观。但是焦虑的情绪的确普遍存在于当今的中国年轻人中。据心理学家称，乐观与自信是健康的心理状态所应具备的要素。焦虑是一种心理问题，它源自对生活中的不确定因素的内在恐惧，或者说是一种不安全感。繁荣的市场经济中躁动的消费需求是某些人焦虑情绪产生的原因。名车、豪宅和优越的生活被人们视作高档的标志。但是，由于多数人难以达到这样的生活标准，有些人就会产生失落感。

然而，这种出于对金钱崇拜而产生的焦虑感并不具有代表性。对于多数人来说，引起焦虑的主要原因是高昂的房价、教育支出和医疗费用。人们生活在巨大的压力之下，但是低廉并且增长缓慢的工资使他们看不到脱离困境的希望。有时似乎是机会多多，人们也会因此而产生焦虑。

---

figuratively 比喻地，象征性地
are critical of 对…持批评意见
lift…out of poverty 使…脱贫
in the first place 首先
disposable income 可支配收入

in a pursuit of 追求
obsession 执迷，迷恋
at the expense of 代价是
personal pursuits 个人追求

32

 **Exercises** 练习

Answer these questions.

1. What are the two boats in the Yangtze River called?
2. What do Westerners feel about the pursuit of fame and wealth by young Chinese people?
3. Where do Western, young people, do their volunteer work?

Translate these sentences into Chinese.

1. Chinese students are in a busy pursuit of fame and wealth.
2. Many Westerners are critical of the obsession with fame and wealth by young Chinese.
3. Every man had an obligation to both their immediate and extended families.
4. China is a developing country with scarce resources and opportunities.
5. His brothers and sisters may have to drop out of school.
6. Young people of a different time period have different pursuits.
7. There wouldn't be any personal wealth without a prosperous country in the first place.
8. I'm not too worried though.
9. As people become more affluent, their sense of responsibility will become stronger.
10. More and more young Chinese people have also signed up as volunteers.

Complete this paragraph with suitable words.

Although many Westerners are __1__ of the __2__ with fame, and wealth, by young Chinese people, __3__ of them understand the __4__ behind it. In traditional Chinese culture, fame and wealth were two __5__ of a family's glory. Every man had an __6__ to both, their immediate, and __7__, families, as well as, to their entire village. His actions would either __8__, or defame, his family.

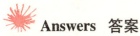 **Answers** 答案

Translate these sentences into Chinese.

1. 中国的大学生们热衷于追求功名。
2. 不少西方人对中国青年追逐名利持批评态度。
3. 每一个人对家庭、家族都有着自己的责任。
4. 中国是一个发展中国家，资源和机会匮乏。
5. 他的弟弟或妹妹也许不得不辍学。
6. 不同年代的年轻人有不同的追求。
7. 只有国家富裕了，个人才能富有。
8. 我倒是不太担心。
9. 随着人们不断富裕起来，他们的责任感也会加强。
10. 越来越多的中国青年报名当志愿者。

Complete this paragraph with suitable words.

1. critical   2. obsession   3. few   4. reason   5. indicators   6. obligation   7. extended
8. glorify

9. Chinese Fans

中国扇子

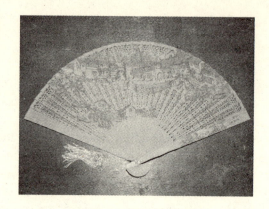

Dialogue

A： Fans seem to have special meanings in Chinese culture. I have received a number of them as gifts from my Chinese friends. The fans are very pretty, so, I assume, they are not meant to be used. Also, they are too **cute** for a man, like me, to use.

B： Fans used to be a **favorite** item for women in China. You may have noticed that nearly all female figures in traditional Chinese paintings carry a silk fan. In the movies of the 1930s, and 1940s, fans are a very visible article for Shanghai women on **the Bund**. Usually, the structure of the fans is made of sandalwood, and the faces are made of silk, or paper. Because the fans are always scented, women who use them appear, even more, attractive. Fans are, probably, one of the most appropriate expressions of female elegance. Men also use fans but, these fans are, usually, much bigger. Men's fans often use valuable materials for their structure but, the faces are always painted with plants, landscapes, or calligraphy, to express the owner's status and **aspirations**.

A： But, none of the fans I have look the same as what you just told me. The paintings are also different. Mine are painted with either Peking opera masks, or Chinese dragons.

B： As a result of the open-door policy, fans have become popular again, not for people to use at home but, as gifts for foreigners. However, unlike fans of the old days, the ones people use as gifts, nowadays, do not take a lot of **craftsmanship** to make. Neither are the materials unique. In some of the popular tourist markets around Beijing, you can buy traditional Zhejiang fans made of blue printed cloth. **Instead of** sandalwood, various scented, substitute materials, are used for the structures. Because fans are small, inexpensive and, typically Chinese, many people like to use them as gifts from their overseas trips. I hope Westerners appreciate these gifts.

A： My Mexican friend told me that Chinese fans are "all over the place" in Mexico. The same is, probably, true in Chinatowns throughout the United States.

B： That reminds me of an article by a Chinese writer. He wrote that two former Soviet Union experts paid a special visit to a fan factory in Suzhou during the 1960s. They wanted to buy some fans to take home. The workers were very excited about their visit. The factory **held a meeting** of its 200 workers to discuss the production plan. They were determined to make the best fans they could for their Soviet friends. Now, although fans are still a very good gift for foreigners, we seem to be using them **excessively**. Someone needs to **alert** the fan factories, and people who go on overseas trips, about the over-supply of fans.

对 话

A： 扇子在中国文化中好像有特别的含意，因为已经有好几位中国朋友送我扇子作礼物。这些扇子做工那么精美，我想一定不是拿来用的吧。而且我是个大男人，不太可能用到那么女性化的东西。

B： 扇子曾是中国女人的至爱。你可以在古代图画中看到，画中的仕女都是手持一把绢扇。上世纪三四十年代拍摄的老电影中，上海滩的女子几乎人手一扇。这些扇子多用檀香木做扇骨，绢或纸作扇面，轻摇之下，香风习习，显出女人的妩媚来。扇子也许是女人用来表现风情的最好的道具。男人也用扇子，但是男人用的扇子要大多了。名贵的扇子用上好的材料作扇骨，扇面的内容多为花卉、山水园林或名人题字等。借着这样的扇子，男人表现的是身价和学养。

A： 但是我收到的那些扇子并不像你所说的这么讲究，而且图案也不同，有京剧脸谱、中国龙等等。

B： 改革开放后，作为传统艺术品的扇子又一次流行，但这次不是给人们自用，而是作为礼物送给外国人。比起过去精细的工艺来，现在普通人用来送礼的扇子有传统的外观，但材料和工艺都已不再讲究。在北京著名的旅游商品市场，还能买到以蓝印花布作扇面的江浙传统扇子。扇骨不再是昂贵的檀香木，上面的檀香味道也是化学香料的结果。因其轻巧易携带、价格便宜且有中国特色，出国的人会带许多这样的扇子作为礼物。在我们看来，洋人肯定会喜欢这种有中国特色的小玩艺。

A： 我的墨西哥朋友说那里的中国扇子已经"臭了街"，在美国的唐人街也随处可见中国扇子。

B： 这使我想起一位中国作家写过的一篇文章。20 世纪 60 年代，曾有两位前苏联专家特地到苏州参观檀香扇制作并打算购买。工人们十分兴奋，召集 200 人举行生产动员大会，制订生产计划，下决心做出最美的扇子送给苏联朋友。这些年，我们又热情地把扇子送给其他国家的朋友，以至于它们在当地"臭了街"。也许应该告诉扇子厂和出国的人们，扇子的产量和供应量可以适当削减了。

Colored Lanterns 花灯

The 15th day of the first lunar month is the Lantern Festival in China. It is the custom to hang red lanterns on the door. Children play with colored lanterns, and people go to squares and streets to view and admire decorative lanterns. It is recorded that lanterns adorned the Lantern Festival at least 3,000 years ago, when they were used in memorial ceremonies for the Heavenly Emperor. By the Tang Dynasty, the court had connected lanterns with Buddhism, and made the lighting of lanterns at the Lantern Festival a part of official protocol.

Colored lanterns in different regions have their own specific feature. Farmers in northern Shaanxi Province make lanterns out of pumpkins, with materials like cotton or in the shape of the head of a goat. In Beijing, which had long been a dynastic capital, the colored lanterns are mainly in the style of imperial palace lanterns.

The shapes of the lanterns hung up at festivals have auspicious implications. Lotus- and fish-shaped lanterns symbolize wealth; watermelon lanterns and pomegranate lanterns symbolize many offspring; chicken lanterns and sheep lanterns symbolize luck; and elephant lanterns symbolize the refreshment of everything. Riddles are often inscribed on the lanterns at lantern fairs. The riddles are composed in elegant language and have ingenious structures. Guessing the answer to a lantern riddle is supposed to be a good omen.

农历正月十五是中国的元宵节，人们习惯在门外悬挂大红灯笼，孩子们提彩色灯笼玩，大人们则上街观赏各式各样的灯笼。据记载，灯笼早在约 3 000 年前就出现在元宵节上，用于祭祀天子。到了唐代，朝廷将灯笼与佛教联系起来，从此点灯笼就成了元宵节官方礼仪的一部分。

不同地区的彩灯风格迥异，陕北的农民用南瓜做灯笼，用棉花等材料做成羊头形状。而北京因为是帝王之都，灯笼一般都做成宫廷灯笼的样子。

灯节上所悬挂灯笼的形状有其各自的寓意，莲花和鲤鱼代表富贵，西瓜和石榴代表子孙满堂，鸡和羊代表好运，而大象则代表万象更新。灯节期间，灯笼上都写有灯谜，这些灯谜的文字优雅工整，猜到谜底往往被认为是好的兆头。

---

cute 小巧玲珑的，非常可爱的	favorite 心爱的，受宠的	The Bund 上海外滩
aspirations 愿望，追求	craftsmanship 工艺，手艺	instead of 除了
hold a meeting 开会	excessively 过度的，极端的	alert 提醒，告诉

 **Exercises** 练习

Answer these questions.

1. What kind of fans did Chinese women carry in the 1930s?
2. What does a typical fan for man look like?
3. Are there many Chinese fans in Mexico?

Translate these sentences into Chinese.

1. Fans have special meanings in the Chinese culture.
2. The fans are too cute for a man like me to use.
3. Fans used to be a favorite item for women in China.
4. Nearly all women figures in traditional Chinese paintings carry a silk fan.
5. People use fans as gifts for foreigners.
6. Nowadays it no long takes a lot of craftsmanship to make a fan.
7. Many people like to use them as gifts on their overseas trips.
8. This reminds me of an article by a Chinese writer.
9. They were determined to make the best fans for their Soviet friends.
10. Someone needs to alert the fan factories about the over-supply of fans.

Complete this paragraph with suitable words.

Fans __1__ to be a favorite item for women in China. You may have __2__ that nearly all women figures in traditional Chinese paintings __3__ a silk fan. In the movies of the 1930s and 1940s, fans are a very __4__ article for women __5__ the Bund in Shanghai. Usually the structures of the fans are __6__ of sandalwood, and the faces are made of __7__ silk or paper. Because the fans are always scented, women who use them look __8__ more attractive.

 Answers 答案

Translate these sentences into Chinese.

1. 扇子在中国文化中有特别的含意。
2. 那些扇子太秀气了，不适合我这个大男人。
3. 扇子曾是中国女人的至爱。
4. 在古代的图画中，画面中的仕女几乎都手持一把绢扇。
5. 人们将扇子作为礼物送给外国人。
6. 现在扇子的做工已经不那么精细了。
7. 许多人出国时用它们作礼物。
8. 这使我想起一位中国作家写过的一篇文章。
9. 他们下决心为苏联朋友做出最美的扇子。
10. 应该将扇子过剩的情况告诉扇子厂。

Complete this paragraph with suitable words.

1. used 2. noticed 3. carry 4. visible 5. on 6. made 7. either 8. even

10. Peking Opera Facial Masks

京剧脸谱

Dialogue

A: Peking Opera is the cream of Chinese culture. **As such**, it has become a must-see item to **entertain** foreigners. But I don't like its shrieking singing and the noisy percussions. I enjoy the costumes and the facial masks better.

B: As a traditional art form, Peking Opera has problems in **appealing** to today's theatergoers. It is very slow and monotonous. Its costumes and facial masks are more attractive. There is a very **distinct** Ming Dynasty influence on Peking Opera costumes. They are very colorful and majestic. Two long pieces of white silk at the end of the sleeves create a graceful feeling during dancing. Different styles of the costumes are used to reflect the status of different characters. There are more decorations in the costumes of the nobles, while those for the poor tend to be simple and less ornamental. But the same materials are used for all costumes to ensure the desired theatrical presentation. Present-day designers are also borrowing from the Peking Opera for their work.

A: Facial masks can reflect the qualities of different characters.

B: Facial masks using different colors are an important way to **portray** a character. There are hundreds of different facial mask designs and each character has its own design. For example, Guan Yu is a very well-known warrior. People believe he had a dark red **complexion** so his facial mask is painted red because red is a color that **represents** loyalty and courage.

A: As the folk saying goes, "All red complexion guys are good guys."

B: The facial mask of the Song Dynasty Emperor Zhao Kuangyin depicts a dragon to show his imperial background. Another hero is Yang Qilang. There is a tiger in his facial mask. The word "tiger" is even written on the forehead to show that he is as courageous as a tiger.

A: So colors become an important expression.

B: Yes. People can tell a hero from a villain by the colors of their masks. In general, white usually represents treachery, black represents righteousness, yellow represents bravery, blue and green represent rebellious fighters while gold and silver represent divinity and Buddhism.

A: I didn't realize that Peking Opera's facial masks are so **complicated**. Although I can't **stand** its shrieking singing, I still like to go to a Peking Opera show. I'll listen to my MP3 while enjoying the facial masks.

B: Then you can have the best of both worlds.

对 话

A: 京剧是中国的国粹，也成了招待外国人必不可少的项目。但是，我不太适应京剧高亢的唱腔和令人发疯的打击乐，我喜欢它的服装和各种各样的脸谱。

B: 作为一门古老的艺术，京剧的确有许多难以被现代人接受的元素，比如它缓慢的节奏。京剧的服装、脸谱更易被人喜爱。京剧的戏服基本上是以明代服饰的样式为基础略加改变，色彩鲜艳华丽。袖口处加了两块长长的白绸，舞蹈时有一种美感。服装也是剧中人物身份的象征。富贵者的服装缀满精美的刺绣；穷困者的服装则简单朴素，少有装饰。但所有服装都选用同样的质地，目的是维护统一的舞台美感。当代的服装设计师也从京剧服装中汲取灵感。

A: 京剧脸谱可以表现人物性格。

B: 脸谱是京剧中塑造人物形象的重要手段，它是用不同的颜色在脸上勾画出来的。京剧的脸谱有几百种，每个角色都有自己专用的谱式。中国有个家喻户晓的武将关羽，传说他面如重枣。他的脸谱就使用了红色，代表仁义忠勇。

A: 所以有俗语说"红脸无坏人"。

B: 宋朝皇帝赵匡胤的脸谱上画了条小龙，以示他有帝王之命。还有一位英雄杨七郎，脸谱的形态是变形的虎面，脑门上也写了一个虎字，寓意他如虎般勇猛。

A: 看来颜色成为十分重要的表现手法。

B: 是啊。脸谱的颜色让人一看便知角色的善恶。比如白色代表奸诈，黑色代表正直不阿，黄色是骁勇凶狠，蓝、绿色多用于绿林好汉，金、银色多用于神佛等。

A: 没想到京剧的脸谱有这么多的讲究。尽管我无法忍受它的唱腔，但是我会戴着MP3去剧场，听着流行歌曲看那些脸谱。

B: 一个中西结合的办法。

The Makeup of Zhong Kui 钟馗的脸谱

The makeup for well-known Peking Opera character Zhong Kui is notable for being in the shape of a bat-symbol of happiness because its Chinese pronunciation is a homonym of that for happiness.

There are various versions of Zhong Kui's story, the most popular of which tells of his winning first place in the highest imperial examination and of the emperor's canceling Zhong's *zhuangyuan* title because of his physical unattractiveness. In despair, Zhong Kui commits suicide by dashing his head against a pillar. The immortal Jade Emperor takes pity on him, and confers on him the post of dispeller of demons. Du Ping, one of Zhong Kui's fellow imperial examinees, and fiancé of his younger sister, buries his late fellow scholar, and Zhong Kui's gratitude moves him to escort his sister to her wedding to Du Ping. He goes on to excel at his post as judge and exorcist of demons and protector of mortals. Despite being the ugliest of all the gods in Chinese mythology, Zhong Kui is the most popular.

The Peking Opera "Zhong Kui Marries off His Sister" is a national favorite. The bat design of Zhong Kui's makeup signifies the happiness he brings to mortals, and the red shoe-shaped ingot on his forehead indicates his death from dashing his head against a pillar as well as his high-principled character. Zhong Kui's black and white lines on his face endorse the character's just uprightness, and the smiling expression reflects his innate good humor.

在京剧中，著名的人物钟馗的脸谱像是一只蝙蝠，因为蝙蝠在汉语中与幸福的福发音相同，是福的形象表意符号。

关于钟馗的故事有不同的版本，流传最广的说法是，他在科举考试中以优异成绩高中榜首。但是因为他相貌丑陋，被皇帝勾掉了状元资格。钟馗一怒之下，撞柱而死。玉帝怜其不幸，封他为捉恶鬼之神。与钟馗一同赴试的杜平出资安葬了他。钟馗感其恩德，带领属下将妹妹送至杜家完婚。钟馗即是法官又是执行者，他惩恶扬善。尽管在民间神话中，钟馗的形象是最丑的，但他也是最受欢迎的神明之一。

京剧曲目《钟馗嫁妹》在全国都很知名。他的化妆中的蝙蝠造型意味着他给人们带来的福气，还有一块红色元宝形的化妆在他的额头上，既表明他的忠正，也暗示他是用头撞柱而亡。用黑白二色描绘的图纹，强化他执法公正的品格，而似带笑形的化妆手法，反映了钟馗特有的幽默。

---

as such 因为如此	entertain 招待	appeal 吸引	distinct 明显的	portray 描绘
complexion 肤色	represents 代表	complicated 复杂	stand 忍受	

 **Exercises** 练习

Answer these questions.
1. What are the differences in the costumes for different characters?
2. What are the differences in facial masks for different characters?
3. Why is Guan Yu's facial mask painted red?

Translate these sentences into Chinese.
1. Beijing Opera has become a must-see item to entertain foreigners.
2. I enjoy the costumes and the facial masks better.
3. Beijing Opera has problems in appealing to today's theater-goers.
4. There is a very distinct Ming Dynasty influence in Beijing Opera costumes.
5. Present-day designers are also borrowing from the Beijing Opera for their work.
6. Facial masks are an important way to portray a character.
7. Red is a color that represents loyalty and courage.
8. Colors become an important expression.
9. People can tell a hero from a villain by the colors of their masks.
10. I didn't realize that Beijing Opera's facial masks are so complicated.

Complete this paragraph with suitable words.
Beijing Opera is the cream of the Chinese culture. As ___1___ , it has become a ___2___ item to entertain foreigners. But, I don't like its ___3___ singing and the noisy percussions. I ___4___ the costumes and the facial masks, better. As a traditional art ___5___ , Beijing Opera has problems in ___6___ to today's theater-goers. It is very slow and monotonous. Its costumes, and facial masks are ___7___ attractive. There is a very ___8___ Ming Dynasty influence on Beijing Opera costumes.

 Answers 答案

Translate these sentences into Chinese.
1. 京剧成了招待外国人必不可少的项目。
2. 我更喜欢它的服装和脸谱。
3. 京剧难以被现代人接受。
4. 京剧的服装有明显的明代文化痕迹。
5. 当代服装设计师也从京剧服装中汲取灵感。
6. 脸谱是塑造人物形象的重要手段。
7. 红色代表忠勇。
8. 颜色成为十分重要的表现手法。
9. 人们可以根据脸谱的颜色分辨角色的善恶。
10. 没想到京剧的脸谱有这么多的讲究。

Complete this paragraph with suitable words.
1. such   2. must-see   3. shrieking   4. enjoy   5. form   6. appealing   7. more   8. distinct

11. Yellow: China's Favorite Color

黄，中国人崇尚的颜色

Dialogue

A: Chinese people seem to like the red and yellow colors a lot. The two colors are used for the Chinese national flag. They are also the **predominant** colors for the cover design of some important books, as well as in the decorations for major events, such as the flower display in Tian'anmen Square during the National Day holidays.

B: The color preferences of the Chinese people are influenced by the five elements of metal, wood, water, fire and earth, in addition to geographical locations and weather. China is a huge and geographically **diversified** country. It is cold in the north so people there like warm colors. But it is just the opposite in the south. Of all the warm colors, the Han people like yellow especially.

A: Maybe because the Hans originated in the Yellow River Plateau, a region where yellow was the **prevailing** color.

B: You are probably right. As far as the five elements are concerned, the corresponding colors are white, green, black, red, and yellow. Yellow is the predominant color and is situated in the center of the diagram. Yellow was also the color representing the imperial court in traditional China. It was established as the authoritative color representing the Emperor during the Han Dynasty more than 2,000 years ago. During the Sui Dynasty, yellow was officially designated as the **exclusive** color for the imperial family. It was used in the Emperor's clothes, the paper on which the Emperor published his decrees, and the **calendar** that was printed by the Imperial Court.

A: People have a tradition of making a "longevity outfit" for the deceased. The inner side of the outfit is always yellow. The bottom of the coffin is also lined with yellow silk.

B: During the 1980s and 1990s, taxis in Beijing were all painted yellow. Those taxis were very popular because of space and low fares. However, they were considered inappropriate for Beijing and were **replaced with** new models. The new taxis use a standard color pattern with yellow at the bottom, which acts as a reminder of Beijing's Imperial tradition.

A： Nowadays, people always refer to **pornography** as "yellow literature" and pornographic films as "yellow movies." That reference can be traced to a newspaper from the 19th century United States, which used to print vulgar paintings in yellow.

B： The word "yellow" in the campaign statement of "Eradicate the yellow and fight against the illegal" refers to pornography. I guess we all need to be very careful with the yellow color since it is used to represent both the Imperial Court and **bad taste**. In olden times, a person could be beheaded for the misuse of yellow. It can also cause trouble today if a person **associates** himself with the wrong yellow.

对 话

A： 中国人似乎很喜欢红黄两色，你看，中国国旗就是由这两种颜色组成的。很多重大场合或重要书籍的装帧总会用到这两种颜色。国庆节天安门广场摆放的花坛，也是以这两种颜色作主调。

B： 中国人对色彩的好恶除了受地理、气候的影响外，也受到传统五行说的影响。从地理方面说，中国是个地域广阔的国家，北方寒冷，人们喜欢暖色；南方炎热，人们喜欢冷色。在暖色中，汉民族最崇尚黄色。

A： 这也许是因为汉民族的发源地是黄土高原，这个地域满目黄土之色。

B： 可能是吧。从五行说来看，金、木、水、火、土所代表的五色分别是白、青、黑、赤、黄，其中黄为主色，位在中央。在中国古代社会，黄色是皇权的象征。在两千多年前的汉代，朝廷就规定"衣尚黄"，确立了黄色的权威地位。从隋朝起，黄色成为皇家专用的颜色。皇帝的龙袍称作黄袍；皇帝的文告用黄纸写成，称黄榜；皇帝颁发的历书用黄纸印刷，称为黄历。

A： 据我所知，按照传统，死者去世后穿的衣服称作"寿衣"，它讲究双层缝制，里面那一层一定要用黄色。棺材的底部也要铺上黄绸布。

B： 上世纪八九十年代，北京街头跑着的出租车就是黄色的面包车。它因为价廉且空间大而广受欢迎。后来这种车型被认为有碍京城市容而被新车型取代。现在的出租车采用统一的颜色，下半部为土黄，以体现北京皇家名城的传统。

A： 现在，人们称色情文学为"黄色小说"，称色情电影为"黄色电影"。这种说法来源于19世纪美国的一家报纸，该报社以黄色印刷趣味低下的漫画。

B： 现在的词汇"扫黄打非"中的"黄"就有色情的意思。这种有时贵为皇家专用，有时又表示低级趣味的颜色，用起来还真要小心。古时用错了黄色会杀头，今天错用了黄色会闯祸。

Background Reading 背景阅读

Tang Tri-color（1） 唐三彩（一）

Tang San Cai, or Tang Tri-color (tri-color pottery of the Tang Dynasty), was created specifically as a burial object. Its existence relates closely to the political system and burial rituals of the Tang Dynasty.

Tang tri-color is the generic name for color-glazed pottery of the Tang Dynasty. Its colors include yellow, green, brown, blue, black and white, but the first three shades of yellow, green and brown are its major tones. The body was made from white clay, and after the clay mold had been fired into a fixed shape, a mineral frit containing such elements as copper, iron, cobalt and manganese was applied. The body would then be fired again at a temperature of around 900 degrees centigrade. Since the frit was high in lead compounds, its fusing degree was low, and it would therefore diffuse while being heated, allowing different colors to permeate. Though tri-color pottery took more time and went through a complex process in its making, it was not as solid and durable as porcelain, and had a high lead content. It was, therefore, used mainly for burial utensils, and rarely for items of daily use.

Since ancient Chinese attached equal importance to their earthly and after life, different types of tri-color were made to represent each aspect of earthly life, and included articles of daily use, human and animal figures, furniture, vehicles, miniature landscapes and buildings. The human and animal figures are notable for their excellence of workmanship.

唐三彩出现时最主要的用途是随葬冥器。它的产生同唐代的政治制度和墓葬仪式密切相关。

唐三彩是唐代彩色釉陶器的总称，它的釉色包括黄、绿、褐、蓝、黑、白等，而以黄、绿、褐三彩为主。其胎质为白色黏土，胚胎经过素烧成形后，再施加含铜、铁、钴、锰等元素的矿物作釉料着色剂，用900度左右的低温进行第二次焙烧。由于釉料中配以铅化合物，降低了釉料的熔融温度，使釉料在受热的过程中向四周扩散。三彩制作费工费时，但其胎质不如瓷器细密坚实耐用，且釉中含铅量过高，因此它很少作实用器皿，而多用作冥器。

由于古人把阴阳二界都视为自己的生活空间，因而唐三彩的器形多样，涉及到社会生活的各个方面，包括生活用具、人物和动物、家具、车马、山水和建筑物等。其中最为精美的是人物俑和动物俑。

---

predominant 主要的，显著的	diversified 多样化的	prevailing 主要的，显著的
exclusive 独有的，专属的	calendar 日历	replace with 由…替代
pornography 黄色	bad taste 低级趣味	associate 与…联合

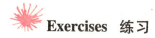 **Exercises** 练习

Answer these questions.

1. Why do Chinese people like yellow and red color?
2. Why Beijing's yellow taxis were replaced?
3. Why is the word "yellow" used to refer to pornography?

Translate these sentences into Chinese.

1. Chinese people seem to like the red and yellow colors a lot.
2. The color preferences of the Chinese people are influenced by the five elements.
3. China is a huge and geographically diversified country.
4. Yellow was the color representing the Imperial Court in traditional China.
5. Those taxis were very popular because of the space and low fares.
6. The newspaper used to print vulgar paintings in yellow.
7. The yellow color is used to represent both the Imperial Court and bad taste.
8. The new taxis use a standard color pattern with yellow at the bottom.
9. A person could be beheaded for the misuse of yellow.
10. It can also cause trouble if a person associates himself with the wrong yellow.

Complete this paragraph with suitable words.

Chinese people's color __1__ is influenced __2__ the five __3__ of metal, wood, water, fire and earth, in __4__ to geographical locations and weather. China is a __5__ and geographically diversified country. It is cold __6__ the north so people there like __7__ colors. It is just the __8__ in the south. Of all the warm colors, the Han people like yellow especially.

 **Answers** 答案

Translate these sentences into Chinese.

1. 中国人似乎很喜欢红黄两色。
2. 中国人对色彩的好恶受到传统五行说的影响。
3. 中国是个地域广阔的国家。
4. 黄色也是皇权的象征。
5. 那些黄色出租因为价廉且空间大而受到欢迎。
6. 该报社以黄色印刷趣味低下的漫画。
7. 黄色既贵为皇家专用，又表示低级趣味。
8. 现在的出租车采用统一的颜色，下半部为土黄。
9. 用错了黄色会被杀头。
10. 错用了黄色也会闯祸。

Complete this paragraph with suitable words.

1. preference 2. by 3. elements 4. addition 5. huge 6. in 7. warm 8. opposite

12. Red: China's Favorite Color

红，中国人崇尚的颜色

Dialogue

A: Chinese people also like the red color a lot. China used to be called the "red country" in the past. Even now Chinese people like to refer ourselves as "*chi zi*", meaning the "red descendent".

B: Traditionally, red represents the motherland and authority. Official uniforms of the Tang Dynasty were red. In the Qing Dynasty, different shades of red were used on the official caps to show different ranking. Even nowadays, headlines of the official documents are still printed in red. This is why they are call "red head documents".

A: Red is also a highly-regarded color among ordinary people.

B: Yes, because it represents happiness. For example, the word "double happiness" used for weddings is red. The bride wears red clothes, which is different from the white gowns of the West. During Chinese Spring Festival, people will give *hong bao*, or red envelopes with money inside to the children as well wishes. Couplets hanging on both sides of the doors are written in red. Even the outfit of Zhong Kui, the door god whose portrait is hung on the door, is red. The word red equals prettiness. The expression *hong yan*, meaning "red color", is a **synonym** of a beautiful girl. Red is also one of the most popular words used in the names of Chinese women.

A: You've talked a lot about how people like the red color. In traffic lights, as well as in soccer, red means stop or elimination.

B: This is how the Westerners like to use the red color. Because red is very bright, it is good for warning purposes. But it doesn't really have any negative meanings. In China, the red color was **abused** during the "cultural revolution" in the 1960s. The country was **overwhelmed** with red flags, posters, arm bands, and Mao's badges, etc. and was therefore called a "red sea".

A: Ironically, although there was a **worship** of red, no one dared to wear red clothes. Everyone was in either blue or grey uniforms. That's why Westerners referred to the Chinese as "blue ants" at that time.

B: I guess red clothes were somehow associated with the meaning of beauty in the red color. During those special years, beauty was considered bourgeois. So anyone who dared to wear red would be drowned in the "red sea".

对 话

A: 中国人也酷爱红色。据说古代中国有"赤县神州"之称，中国人自称"赤子"，赤就是红色。

B: 红色在传统上就是祖国和权力的象征。唐朝的官服是红色的；清朝官员帽子顶戴的颜色是不同色调的红，以此区别官阶的大小。直到现在，公文的标题还是选用红色，称作"红头文件"。

A: 中国民间对红色也很推崇。

B: 对，红是喜庆的象征。比如结婚时的双喜字是红色的，新娘要穿红色的嫁衣，这与西方穿白色婚纱不同。年节时，送晚辈压岁钱要用红纸包了，称"红包"，以示吉祥；对联也是用红纸书写，贴在大门两侧；年画中的门神钟馗也穿大红官袍。红还与美丽同义，"红颜"指美丽的女子。在中国女性的名字中，"红"是使用频率最高的字之一。

A: 你讲了红色诸多的正面因素，但是在交通标志中，红灯是停止的意思；在足球场上，红牌是罚下场的表示。

B: 这是西方人对红色的运用，因为它醒目，有警示的作用，但不能算作负面意思。中国人有过滥用红色的时候，那就是 20 世纪 60 年代的"文化大革命"。到处是红色的旗帜、标语、袖标、像章。当时的中国被称为"红海洋"。

A: 奇怪的是，在那个尚红的年代，却没有人敢穿红色的衣服。当时的人们不分男女都穿着蓝色或灰色的制服，西方人称之为"蓝蚂蚁"。

B: 红衣服大概与红色所代表的美丽之意相关。在那特殊的年代里，美丽是资产阶级的代名词，穿了红衣服，必定会被"红海洋"所席卷、淹没，谁还敢尝试呢?

Tang Tri-color（2） 唐三彩（二）

Most of the tri-color human figures are female. They range in size from a dozen centimeters to over one meter tall, and wear gorgeous, fashionable costumes whilst emanating grace and refinement. Their full figure and round face are in conformity with the criteria of beauty in the Tang Dynasty. Human figures also include depictions of Hu people (a general term for people of non-Han origin), which make them a unique feature of the Tang Dynasty.

Of the animal figures, horses and camels account for the greatest number. The Tang Empire was won on horseback, so the Tang people had a special affection for horses. No artisans of any other dynasty were so skillful in their vivid representations of horses. Such works are consequently admired and avidly collected by people all over the world. In 1989, for instance, a Tang Tri-color horse (known as number 56) sold for 3. 4 million pounds at a Sotheby's auction in London. A simple standing figure could be imbued with a distinctive and irresistible charm by Tang Tri-Color artisans.

The camel was also an important means of transportation on the Silk Road during the Tang Dynasty, over 1,300 years ago. Many camel figurines of the Tang are described in a walking position, or with their heads held high, as if whinnying.

三彩人物俑中女性占多数，这些俑人大小不一，从十几厘米到一米多的都有。她们身着华美的服饰，形态端庄大方，形体和面部都十分丰满，这是唐代偶像的风格。人物俑中还有众多的胡人俑（唐代对非汉族人的通称），从而成为盛唐独一无二的特征。

动物俑以马和骆驼形象为最多。唐人爱马，因唐朝的天下得自马上。在生动地刻画马这方面，其它朝代的艺术家无一能与唐代艺术家相比，因此，唐代有关马的艺术品受到世界各国收藏者的喜爱。1989 年，苏富比拍卖行在伦敦举行的拍卖会上，一尊编号为 56 的唐三彩马以 340 万英镑成交。唐三彩的艺人们可以将独特而令人难以抗拒的美妙注入一个简单的站立塑像中。

骆驼是一千三百多年前，唐代丝绸之路上的重要交通工具。唐人塑造的骆驼有许多呈现昂首嘶鸣状，或勇往直前的姿态。

---

synonym 代名词，同义词   abuse 滥用   overwhelm 淹没，压倒   worship 崇拜

 **Exercises　练习**

Answer these questions.

1. What did the color red represent in the past?

2. How do ordinary people use the red color?

3. How was the red color abused during the "cultural revolution"?

Translate these sentences into Chinese.

1. Traditionally, red represents the motherland and authority.

2. Different shades of red were used to show different ranking.

3. Red is also a highly-regarded color among ordinary people.

4. The bride wears red clothes.

5. Because red is very bright, it is good for warning purposes.

6. The red color was abused during the "cultural revolution" in the 1960s.

7. Everyone was in either blue or grey uniforms.

Complete this paragraph with suitable words.

Red ___1___ happiness. For example, the word "double happiness" ___2___ for weddings is red. The bride wears red clothes, which is different ___3___ the white gowns of the West. ___4___ Chinese Spring Festival, people will give *hong bao*, or red packets with money ___5___ to the children as well wishes. Couplets hanging on ___6___ sides of the doors are ___7___ in red. Even the outfit of Zhong Kui, the door god ___8___ portrait is hang on the door, is red.

 **Answers　答案**

Translate these sentences into Chinese.

1. 红色在传统上就是祖国和权力的象征。

2. 不同色调的红表示不同的官阶。

3. 民间对红色也很推崇。

4. 新娘身穿红色的嫁衣。

5. 红色很醒目，有警示作用。

6. 在 20 世纪 60 年代的"文化大革命"期间，红色曾被滥用。

7. 人们都穿着蓝色或灰色的制服。

Complete this paragraph with suitable words.

1. represents　2. used　3. from　4. During　5. inside　6. both　7. written　8. whose

13. The Importance of Chopsticks

筷子的重要性

Dialogue

A： In the 17th century, when a British businessman heard that there were 100 million people in China, he was determined to go there and sell spoons. He thought, **even if** a spoon would only sell for one penny, he would still make 100 million pennies, but he didn't succeed. The Chinese people used chopsticks, not spoons.

B： Some people did some research on the origin of China's chopsticks compared to the knife and fork of the West. One theory is that China was an agricultural society and **relied on** vegetables for food. Chopsticks were very convenient tools for eating. The Westerners, on the other hand, were nomads and lived on meat. The knife and fork were more practical. Others believe that China did not have much industry and, therefore, people used chopsticks. The West was an industrial society, so their eating **utensils** were made of metal.

A： Sounds interesting! When I first learnt that the Chinese use **a pair of** sticks to eat with, I was curious how they would drink soup. Just like the Indians who use their fingers to eat, do they also use their fingers to drink soup?

B： Whatever the reasons why the Chinese use chopsticks and Westerners use a knife and fork, it is the result of their respective cultures. Chinese culture is developed around collectivism which stresses communion and harmony. Western culture emphasizes individualism. **In terms of** eating customs, chopsticks and knives and forks are two disparate expressions of this cultural difference. The Chinese like to have communal meals where everybody eats out of the same bowl of food. Chopsticks were used in order to discourage people from eating more than others. This was not only a good way to preserve collectiveness, but also to limit individualism. It is more straightforward in the West. People eat their meals **on their own** and there is no restriction on how to eat.

A： That's sounds quite reasonable.

B： **In addition**, **table manners** are very strict during a Chinese meal. Respect has to be given to the elderly. Each time a dish is served, everyone has to wait until the elder person starts or, "to cut the ribbon," as it is now called. The Westerners will simply say, "Help yourself," to start. The food is brought to the table all at the same time so everybody is on the same starting line. This lacks the warm atmosphere which prevails at a Chinese dinner.

A： This may be the reason why it is always very noisy at a Chinese dinner but quiet in a Western restaurant.

对 话

A： 17世纪的时候，一个英国商人得知中国有一亿人口时，就想把他的勺子卖到中国来。他的算盘是：一亿中国人一人一只，就算一把勺子只卖一个便士，也能大赚一亿个便士。但是他没有成功，因为中国人用筷子而不是勺子。

B： 说到中国的筷子和西方的刀叉，学者们对此还做过一些追根溯源的研究。有人认为，中国是农耕民族，食物以植物为主，用筷子适宜取食。而西方人是游牧民族，以肉食为主，刀叉就来得更方便。也有人认为中国是农业社会，工业发展晚，木筷正是这种情形的产物。而西方是工业化社会，金属制品做餐具是其必然。

A： 听起来很有趣。不过最初知道中国人用两根棍子吃饭时，我感兴趣的是他们怎么喝汤。就像印度人用手抓饭，他们也用手抓汤来喝吗？

B： 无论如何，中国人用筷子、西方人用刀叉是特定文化的产物。中国文化推崇集体主义，崇尚共有、融合；西方文化崇尚个体。体现在吃饭的方式上就是筷子和刀叉的不同。中国人实行合餐制，用餐的人在同一个盘中取食，用筷子可以限制个别人大量取食。如此一来，既保留了集体主义的形态，个人利益又不会受太大影响。西方人就简单一些，每个人吃自己盘里的食物，吃法也没有什么严格限制。

A： 你这种分析有些道理。

B： 不仅如此，中餐还有严格的餐桌礼仪。长辈要受到尊重。一盘菜上来，大家要先让长者举筷，这被称作"剪彩"。不像西方人，只一句"祝你好胃口"就自顾自吃了起来。西餐中每个人点的菜都同时端上，大家在同一时间开始用餐，缺少了中国人相互礼让的过程，友好的气氛就差了许多。

A： 这也许就是中国人吃饭热热闹闹，西方人的餐桌相对安静的原因吧。

Background Reading 背景阅读

Taboo of the Chopsticks 使用的筷子的禁忌

In ancient China, chopsticks signified far more than tools that take food to the mouth; they also signified status and rules, "can" and "can't." During the Northern Song Dynasty, an official named Tang Su once had dinner with the emperor. He was not well informed in noble table etiquette and so laid down his chopsticks horizontally on the table before the emperor did. As a result, he was expatriated to a frontier area for penal servitude.

In ancient eating etiquette, there were over a dozen taboos concerning chopsticks. For example, they could not be placed vertically into a dish, as this was the way of making sacrifices to the dead. Diners could not tap or push a dish with chopsticks, nor use a chopstick as a fork by poking it into a piece of food. When taking food, they could not go from one dish to another or let their chopsticks cross over those of others. When diners wanted to put down their chopsticks during a meal, they would place them lengthways on a chopstick holder, or on the plate, or spoon on their right hand side. Many of these chopstick taboos are valid to this day and accepted as a norm in today's table etiquette.

在古代中国，筷子不仅仅是把食物送到口中的餐具，它被赋予了重要的内涵和"能"与"不能"的规矩。北宋朝时，一个叫唐肃的官员陪皇帝进膳。他不了解用餐时使用筷子的礼制，在皇帝还没有吃完时，他就把筷子横放在桌子上，表示他不想再吃了。结果这位官员被发配边疆。

在古代的饮食礼仪中，筷子使用方法的禁忌有十多种。比如，忌将筷子竖直插入菜盘或饭碗中，因为这代表为死人上坟。在餐桌上不要用筷子敲打或推动盘碗，也不要把筷子当叉使用。在夹菜时，不可从一个盘子到另一个盘子拿不定主意地移动，或者在盘子上把自己的筷子与别人的筷子相交叉。在用餐过程中，筷子暂时不用应竖直搁在专用的筷子架或食碟上，筷子和调羹一般应放在右侧。许多用筷的禁忌如今已变成人们普遍认同的习俗，大多沿用至今。

---

even if 即使	rely on 依靠	utensils 餐具（尤其指刀叉）
a pair of 一副，两个	in terms of 就…而言	preserve 保持，维护
on their own 自己，独自	in addition 除此之外	table manners 餐桌上的规矩

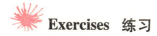 **Exercises** 练习

Answer these questions.

1. What did the 17th century British businessman want to do?
2. Why do Chinese people use chopsticks to eat?
3. What are the table manners at a Chinese meal?

Translate these sentences into Chinese.

1. He was determined to sell spoons to China.
2. The Chinese people used chopsticks, not spoons.
3. Chopsticks were very convenient tools for eating.
4. China did not have much industry and, therefore, people used chopsticks.
5. I was curious how they would drink soup.
6. It is more straightforward in the West.
7. Table manners are very strict during a Chinese meal.
8. Everybody is on the same starting line.
9. A Western meal lacks the warm atmosphere which prevails at a Chinese dinner.
10. This may be the reason why it is always very noisy at a Chinese dinner.

Complete this paragraph with suitable words.

In __1__ , respect has to be given to the elderly. Table manners are very __2__ during a Chinese meal. Each time a __3__ is served, everyone __4__ to wait until the elder person starts or, "to __5__ the ribbon," as it is now called. The Westerners will __6__ say "Help yourself" to start. The food is brought to the table all __7__ the same time so everybody is on the same __8__ line. This lacks the warm atmosphere which prevails at a Chinese dinner.

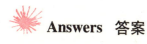 **Answers** 答案

Translate these sentences into Chinese.
1. 他决心要把他的勺子卖到中国来。
2. 中国人用筷子而不是勺子。
3. 用筷子吃饭很方便。
4. 那时中国没什么工业，因此人们用筷子。
5. 我感兴趣的是他们怎么喝汤。
6. 西方人就简单多了。
7. 中餐有严格的餐桌礼仪。
8. 大家在同一时间开始。
9. 西餐缺少了吃中餐时的热闹气氛。
10. 这也许就是中国人吃饭热热闹闹的原因。

Complete this paragraph with suitable words.
1. addition   2. strict   3. dish   4. has   5. cut   6. simply   7. at   8. starting

14. The Elegance of Tea-Drinking

茶的格调

Dialogue

A: In classical novels, if someone drinks tea out of a big cup to quench his thirst, the word used to **illustrate** this action is "drink", like a cow drinking water. Scholars would use fine cups to drink tea and the word to use is "savour".

B: Tea drinking is a very sophisticated **pastime**. It starts with the environment. In the past, tea drinking should take place in a **setting** where "spring water runs on marbles" or "in a monastery in misty spring" or "in the woods during **sunset**." Nowadays, in order to **recreate** such an ambience, tea houses are always decorated with traditional paintings, calligraphy and furniture, with a girl in traditional costume playing the *gu zheng*, a traditional Chinese musical instrument.

A: How about the tea sets?

B: In the old days, people used iron kettles to boil water. Tea was placed in a paper bag. Porcelain cups were used for drinking. The water came from melted snow which was collected from plum blossom trees the **previous** winter and stored underground in a jar. Today people use different tea sets but the most popular ones are the pots made in Yixing. No one collects snow any more because of pollution so people use **bottled water** instead.

A: Is there any difference in the tea?

B: Tea has categories: red tea, green tea, Wulong tea and Pu'er tea. The first three types of tea are processed using similar methods but Pu'er tea uses a totally different method. It **contains** a kind of fungus which is believed to be healthy. The fungus will ferment on its own after the tea is processed. This is why expensive Pu'er tea is always quite old.

54

A： Is tea drinking very expensive?

B： Yes, it is a commercialized hobby now. This is different from the way ancient scholars enjoyed themselves, by savouring tea among bamboos or in the moonlight. People nowadays **talk business** in expensively-decorated tea houses. Ordinary people go to the inexpensive tea houses where they can play games or simply chat with friends. It's more personal. Although such tea houses may not look elegant, they certainly have a relaxed atmosphere and are good fun.

A： Different tea houses can meet different needs and, you are right, people's taste preferences are not always swayed by money.

对 话

A： 在古典小说中，某人用大杯喝茶解渴被称为"饮"，指此人像牛般饮水；而雅士用精致的茶具喝茶被称为"品"。

B： 饮茶是一种很讲究格调的消遣。首先是环境，在古时，饮茶要在有"石上清泉"、"春烟寺院"或"夕照林间"这样的环境中。今天的店家们就设法把茶馆用字画和古典家具装饰起来，再安置个穿古装、弹古筝的女子，营造出一个雅致的情景。

A： 茶具怎么样呢？

B： 古人用铁壶烧水，用纸袋装茶，用瓷杯饮茶。泡茶的水是前一年冬天从梅花树上收集起来、装在瓷坛中埋入地下的雪水。现在的茶具五花八门，但最受宠的要算宜兴的陶器。因为污染，没有人再收集雪水泡茶，取而代之的是瓶装矿泉水。

A： 茶有什么不同吗？

B： 茶大概分为这样几种：红茶、绿茶、乌龙茶和普洱茶。前三种茶的制作方法是一样的，普洱茶的制作方法则不同。普洱茶本身含有一种有益的霉菌，在制成后会随着时间而自然发酵。这也是普洱茶年头越长越值钱的原因。

A： 这样一来，喝茶的花费一定不少吧？

B： 对，格调被商业化了。古人在竹间月下品茶论道，如今，人们在装修豪华的茶馆中谈生意，这真是大异其趣。平民百姓常常光顾小茶馆，打牌、闲谈，不多的茶钱，更多的人情味。格调当然谈不上，气氛却是轻松随意，多了几分趣味。

A： 不同的茶馆适合不同的人。格调其实不是金钱决定的。

Background Reading 背景阅读

A Civilized Pleasure 享受之文明

Observers have long lauded the Chinese custom of drinking boiled water on its own. Alan Macfarlane (the author of the book *Green Gold: the Empire of Tea*, and a professor of social anthropology at Cambridge University) believes this custom arose as a kind of poor man's tea. He credits the sterilizing and civilizing effects of tea with a major role in animating the cultural and economic vigor of epochs as disparate as China's Tang dynasty and Britain's Industrial Revolution.

In Macfarlane's mind, tea is the ultimate drink—a mild stimulant that is cheap and easy to produce. Coffee may be stronger, but it lacks the proven medicinal properties of tea. A glass of beer accelerates mental activity for 20 minutes, but is followed by a depression lasting twice as long.

For Buddhists, preparing and drinking tea is one of four ways of concentrating the mind, alongside meditating, walking and feeding fish. For workers in the satanic mills of 19th-century Britain, the afternoon tea break was the single beacon of relief in a long day of monotonous drudgery.

In China, the social ritual of tea drinking spurred porcelain makers to new heights of perfection and refinement. And during the British frenzy for tea in the 19th century, competition between importers produced the most beautiful ships the world has ever seen—the tea clippers.

观察家们一直对中国人饮用开水的习惯予以赞赏。《绿金：茶之帝国》一书的作者、剑桥大学社会人类学教授艾伦·麦克法兰认为这产生于穷人以水代茶的习惯。在他看来，茶所具备的卫生和文明的作用，对于刺激中国唐代和英国工业革命时期的文化和经济有着重要的作用。

在麦克法兰看来，茶是极佳的饮品——带有温和的提神作用，而且廉价、易于生产。咖啡的提神作用也许更强，但它缺少茶中已被公认了的有益成份。一杯啤酒能够使精神兴奋 20 分钟，但随之而来的精神低落期会加倍。

对于佛教徒来说，备茶和饮茶是集中精神的四种方式之一，其它包括冥思、步行和喂鱼。在 19 世纪英国噩梦般的工厂中，下午茶是工人们在每天单调漫长的苦力劳作中唯一的一点儿解脱。

在中国，茶道促使瓷器日臻精致和完美。而在英国对茶极为着迷的 19 世纪，进口商的竞争创造出了世界上前所未有的最漂亮的运茶船。

---

illustrate 描述	pastime 消遣	setting 氛围，环境
sunset 日落，傍晚	recreate 再现	previous 先，前一个
bottled water 瓶装水	contain 包含，包括	talk business 谈生意

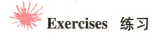 **Exercises 练习**

Answer these questions.

1. What kind of an environment did tea drinking take place in the past?
2. What tea sets were used?
3. Why is it expensive to drink tea nowadays?

Translate these sentences into Chinese.

1. Scholars would use fine cups to drink tea and the word to use is "savour".
2. Tea drinking is a very sophisticated pastime.
3. Tea houses are always decorated with traditional paintings, calligraphy and furniture.
4. In the old days people used iron kettles to boil water.
5. Water came from melted snow collected from plum blossom trees the previous winter.
6. No one collects snow any more because of pollution.
7. The first three types of tea are processed using similar methods.
8. The fungus will ferment on its own after the tea is processed.
9. Ancient scholars enjoyed themselves by savoring tea among bamboos or in the moonlight.
10. People nowadays talk business in expensively decorated tea houses.

Complete this paragraph with suitable words.

Tea drinking is a very __1__ pastime. It starts __2__ the environment. In the past, tea drinking should take __3__ in a setting where "spring water runs __4__ marbles" or, "in a monastery in misty spring" or, "in the woods __5__ sunset." Nowadays, in __6__ to recreate such an ambience, tea houses are always decorated __7__ traditional paintings, calligraphy and furniture, with a girl, __8__ traditional costume, playing the *gu zheng*, a traditional Chinese musical instrument.

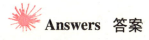 **Answers 答案**

Translate these sentences into Chinese.

1. 雅士用精致的茶具喝茶被称为"品"。
2. 饮茶是一种很讲究格调的消遣。
3. 茶馆往往用字画及古典式家具装饰起来。
4. 古人用铁壶烧水。
5. 水是前一年冬天从梅花树上收集起来的雪水。
6. 因为污染,没有人再收集雪水泡茶。
7. 前三种茶的制作方法是一样的。
8. 在制成后,霉菌会随着时间而自然发酵。
9. 古人在竹间月下品茶论道。
10. 如今,人们在装修豪华的茶馆中谈论生意。

Complete this paragraph with suitable words.

1. sophisticated　2. with　3. place　4. on　5. during　6. order　7. with　8. in

15. Beijing's Identity

北京人的身份

Dialogue

A： Are you a Beijinger?

B： Not really. I was born in Shandong but was raised in Hubei. I came to Beijing when I was ten and have lived here ever since. So **you tell me** if I qualify as a Beijinger.

A： No, you are not a real Beijinger.

B： It's now hard to find a family that has lived in Beijing for more than three generations.

A： Some people say that Beijingers are very generous and open-minded. Do you agree?

B： Generous, maybe. A friend of mine had a small accident once. Her car **got stuck** in a ditch. Four young men, all non-Beijingers, **happened to** pass by, but they refused to help. Then an old man came over. He was a Beijinger. **Without any hesitation**, he helped my friend pull the car out. He also told her to drive carefully.

A： That's a typical Beijinger. Such a person is always ready to help when someone is **in need**.

B： I guess this **has something to do with** the fact that Beijing has been a capital city for several dynasties. People living here always feel obligated by a **sense of honor**. Also, face is very important for a Beijinger. When doing business, especially with a friend, a Beijinger doesn't want to appear too **fussy** about a contract or making concessions. He cares more about friendship and esteem.

A： "Tolerant" may not be the right word to describe a Beijinger. About 20 years ago, Beijing residents usually **looked down upon** non-Beijingers, believing them to be rustic and ignorant.

B： That's true. Beijingers used to look down upon outsiders. In the past, due to strict residential permit requirement, it was extremely difficult to become a Beijing resident. There's more mobility now and anyone can find a job in Beijing. Pick someone in the street and most likely that person is not a real Beijinger. True Beijingers do not have a feeling of superiority and that may be why they appear to be more tolerant nowadays.

A: This is quite similar to New York. There are fewer and fewer real Americans there. Some say New York is no longer a city of Americans. I think the same is true with Beijing.

对 话

A: 你是北京人吗?

B: 严格地说,我不是。我出生在山东,长在湖北,10 岁时到了北京,一直到现在没有离开这里。你说我算不算北京人?

A: 你不是地道的北京人。

B: 事实上,三代均生长在北京的本土北京人真是少而又少。

A: 有人说北京人很大气,也很包容,你认为呢?

B: 的确是大气。我有一个朋友开车不小心掉进一个沟里,这时候有四个外地人模样的小伙子正好路过,但他们拒绝帮忙。过一会儿来了一位老者,一个北京人,他二话没说就帮我的朋友把车推出来,还叮嘱她开车要小心。

A: 北京人就是这样,当别人有麻烦时,他们最乐于帮忙。

B: 我想这也许是因为北京是历代都城,这里的居民总有一种荣誉感。此外,对于北京人来说,面子最重要。做生意时,特别当对方是朋友时,他们不太在乎合同怎么签,或自己是否吃亏,他们在乎的是别伤了和气,让人看不起。

A: 说北京人包容也许并不准确。20 年前,北京居民往往看不起外地人,嫌他们土气和无知。

B: 是这样,北京人那时是瞧不起外地人。当时,由于户籍制度的限制,北京成为可望而不可进的圣地。现在流动性大了,什么人都可以在北京谋到职业。大街上随便找人一问,大多是外地人。北京人少了优越感,这也是人们感觉北京人越来越包容的原因。

A: 这有点儿像纽约,这个城市里真正意义上的美国人越来越少。有人说,纽约已不再是美国人的纽约。也许北京也不再是北京人的北京。

Changing Beijing 变化中的北京

Beijing is undergoing an extraordinary transformation. The city is littered with cranes and construction sites—physical symbols of the nation's growing prosperity. Yet Beijing is also a place of great antiquity and only 60 years ago contained one of the best preserved imperial cities to be found anywhere. The Beijing of today is a sprawling city of 15 million people, stretching out nearly 200 km east to west, and north to south.

But at its heart lies a 62 sq. km. area that was the city in ancient times—a place of distinctive courtyard homes, narrow alleyways called *hutongs*, and temples and parks. But it's valuable land in heart of Beijing today and fast disappearing under the wrecking ball to make way for a more modern city of wide roads and tall buildings. When the PRC was founded in 1949, the new government quickly set about destroying Beijing's encircling city wall. It was necessary, it said, for a modern capital. UNESCO estimates that just in the past 20 years, a third of what was left of the old city has been demolished, including over 1,000 *hutongs* and courtyard homes.

A long-awaited regulation to protect Beijing's historical and cultural heritage is now in effect. The Beijing Regulation for Historical and Cultural City Protection stipulates that the city will protect not only its more than 3,500 listed heritage sites, but also unlisted sites deemed to be of historical or cultural value. The 41-article regulations also guarantee protection for all areas of the 850-year-old capital within the Second Ring Road.

北京正经历着一场不同寻常的变化。国家繁荣发展的外部象征就是这个城市充斥着的吊车和建筑工地。北京是著名的古都，仅仅在60年前，这里还保留着许多古代皇城的遗迹。今天的北京已经成为拥有1 500万人口、到处是拥挤的住宅的城市，它从东到西，从南向北扩展了近200公里。

但是，在城中心62平方公里的地区曾是古代时的城区——这里有独一无二的四合院和被称作胡同的窄巷，还有古塔和公园。但是这块中心区极具价值的区域正在消失，让位于现代化的宽阔道路和高大建筑。1949年建国时，中央政府立即决定推倒城区周边的城墙。据说，这是现代化城市必要的步骤。联合国教科文组织估计，仅仅过去20年，尚存的旧城中的三分之一已经被破坏，包括一千多条胡同以及其中的四合院。

保护北京历史文化遗产的规定终于生效。《北京历史及文化城市保护条例》规定，它不仅要保护3 500个已列入名单的遗迹，同时也要保护具有历史和文化价值的未列入名单的遗迹。条例中41条规定要对二环路以内有850年历史的古都城进行保护。

---

you tell me 那你说…	get stuck 卡住
without any hesitation 不犹豫，二话不说	happen to 碰巧
have something to do with 与…有关	in need 需要时
fussy 小题大做	sense of honor 荣誉感
	look down upon 瞧不起

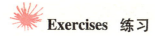 **Exercises** 练习

Answer these questions.

1. What happened to the author's friend?
2. Why are Beijingers always ready to help people?
3. Why did Beijingers look down upon outsiders in the past?

Translate these sentences into Chinese.

1. I was born in Shandong but was raised in Hubei.
2. It's hard to find a family that has lived in Beijing for more than three generations.
3. Four people happened to pass by but they refused to help.
4. Without any hesitation, he helped my friend pull the car out.
5. A typical Beijinger is always ready to help when someone is in need.
6. People living here always feel obligated by a sense of honor.
7. Face is very important for a Beijinger.
8. A Beijinger does not want to appear too fussy about a contract.
9. Beijingers used to look down upon outsiders.
10. Most likely, that person is not a real Beijinger.

Complete this paragraph with suitable words.

Beijingers __1__ to look down __2__ outsiders. In the past, __3__ to strict residential permit requirement, it was __4__ difficult to become a Beijing resident. There is more mobility now and anyone can __5__ a job in Beijing. Pick someone in the street and, __6__ likely, that person is not a real Beijinger. True Beijingers do not have a feeling of __7__ and that may be why they __8__ to be more tolerant nowadays.

 **Answers** 答案

Translate these sentences into Chinese.

1. 我出生在山东，长在湖北。
2. 很难找到三代均生长在北京的家庭了。
3. 四个人正好路过，但他们拒绝帮忙。
4. 他二话没说就帮我的朋友把车推出来。
5. 当别人有麻烦时典型的北京人最乐得帮忙。
6. 住在这儿的人总有一种荣誉感。
7. 对于北京人来说，面子最重要。
8. 北京人不愿意让别人看到他很在乎是否签合同。
9. 北京人曾看不起外地人。
10. 很可能那人不是真正的北京人。

Complete this paragraph with suitable words.

1. used 2. upon 3. due 4. extremely 5. find 6. most 7. superiority 8. appear

16. Trendy Shanghai

时尚的上海

Dialogue

A: Some MNC employees in Shanghai prefer speaking English than Chinese. Many people disapprove of this phenomenon as **a blind worship** of Western culture.

B: I'm not surprised that this could happen in Shanghai. As a port city, Shanghai was heavily influenced by Western culture, beginning in the 1920s and 1930s. It was called "a paradise of the adventurers." A lot of Western companies opened offices there as trade and commerce began to develop. New ideas were brought in, together with the arrival of businessmen and foreigners. Shanghai residents were **overwhelmed** with imported merchandise, foreign languages, and jobs at foreign companies. As a result, Shanghai people are very open-minded and **receptive** to new things.

A: I know many Westerners like Shanghai because of its cosmopolitan atmosphere. Shanghai people are both smart and pragmatic. They are **business-minded** and have a high standard of ethics. For example, you seldom hear people **accuse** Shanghai taxi drivers **of** cheating. If you ask a Shanghai person for directions, he or she will show you the most efficient routes to your destination.

B: Many new things were initially introduced to China through Shanghai. In the 1920s, some Shanghai art schools were the first in the country to use human models. Shanghai was also the first city to have movies. In the late 1970s, Shanghai was again among the first cities to send students to study abroad. Shanghai-made products, such as watches, bicycles, and sewing machines, enjoyed a very favorable reputation throughout the country even during the years of central economic planning. This reputation still benefits Shanghai today.

A: People from other cities always feel that Shanghai people are biased against them.

B: This is indeed very perplexing. A city as open and developed as Shanghai doesn't have the capacity to accommodate others. In the past, an outsider who didn't speak the Shanghai dialect was always ignored by the shop assistants. Now as more and more MNC employees prefer speaking English, will non-English speakers feel disadvantaged?

A： Some people say Shanghai doesn't look like a Chinese city. It is more like New York.

B： People used to make that comment in the 1930s. In many ways, Shanghai does look like New York but it's not New York. It is a Chinese city, **no matter what**.

对 话

A： 在上海的一些跨国公司里，中国职员几乎不说中文而说英文。许多人不认同这种现象，认为是在盲目崇拜西方文化。

B： 这种事情发生在上海是再自然不过的了。作为一个港口城市，上海在上世纪二三十年代就深受西方文化的影响，被称为"冒险家的乐园"。随着商业的发展，大量外国公司在此落户。新的观念也随着商人和洋人的到来而传入。上海人用洋货，讲洋文，在洋行做事。这一切造就了上海人观念开放、敢于尝试新鲜事物的特点。

A： 我知道很多西方人喜欢上海，因为它有现代都市的氛围。上海人精明、务实。他们看重金钱，也重诚信。比如，上海的出租车司机很少欺骗外来客。向上海人问路，他们会告诉你最省钱的乘车路线。

B： 很多的新生事物都是从上海开始的。上世纪 20 年代，这里的美术学校率先使用人体模特；上海也是第一个放电影的城市。上世纪 70 年代末的出国留学热源于上海。在计划经济时期，上海的产品就在全国拥有良好的口碑，包括手表、自行车、缝纫机等。这种信誉一直延续至今。

A： 其他城市的人认为上海人看不起他们。

B： 这个确实令人费解，一个开放很早、发展很快的城市，反而缺少大都市应有的包容。在过去，一个不会讲上海话的外来者会遭到售货员的白眼。在大公司职员们热中于讲英语的今天，不会英文的人是不是会被人看不起呢？

A： 有人说上海不像中国的城市，而像纽约。

B： 这种话在上世纪 30 年代就有人说过。的确，上海在很多方面像纽约，但它不是纽约。它依然是中国的一个都市。

Background Reading 背景阅读

New Bund 新外滩

The New Bund lies along the west bank of the Huangpu River between Waibaidu Bridge and Nanpu Bridge. The four-kilometer-long thoroughfare was listed as one of the top 10 new scenes and tourist attractions in the city in the past decade. Along the Bund, there are buildings of different Chinese and western architectural styles, nicknamed the contemporary world expo of architectures. This cultural heritage of mankind has epitomized the modern history of Shanghai. At night, with lights on, they look just fantastic.

新外滩地处黄浦江西岸的外白渡桥和南浦大桥之间。10 年来，这一约 4 公里长的街景已经成为上海十大旅游新景点之一。这里有中西风格迥异的建筑，因此外滩也被称为现代建筑万国博览会，这些人类文化遗产已经成为新上海的象征。夜幕降临，彩灯初上，这些建筑越显华丽。

Shanghai Xintiandi 上海新天地

An old city block, featuring the city's unique stone-framed-gate residential buildings, has been renovated and turned into a catering, commercial, entertainment, cultural and leisure center and one of the top tourist attractions in downtown Shanghai. It's a successful combination of the old and new, east and west, the traditional and the trendy. It is mow frequented by overseas tourists and local visitors.

这里原本是一片石库门建筑旧区，现已改造为上海市中心以餐饮、商业、娱乐、文化和消遣为特色的新景点，成功地融合了新与旧、中与西、传统与现代的特点，是中外游客的必到之处。

Jin Mao Tower 金茂大厦

As the tallest building in China and the third tallest building in the world, Jin Mao Tower is located in the Lujiazui Finance and Trade Zone in Pudong. It is an intelligent building offering service for business, hotel, recreation, sightseeing and shopping. Jin Mao Tower is not only a new tourist attraction, but also a window through which people from other parts of the world may get a better understanding of Shanghai and Pudong.

金茂大厦是中国最高，世界第三高的建筑，位于浦东陆家嘴金融贸易区，是一座集商务、酒店、娱乐、观光和购物的智能型大厦，金茂大厦不仅是一个新的旅游景点，同时也是世界各地的人们了解上海，了解浦东的一个窗口。

a blind worship 盲目崇拜	overwhelmed 招架不住，不知所措
receptive 接受能力强的	business-minded 很强的经济头脑
accuse... of 指责…	no matter what 不管怎样，无论如何

 **Exercises** 练习

Answer these questions.

1. Why do people disapprove of Shanghai, MNC employees, speaking English?
2. Why do many Westerners like Shanghai?
3. Does Shanghai look like New York?

Translate these sentences into Chinese.

1. Many people disapprove of this phenomenon as a blind worship of Western culture.
2. Shanghai was heavily influenced by Western culture beginning in the 1920s and 1930s.
3. New ideas were brought in, together with the arrival of businessmen and foreigners.
4. Shanghai people are very open-minded and receptive to new things.
5. You seldom hear people accuse Shanghai taxi drivers of cheating.
6. He or she will show you the most efficient routes to your destination.
7. Many new things were initially introduced to China through Shanghai.
8. This is indeed very perplexing.
9. Will non-English speakers feel disadvantaged?
10. Shanghai does look like New York in many ways.

Complete this paragraph with suitable words.

Many Westerners like Shanghai __1__ of its cosmopolitan __2__ . Shanghai people are __3__ smart and pragmatic. They are business-minded and have a __4__ standard of ethics. For example, you __5__ hear people __6__ Shanghai taxi drivers __7__ cheating. If you ask a Shanghai person __8__ directions he, or she, will show you the most efficient routes to your destination.

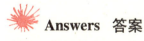 **Answers** 答案

Translate these sentences into Chinese.

1. 许多人不认同这种现象,认为是在盲目崇拜西方文化。
2. 二十世纪二三十年代,上海就深受西方文化的影响。
3. 新的观念也随着商人和洋人的到来而传入。
4. 上海人观念开放、敢于尝试新鲜事物。
5. 很少有人指责上海的出租车司机欺骗外来客。
6. 他们会告诉你最省钱的乘车路线。
7. 很多的新生事物都是从上海开始的。
8. 这确实令人费解。
9. 不会英文的人是不是会被人看不起呢?
10. 上海在许多方面像纽约。

Complete this paragraph with suitable words.

1. because   2. atmosphere   3. both   4. high   5. seldom   6. accuse   7. of   8. for

17. Happy-Go-Lucky Chengdu

幸福的成都

Dialogue

A： People like to call Beijing a political city because it's the capital and there are lots of bureaucrats. Even taxi drivers talk politics. Shanghai, on the other hand, is viewed as a city of fashions. Ever since the 1930s, when Shanghai was under Western rule, it has always been **at the forefront of** fashion. Guangdong is the center of the economy where business has **priority**. As the saying goes "whether a cat is black or white, it is a good cat as long as it catches mice." Chengdu is a happy-go-lucky city. Do you know anything about Chengdu?

B： Chengdu is a major city in Sichuan Province. The temperature is mild and the land is very productive; in fact so fertile that even a stick will grow. The favorable environment has **given rise to** a very easy and relaxed lifestyle. According to a 2005 survey, people's **expectation** for a monthly salary is 3,000 yuan. They believe that amount of money is enough to lead a happy life in Chengdu. Many Chengdu people drive a small, fuel efficient car called Auto. The car didn't sell well in Beijing because Beijingers thought it was too shabby. In fact, Autos were not even allowed on Beijing's Chang'an Avenue for some time.

A： Chengdu is also known for its teahouses.

B： Yes. There are teahouses everywhere. Unlike some other big cities, where teahouses are graded to serve different customers, teahouses in Chengdu offer a whole range of products. Everyone, be it a businessman, a migrant worker, or a student, can find something they want. People can spend a day in the teahouse, either to talk business or simply relax.

A： Are there any other interesting games there?

B： Mahjong is a popular game among teahouse goers in Chengdu. There was a joke on the Internet that says: as soon as a plane enters the Chengdu **airspace**, passengers can hear the sound of mahjong shuffling. Chengdu is also known for its **snacks**. There are plenty of culinary and entertainment outlets. You don't always find the kind of **restlessness** in Chengdu as in other cities but this doesn't mean Chengdu people have closed minds. On the contrary, they are very open-minded.

A: It's good for a person to be happy and forget about fame and wealth but we still have to worry about social progress. Right?

B: In fact, Chengdu has made great progress. It ranked fourth in terms of economic growth in 2005, after Beijing, Shanghai and Guangzhou. During the National Day golden week holidays, Chengdu ranked eighth of the top ten most popular tourist **destinations**.

A: This reminds me of a Chinese saying, "a lucky person doesn't have to chase luck".

对 话

A: 人们都说北京是政治之城,这里是首都,政府工作人员多,出租车司机都能大谈政治;上海是时尚之城,在 20 世纪 30 年代就是十里洋场,一直引领着中国的时尚;广东是经济之城,崇尚"不论黑猫白猫,捉住耗子就是好猫",以赚钱为重;成都是幸福之城,你如何理解这个城市?

B: 成都是四川省的一个大城市。这里气候温润,物产丰富。人们说这里插只木棍都能发芽。这种得天独厚的自然环境使得人们谋生比较容易,生活因此而安逸、轻松。2005 年的一个调查表明,成都人对月收入的期望值是 3000 元,他们认为达到这个数字就会感到幸福。成都街头跑得最多的汽车可能是奥拓,它小巧、省油。北京人却不能接受这种款型的车,觉得它不够体面。有一段时间这种车型甚至不能上长安街行驶。

A: 成都的茶馆也很有名。

B: 是的,可以说处处有茶馆。其他大城市的茶馆等级分明,而成都的茶馆里价格有高有低,打工仔、学生、商人都可同处一馆。人们可以在茶馆里泡一天,或谈生意或休闲。

A: 茶馆里有什么好玩的吗?

B: 打麻将是成都茶馆里的一景。网上有一个笑话:飞机飞到成都时,可以听到下边"哗哗"搓麻的声音。此外,成都小吃也很有名,餐饮娱乐随处可见。成都人少有其他城市人的浮躁,但他们并不保守,观念非常开放。

A: 一个人活着不为升官发财,而是图一份好心情,这也挺好。但是社会如何进步呢?

B: 成都的进步是有目共睹的。论经济发达程度,在 2005 年成都已经成为继北京、上海、广州之后的第四城。在当年的黄金周,成都名列全国人气最旺的"十佳旅游城市"的第八位。

A: 这应了中国的一句老话"有福之人不用忙。"

Background Reading 背景阅读

Backpacking in China 中国的背包旅游一族

Technically, they should be called friends of backpackers, but pronounced in Chinese, the name of this popular group of outdoor enthusiasts means "friends of donkey".

No one knows the exact origins of the backpacker phenomenon, yet tens of thousands of people have joined in this eco-centric activity. Backpackers in China are not necessarily young or affluent; many are impoverished students budgeting their travels very carefully, some are middle-aged parents or senior citizens. They go hiking in remote places for months, tour suburban sights on weekends, and are always ready to discover new paths and surprises on their journeys.

Escaping concrete and steel-heavy city vistas, these adventurers embrace individualism and self-reliance, but are welcoming and helpful to their fellow travelers. What began as a small group of like-minded people has spilled onto the Internet, where large communities, clubs and organizations have formed.

专业上他们被称作"旅友",但人们借用中文的谐音,给这群充满朝气的背包旅行者取了一个更为可爱的头衔——"驴友"。

现在要给中国的背包旅行现象找一个确切的渊源,恐怕不是件太容易的事,不过这种生态自助型的新旅游方式,业已吸引了成千上万的爱好者。而想要成为"驴友",你不一定要年轻力强,也不一定要囊中富足。"驴友"们很多不过是口袋空空的学生,每一次旅途都需要精打细算,而另一些人则可能已到了中老年。有的人徒步到"海角天边"泡上好几个月,有的在周末来一次远足。在路线上,他们基本上有着共同的嗜好——探索未知!

离开了钢筋混凝土建构的"怪兽"城市,他们通过旅行追寻着自立自强的精神,也在旅行中相互关爱。最初,一小群志同道合者在因特网上汇集,一些更大规模的网上社区、俱乐部和组织也随之建立起来。

---

at the forefront of 在…前沿	priority 优先权	give rise to 引发,导致
expectation 期望值	airspace 空域,领空	snacks 小吃
restlessness 浮躁,焦虑不安	destinations 目的地	

 **Exercises 练习**

Answer these questions.
1. Why is Chengdu a happy-go-lucky city?
2. What do people do at teahouses in Chengdu?
3. Why do people in Chengdu like to drive an Auto?

Translate these sentences into Chinese.
1. Even taxi drivers talk politics.
2. It has always been at the forefront of fashion since the 1930s.
3. The favorable environment has given rise to a very easy and relaxed lifestyle.
4. Autos were not even allowed on Beijing's Changan Avenue for some time.
5. People can spend a day in the teahouse, either to talk business or simply relax.
6. Mahjong is a popular game among teahouse goers in Chengdu.
7. Passengers can hear the sound of mahjong shuffling.
8. Chengdu is also known for its snacks.
9. You don't always find the kind of restlessness in Chengdu as in other cities.
10. Chengdu ranked the eighth of the top ten most popular tourist destinations.

Complete this paragraph with suitable words.
Chengdu is a __1__ city in Sichuan Province. The temperature is __2__ and the land is productive. The land is so __3__ that even a stick will grow. The favorable environment has given __4__ to a very easy and relaxed __5__ . According to a 2005 __6__ , people's expectation for a __7__ salary is 3,000 yuan. They believe that amount of money is __8__ to lead a happy life in Chengdu.

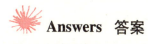 **Answers 答案**

Translate these sentences into Chinese.
1. 连出租车司机都能大谈政治。
2. 自 20 世纪 30 年代以来上海就一直引领着中国的时尚。
3. 这种得天独厚的自然环境使人们生活得安逸、轻松。
4. 有一段时间，奥拓车甚至不能上长安街行驶。
5. 人们可以在茶馆里泡一天，或谈生意或休闲。
6. 打麻将是成都茶馆里最受欢迎的娱乐项目。
7. 人们可以听到下边"哗哗"搓麻的声音。
8. 成都小吃很有名。
9. 成都人少有其他城市人的浮躁。
10. 成都名列全国人气最旺的"十佳旅游城市"的第八位。

Complete this paragraph with suitable words.
1. major 2. mild 3. fertile 4. rise 5. lifestyle 6. survey 7. monthly 8. enough

18. Chinese Beauty

中国美女

Dialogue

A: I heard there were four beautiful women in Chinese history, Xi Shi, Wang Zhaojun, Diao Chan and Yang Yuhuan. Were they really so beautiful?

B: None of the 1,000 to 2,000 year old portraits of these four women are reliable because there are no photographs to verify their accuracy. These four women are known not just for their pretty looks but also because each of them played **a critical role** during their times.

A: That's amazing! What did these beautiful women do?

B: Both Diao Chan and Xi Shi gave their lives for the removal of some tyrants in the Imperial Court. Wang Zhaojun offered to marry a man from a far away tribe **for the sake of** peace and harmony amongst people of different ethnic backgrounds. Yang Yuhuan was a concubine who hanged herself during a mutiny, for the benefit of the overall situation. So these women are remembered not just for their good looks, but also for their intelligence, bravery and dedication.

A: Is there any change in people's perception of a beautiful woman today?

B: I heard that the Chinese Film Academy likes to recruit female students in Qingdao and Harbin. Girls from these places are pretty, with round and sexy body curves. Gong Li is a typical example. She is regarded as beautiful both in China and in the West. Traditionally, Hangzhou is known for its pretty women. Hangzhou is situated in the **picturesque** southern China. Women there are cute and elegant. Film actress Zhou Xun is an example. She is good at acting as a traditional girl who is restricted by established values but who is ready to die for love.

A: Which of the above categories does the international star Zhang Ziyi fit in?

B: Zhang Ziyi is from Beijing, so she is **unrelated** to any of the above. She rose to stardom through hard work rather than God's blessing. Initially, Americans thought she was sexy and beautiful, but many Chinese did not agree because she did not meet any of the traditional criteria. Subsequently some patriots **accused** these people as being jealous. They said that China does not have many people who have earned international recognition. Zhang Ziyi is one of a few that has and, therefore, it is unpatriotic not to accept her.

A： This is quite like the four beautiful women in Chinese history. As soon as their looks were linked to national interest, they were accepted by all as beautiful.

对 话

A： 我知道中国历史上有四大美女：西施、王昭君、貂婵和杨玉环。她们真的有无比的美貌吗？

B： 古代绘画对这四位活在一二千年前的美女的描绘是不可靠的，因为当时没有照相术。事实上，这四位美女能流芳百世并不仅仅因为容貌美丽，更多是因为她们在历史上起过非同一般的作用。

A： 有意思！这些漂亮女人都干了什么？

B： 貂婵和西施为铲除朝廷中的奸臣而献身；王昭君为了边境安宁及汉族与其他民族的和睦关系而远嫁异族；杨玉环身为皇帝的妃子，在叛乱中为保全大局而自缢身亡。正是她们的聪明机智和侠肝义胆，才使她们的美貌有了依附而得以传世。

A： 今天中国人对美女的观念有什么变化吗？

B： 据说中国的电影学院偏好到青岛和哈尔滨招收表演系的女生，因为这两个地方的女孩子容貌端正，身形健硕。巩俐算得上是代表人物，她在中外都获得美女之名。杭州出美女也是传统的说法。杭州地处中国南方，山灵水秀，这里的女子以玲珑温婉著名，代表人物是周迅。她长于饰演传统礼教束缚下随时准备为爱殉情的古典女子。

A： 现在最有国际名声的章子怡算哪路美女呢？

B： 北京美女。她可以说在各方面都与上面提到的中国典型美女不搭边。她的星途不得自然天成却得自身努力。美国人奉她为性感美女。很多中国人不买账，因为她不合传统的审美标准。结果被一众国人骂作嫉妒。有人说很少有中国人享有如此的国际名声，而章子怡深得洋人推崇，骂她实在不是爱国之举。

A： 事情说到这一步，就有点儿像古代的四大美女。美貌一旦与国家利益相关联，她们必然要成为当代的美女典范了。

Background Reading 背景阅读

Sexy Woman 性感美女

Beauty is more than what we look like. Some people may define beauty as an actress at the Oscars in her stunning gown, or it could be that action hero on the big screen that takes another person's breath away. In reality, beauty is what appeals to our hearts.

Beauty begins from within. As we often say, beauty is the reflection of one's inner spirit. In a recent study, a spirit full of zest, a passion for life and a healthy dose of self-confidence were ranked as three of the highest qualities that men found "sexy" in a woman. In addition to a woman's physique, half of those surveyed said that a woman's smile was the first thing they noticed. And we'd like to add that a smile is contagious. When you smile at someone, they can't help but smile back at you.

美丽不完全是表面的。有些人可能将美丽定义为在奥斯卡颁奖礼上身着华美礼服的女演员，或者是在大银幕上，令人惊异的动作英雄。事实上，美丽是我们内心的写照。

美丽始于内在。如同我们常说的，美是一个人内心气质的反映。在最近的研究中发现，男人认为最性感女性所应具备的前三个条件是，充满热情的精神状态，对生活的激情和自信的健康状态。除了女性自然的身体条件，被调查者中，一半人表示男人首先注意到的是女人的微笑。而且微笑是可以相互传染的——当你对别人微笑，他们也会禁不住地报你以微笑。

Curves Beat Bones 丰满打败骨感

Thin is no longer in and real women do have curves. "I don't want skeletons on the catwalk," show director Leonor Perez-Pita said. "Clothes look much better on a lovely girl than on a clothes hanger."

As the debate over size zero models rages on, a poll revealed that the majority of people would prefer to see fashions modeled by fuller figured celebrities. According to the survey, Curvy Kelly Brook is the woman they would most like to see on the catwalk; Actress Kate Winslet came second, followed by Charlotte Church and Coleen Mcloughlin. Ultra-skinny Victoria Beckham was bottom of the poll.

骨感不再时髦，真正的女人应该曲线玲珑。"我不想让瘦骨架走台，"时装秀导演列奥纳·佩瑞兹-皮塔说。"衣服穿在一个可爱的姑娘身上比挂在一幅衣架上好看多了"

正当关于"零尺码"瘦模的争论炒得沸沸扬扬之际，一项民意调查显示，大多数人更喜欢看到身材丰满些的名模演绎时装作品。根据调查，曲线玲珑有致的凯莉·布鲁克是最受欢迎的模特；女演员凯特·温斯莱特名列第二，接着是夏洛特·丘奇和科琳·麦克洛林。骨瘦如柴的维多利亚·贝克汉姆位列倒数第一。

---

a critical role 至关重要的作用	for the sake of 为了	picturesque 风景如画的
unrelated 无关，不搭界	accuse 指责	

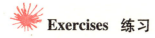 **Exercises** 练习

Answer these questions.
1. Why are the four women considered beautiful?
2. What did Yang Yuhuan do?
3. Why is Gong Li regarded as beautiful both, in China, and in the West?

Translate these sentences into Chinese.
1. None of the portraits are reliable.
2. These four women are known not just for their pretty looks.
3. These women are remembered for their intelligence, bravery and dedication.
4. Girls from these places are handsome, with sexy body curves.
5. She is regarded as beautiful both in China and in the West.
6. A number of people from this area have become popular film stars.
7. They have been recognized as another type of elegance.
8. She rose to stardom through hard work.
9. China does not have many people that have earned international recognition.
10. This is quite like the four beautiful women in Chinese history.

Complete this paragraph with suitable words.
____1____ of the portraits of these four women, of 1,000 to 2,000 years ___2___, are reliable, because there are no photographs to ___3___ their accuaracy. These four women are known, not just ___4___ their pretty looks. Each of them played a ___5___ role during their time. Both Diao Chan and Xi Shi ___6___ their lives for the ___7___ of some tyrants in the Imperial Court. Wang Zhaojun ___8___ to marry a man from a far away tribe for the sake of peace, and harmony, amongst people of different ethnic backgrounds.

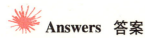 **Answers** 答案

Translate these sentences into Chinese.
1. 这些描绘都不可靠。
2. 这四个女人并不仅仅是因为漂亮而出名。
3. 这些女子以其智慧、勇敢和奉献而被后人纪念。
4. 这些地方出来的女人端庄秀丽，并且有性感的曲线。
5. 无论是在中国，还是西方，人们都认为她漂亮。
6. 这里出来的相当一批人都已经成了电影明星。
7. 人们将其看成是另外一种美。
8. 她是靠着自身的努力而成为明星的。
9. 获国际认可的中国人不多。
10. 这与中国历史上的四个美女差不多。

Complete this paragraph with suitable words.
1. None   2. ago   3. verify   4. for   5. critical   6. gave   7. removal   8. offered

19. Shanghai Men

上海男人

Dialogue

A: "You don't act like a typical man from Shanghai." For a man from Shanghai, such a comment is both a **compliment** and an offense. Usually, he doesn't know how to respond.

B: Why?

A: Because, in northern China, men from Shanghai are usually perceived as "womanly." They are extremely **detail-oriented** and spend too much time doing housework, which, in the eyes of a Northerner, should only be done by women. In other words, Shanghai men have too much respect for women. **In comparison**, men from Northern China are the **hands-off** type. They don't like house chores and they'd feel embarrassed to be subservient to their wives. The worse nickname for a Northern man is *qi guan yan*, meaning henpecked.

B: What kind of a man does a Chinese girl like to marry?

A: It depends. Currently, more women like to marry Shanghai men because they are more understanding, considerate, and helpful. Have you ever seen the film, *What Women Want?* The main character of the movie is Nick Marshall. He was struck by lightning and, as a result, he acquired the extrasensory ability of reading a women's mind. He got a tremendous benefit from this ability both in his career of advertising women's products and in his private life. Understanding women has become a new criterion for an ideal man. There is certainly no need for a Shanghai man to be hit by lightning to become an ideal husband.

B: Is this part of the local culture in Shanghai?

A: Shanghai has been a very open and commercial city for many years, as a result of its longstanding Western influence. People tend to be more practical and chivalrous. You don't find a lot of **male chauvinism** there. Before the 1980s, Shanghai men used to be laughed at for their lack of manly character, but now they have become examples of an ideal husband. For men in the North, especially in Beijing, the reason for their male chauvinism is the bureaucratic environment associated with the Imperial Court. They want to **look important**, even in front of their wives. Of course, I'm only making **a general comment**. Men in the North can also be very tender and considerate. If you run into a man carrying a lady's hand bag next to a woman in a supermarket, most likely he is a Northerner.

B: It's good for men to be chivalrous but I'm not too keen on carrying a woman's handbag. A man is a man **after all**, no matter where he's from.

对 话

A: "你不像典型的上海男人"，对于一个上海男人来说，这个评价像是褒奖，也带些冒犯，常常让他不知所措。

B: 为什么？

A: 因为在北方人眼里，上海男人有点儿"娘娘腔"。他们对小事精于算计，在家里买菜烧饭，干那些在北方男人眼里应该是女人的活儿。而且他们对女人过于迁就。相比较，北方男人都是甩手掌柜，他们以屈从于妻子为耻，不屑于做家务。对北方男人来说，最大的侮辱莫过于给他一顶"妻管严"的帽子。

B: 女孩更愿意嫁给哪种男人呢？

A: 时代不同，选择不同。现在的女孩更愿意嫁给上海男人，他们温存体贴，能够分担家务。你看过梅尔·吉布森主演的电影《男人百分百》吗？他饰演的尼克·马歇尔因为偶遭电击而有了洞悉女人心思的特异功能，并因此在他的女性用品广告事业和家庭生活中受益。了解女人是当代新好男人的必备素质。上海男人无需电击，他们天生就是百分百的理想丈夫。

B: 这来自于上海特定的文化吗？

A: 上海是一个开放很早的商业化城市，深受西方文化的影响。人们讲究实际，尊重女性。大男子主义很少见。在20世纪80年代以前，上海男人这种欠阳刚的形象一直被人嘲弄。今天，上海男人却成为女人心目中的新好男人。北方男人，特别是北京男人的大男子主义，与他们生活其中的天子脚下的官僚氛围有关。男人自以为是，在老婆面前也放不下架子。当然，我这是指一般的情形。北方男人也有体贴细致的一面。你在超市里遇到的背着女式挎包走在女人身旁的男人，十有八九是个北方人。

B: 体贴女人是现代男人应有的素质，但是，给女人背包，我看还是免了罢。无论来自何方，男人总归是男人嘛。

Metrosexuals's Magazine 都市男的杂志

It's almost impossible to find a bottle of men's deodorant in most Chinese cities. Chinese men are not renowned as Metrosexuals. But several publishing houses are banking on their ability to turn local men into sophisticates in shopping, and sex. Publishers of men's magazines have identified Asia as the biggest market of the future, banking on the change in lifestyle and habits of local men.

FHM magazine managed to get a lot racier with a recent cover featuring Hong Kong actress Christy Yung in a see-through negligee. Cover girl for the previous issue was Britney Spears dressed in clingy rubber. FHM China's first cover girl was actress Zhao Wei, featured below the large headline, Zhao Wei, Opium of the Youth. About 30 percent of FHM China's articles are locally produced, the rest being lifted from international editions of the magazine. Recent imported articles have included an illustrated list of 50 extreme sports, pieces on off-road vehicles and orienteering equipment, as well as a special on digital cameras and the results of an FHM sex survey of Britain. Locally written features ranged from a pull-out map of Shanghai parking spaces to a spread on Beijing celebrities' favorite bars. Local fashion shoots and locally produced comic-strip guides for camping and cooking fill a good portion of the magazine.

在中国的绝大多数城市里，要想买到一瓶男用除臭剂都非常困难。中国男人从来不以"都市玉男"著称。但是，一些出版公司正努力让中国男人在购物和展露性魅力方面成熟起来。在寄希望于中国男人改变生活方式和生活习惯的前提下，男性杂志的出版商们已经将亚洲地区确立为最大的目标市场。

不久前，《男人帮》杂志用身着透明睡衣的香港女星钟丽缇的玉照做封面，打算吸引更多读者。还有一期的封面女郎是穿着贴身橡胶衣的布兰妮·斯皮尔斯。中国《男人帮》杂志第一期封面女郎是女明星赵薇，在照片下面用了一个醒目的标题：赵薇，青春鸦片。大约有三成的中国《男人帮》杂志内容来自中国本土，其余由该杂志其它文版的内容编辑而来。最近的外来文章汇聚了50种附带有图片说明的极限运动、越野和赛车装备、数码相机和英国《男人帮》性调查结果。来自中国本土的文章内容涵盖面也相当广泛，既有上海的停车场分布情况介绍，也有名人们时常光顾的北京酒吧活页地图。中国的时尚摄影和作为露营和野炊向导的连环画是该杂志里面颇为吸引读者的部分。

---

compliment 夸奖，恭维	detail-oriented 细心，关注细节
in comparison 相比之下	hands-off 不插手，甩手掌柜
male chauvinism 大男子主义	look important 显得很重要，自以为是
a general comment 泛泛地讲	after all 毕竟

 **Exercises 练习**

Answer these questions.

1. What is Shanghai man like?
2. What is a man from Northern China like?
3. Do women like to marry Shanghai men?

Translate these sentences into Chinese.

1. You don't act like a typical man from Shanghai.
2. They are extremely detail-oriented.
3. In comparison, men from Northern China are the hands-off type.
4. He was struck by lightening.
5. He benefited tremendously from this ability.
6. You don't find a lot of male chauvinism in Shanghai.
7. They want to look important, even in front of their wives.
8. I'm only making a general comment.
9. Most likely the person is a Northerner.
10. A man is a man after all, no matter where he is from.

Complete this paragraph with suitable words.

Shanghai has ___1___ a very open, and commercial, city for a long time. It has been under ___2___ Western influence. People ___3___ to be more practical and chivalrous. You don't ___4___ a lot of ___5___ chauvinism there. Before the 1980s, Shanghai men ___6___ to be laughed ___7___ for their lack of manly character, but now, they have become ___8___ of an ideal husband.

 Answers 答案

Translate these sentences into Chinese.

1. 你不像典型的上海男人。
2. 他们对小事精于算计。
3. 相比之下，北方男人属于甩手掌柜型。
4. 他遭遇了雷击。
5. 他深深受益于这个本领。
6. 在上海很难看到大男子主义。
7. 他们自以为是，在老婆面前也放不下架子。
8. 我这是指一般的情形。
9. 那人十有八九是个北方人。
10. 无论来自何方，男人总归是男人。

Complete this paragraph with suitable words.

1. been   2. tremendous   3. tend   4. find   5. male   6. used   7. at   8. examples

20. Family Relations

家庭关系

Dialogue

A: I heard that one of the **criteria** some girls use when looking for a boyfriend is that the boy doesn't have any parents. Is this correct?

B: It's an **overstatement**, but it certainly reflects the sensitive relationships in a Chinese family. In a traditional household, a man is both a son and an elder brother. There are certain **obligations** that he can never **shun**. Even his marriage is a duty to produce the next generation. The obligations of the wife are less important, as the old saying goes: "Brothers are as indispensable as hands and feet, while the wife is like a coat." Under this influence, a man would have to treat his parents and brothers or sisters with priority even if he was married. If the man happened to be the eldest son, his obligations would be even more important. Such a unique role of the man makes the relationships within a family very complicated. This is why some well-educated young women would rather marry a husband whose parents have **passed away**.

A: An American woman who was teaching in China once asked her students to put themselves in a situation where a man fell into a river together with his mother, wife and son. If the man was only able to save one person, whom would that person be? Some students replied that he should save the mother, out of **gratitude** for her motherhood. Others said that he should save the son because the child represented the future. The American teacher was very unhappy with the answers. "None of you even thought of saving the wife; why?" she asked. The students **fell silent**. She explained, "I think he should save the wife first. The mother is old and has already spent most of her life. The child is too small to feel much pain. The wife has come through a lot with him. After this incident the couple will be bound even closer together, and they can produce another child."

B: Between the Chinese and the Westerners, there are some obvious differences in dealing with family relations. In China, a family is headed by the most senior person, either the grandparents or parents. Children come next, followed by brothers. Husband and wife relations come at the bottom. In the West, the order is husband and wife, children, parents, and brothers and sisters. The husband and wife relationship is the foundation of a family. Under Christianity, a man is required to leave his parents and stay together with his wife. Under Confucianism, the man is required to stay with his parents.

A: The one-child family has freed the man from obligations to his brothers and sisters but he can not escape from duties to his parents. Although it is not the best solution for the girl to choose a husband without any parents, sometimes she doesn't have a better **alternative**.

对 话

A： 据说现在有些女孩择偶的条件之一是男方没有父母，是这样吗？

B： 这是夸张的说法，但它反映了中国家庭关系中的一个侧面。传统的大家庭中，男人作为儿子和兄长，有着难以摆脱的职责。他们娶妻也是为了履行延续后代的责任。对妻子的责任反倒不那么重要了。中国古话说："兄弟如手足，妻子如衣服。"受传统观念的影响，一个已婚男人依然会以其父母和兄弟姐妹为重。如果这个男人是家中的长子，其职责就更大。男人的这种角色定位，使得家庭关系变得复杂起来。这也是有些受过高等教育的女子为什么宁愿嫁一个无父无母的男人的原因。

A： 一位在中国教书的美国女教师给班上的中国学生提了这样一个问题：一个丈夫和他的母亲、太太及儿子一同落入水中，如果只能救一个人，你认为他应当救谁？有人说应当救母亲，这正是报效养育之恩的时候；有人认为救孩子要紧，因为孩子代表着未来。听着大家的发言，女教师不满地责问："你们中间居然没人愿意救自己的太太，为什么？"同学们沉默起来。女教师说："我认为应该先救妻子，因为母亲年事已高，已经走完大部分人生之旅；孩子尚小，不足以感受巨大的痛苦。而妻子与你患难与共，经历了这场灾难，你们会更加亲密无间，并且还可以再生孩子。"

B： 在家庭成员关系的处理上，显然是有中西差异的。在中国，最年长的祖父母或父母在家中占据首位；第二位是子女；然后是兄弟；最后才轮到夫妻。在西方则不同，其家庭关系的排序是：夫妻、儿女、父母、兄弟姐妹，夫妻成为家庭的基础。基督教要求成年男子离开父母，固守妻子；儒教则要求人们固守父母。

A： 独生子女政策使男人少了一重对兄弟姐妹的责任，但是对父母的责任是难以放弃的。年轻的女孩子们选择无父无母的男人作老公，也许是不得已之举。

One Child Much Money 孩子一个，开销不少

As more young people born in the 1980s begin to marry, the formerly widespread belief in *duozi duofu* (more children more happiness) diminishes. To today's urban youth, establishing a career is a far more pressing priority than having children.

Raising children in China today is not cheap, particularly in big cities. The expenses start long before a baby is born. During her nine months of pregnancy, a mother-to-be spends around RMB 5,000 on regular medical check-ups, tests, quality nourishment and clothes. In some cases expenses are as high as RMB 20,000. Each month some families spend around RMB 1,500 on food, baby care, and medical costs.

Putting their children through school is a lesson in economics for many parents. As the cost of study for the 12 years at school from the age of 7 to 19 increases with every grade, not all parents in China can afford well-educated children. Primary education is compulsory, but there are still a high number of drop-outs in poor rural areas. Many parents are convinced that wide interests should be encouraged in an only child. Xu Baoyu, who works at a Beijing scientific research institute, accompanies her seven-year-old daughter Fu Lin to a music school every Saturday. Piano lessons are costly, at around RMB 500 a month, but Xu wants her child to get the best of everything.

当越来越多的生于 20 世纪 80 年代的年轻人开始结婚，从前流行的"多子多福"的观念渐渐消失。对于今天的城市年轻人来说，成就事业远比结婚生子来得急迫。

在当今中国，尤其是在大城市，抚养孩子的费用很昂贵。早在小孩子出生前，费用的支出就开始了。在怀孕的 9 个月里，准妈妈差不多要花去 5 000 元人民币做产前检查、补充营养以及购买服装。有些人甚至要花去 20 000 元人民币。有些家庭每个月花在食品、托儿费和医药费上的钱大约是 1 500 元。

把孩子送进学校，对于许多父母来说好比一堂经济学的课程。从 7 岁到 19 岁这 12 年的学费随着不同年级而增长，不是所有的中国家长都能负担得起孩子接受良好的教育。初级教育是义务的，但是在贫困地区还是有很高的辍学率。许多家长确信广泛的兴趣对孩子是一种激励。每个星期六，就职于北京某科研所的徐宝玉都会陪着她 7 岁的女儿付琳去音乐学校上课。钢琴课的收费很贵，一个月大约要 500 元人民币，但是徐希望她的孩子处处领先。

---

criteria 标准	overstatement 言过其实	obligations 职责，责任
shun 逃避，躲避	pass away 故去，过世	gratitude 感激
fall silent 安静下来	deal with 打交道	alternative 另外的选择

 **Exercises 练习**

Answer these questions.

1. Why would a young woman want to choose a husband without any parents?
2. Do you agree with the American teacher? Why?
3. What are the differences between the Chinese, and Western way, in dealing with family relations?

Translate these sentences into Chinese.

1. There are certain obligations that he can never shun.
2. Even his marriage is a duty to produce the next generation.
3. The obligations of the wife are less important.
4. A man would have to treat his parents and brothers or sisters with priority.
5. The American teacher was very unhappy with the answers.
6. You two will be bound even closer together.
7. In China, a family is headed by the most senior person.
8. A man is required to leave his parents and stay together with his wife.
9. He cannot escape from duties to his parents.
10. She doesn't have a better alternative.

Complete this paragraph with suitable words.

It's an ___1___ but, it certainly ___2___ the sensitive relationships in a Chinese family. In a traditional household, a man is ___3___ a son and an elder brother. There are ___4___ obligations that he can ___5___ shun. Even his marriage is a ___6___ to produce the next generation. The obligations of the wife are ___7___ important. As the old saying ___8___ , "Brothers are as indispensable as hands and feet, while the wife is like a coat."

 Answers 答案

Translate these sentences into Chinese.

1. 他有着难以摆脱的职责。
2. 他们娶妻也是为了履行延续后代的责任。
3. 对妻子的责任就不那么重要了。
4. 他必须以父母和兄弟姐妹为重。
5. 美国教师对回答非常不满。
6. 你们俩会更加亲密无间。
7. 在中国，最年长者在家中占据首位。
8. 男子应该离开父母，固守妻子。
9. 他不能放弃对父母的责任。
10. 她没有更好的选择。

Complete this paragraph with suitable words.

1. overstatement   2. reflects   3. both   4. certain   5. never   6. duty   7. less   8. goes

21. Neighborhood Relationship

邻里关系

Dialogue

A： Neighbors seem to be an important part of community relationship in China.

B： I can give you examples to **illustrate** this importance. For instance, if a couple had a noisy fight and the neighbors heard it, they would come over to calm them down. Or, if both the husband and the wife are working, they will give their house key to the old woman next door so she can help look after the children after school. The "bound feet security guards" was a very popular expression in the last century. It refers to the retired people, usually old women, who would walk around their neighborhood to ensure its security. These people **played a** key **role** in stabilizing social order during that time.

A： I wonder how these special community relations are developed.

B： In a traditional, agricultural society there was almost no population mobility. People lived in one place for generations with no interaction with the outside world. Everyone knew everyone else, and this led to a lot of **mutual** understanding and interdependence. Whenever someone needed any help, the first solution was to ask the neighbors. This is where the expression, "a neighbor is more dependable than a distant relative" came from.

A： I see. I know that such an intimate community relationship was still very popular **as recently as** the 1990s.

B： There is an old joke that goes like this: A newly-wed couple lived together with four other families in a big courtyard. One morning, they slept in until midday. Their neighbors thought something might have **gone wrong** and knocked on the door to check it out. You can imagine how embarrassed the young couple was.

A： Exactly! Now that people live in high-rise apartment buildings, will this relationship be affected?

B： Yes. The closeness that was typical in a traditional courtyard is gone. People live behind closed doors and often do not even know the next-door neighbor. The older people, in particular, have problems **adapting** to this change. This is why you always see groups of old people socializing in public green areas. They miss the intimate community relationship of the past. In fact, even though young people are very protective of their private life, they also appreciate a friendly neighborhood.

A: What can they do to address this issue?

B: Some neighborhoods have started to rebuild the community relationship using the Internet. Through a LAN network, as in the case with a neighborhood in suburban Beijing, they share information with each other. In another place, residents produced a TV drama of their everyday life.

A: This may be one reason why Chinese people are happier and feel more secure.

对 话

A: 街坊邻居似乎是中国社会人际关系中重要的一部分。

B: 邻里关系有多重要呢？这里有一些例子：夫妻吵架，动静闹大了，一定会有邻居来劝说，直到两个人火气平息；夫妻俩都有工作的家庭，会把房门钥匙交给邻居老人，请她帮忙照顾放学回来的孩子。居委会里有"小脚侦缉队"，由一群退休老人组成，多数是老太太，在上个世纪曾经非常有名气。他们在居民区巡逻，在当时是治安力量的重要部分。

A: 这种特有的邻里关系是如何形成的？

B: 传统的农业社会人口流动性小。人们世代居于一地，与外界甚少往来。人与人之间互相了解、互相依存。有了困难首先想到的是求助于邻居，所以有"远亲不如近邻"的说法。

A: 明白了。我听说直到 20 世纪 90 年代，这样的邻里关系在中国还是普遍存在的。

B: 有一个笑话：一对新婚夫妇，住在一个三四户人家共居的大杂院中。将近中午，小两口窗帘未启，大门未开。邻居们以为出了意外，不断去敲门。你能想像两个年轻人多么不好意思。

A: 那当然了。现在人们都住进了高楼，这种关系会发生变化吗？

B: 大杂院中亲密的邻里关系已经不复存在。各家关门闭户，常常不知隔壁所住何人。老人尤其不适应这种变化。你常常可以看到在公用绿地里聚集着许多老人，他们怀念以往亲密的邻里关系。事实上，年轻人尽管喜欢保护隐私，他们也需要好邻居。

A: 那他们怎么办呢？

B: 一些居民利用电脑网络沟通社区情感。北京郊区有一个住宅区的住户建立了自己的社区网络，互通信息。还有的社区居民把他们的生活拍成电视剧。

A: 我想这也许是中国人生活得更快乐和更有安全感的原因之一。

Background Reading 背景阅读

Si He Yuan in North China 中国北方的四合院

In north China, *si he yuan* are the most popular housing buildings in traditional style. A *si he yuan* is a rectangular compound with traditional one-story houses of gray tiles and bricks built on the four sides of it. The most typical *si he yuan* compounds are found in Beijing.

Si He Yuan compounds can be large or small, depending on the social status and financial capabilities of their owners. A *si he yuan* can be very small and crowded, a simple courtyard occupied by several or even scores of families. A large, rich family with three or more generations "living under the same roof" may, however, own a mansion consisting several *si he yuan* compounds standing side by side or one after another, often with a family garden.

Sandwiched in between two rows of *si he yuan* compounds, large or small, is an alley, or *hutong* as it is known to Beijing residents. Both ends of the *hutong* are connected with busy streets. Look at an old map of Beijing you'll find the entire city cut into neat blocks by webs of *hutongs*, each block being a residential area. Beijing is rapidly modernizing, and many old *si he yuan* compounds are gone, along with numerous *hutongs* that have been widened. Tours of the remaining *hutongs* on a rickshaw are becoming popular, reminding people of those long, long years when *hutongs*, long or short, narrow or relatively wide, were alive with small traders hawking their goods including even "sweet water" or buying secondhand clothing for resale. The centuries-old *hutong* culture cries for preservation. Let's hope for the best.

中国北方，四合院是最普遍的传统建筑。四合院是一个由灰砖灰瓦平房组成的长方形院落，北京有最典型的四合院。

四合院可大可小，这取决于其主人的社会地位和经济实力。有的四合院很小，很拥挤，由几户甚至几十户人家共用。大户人家三、四代人"同住一个屋檐下"，拥有一组由几个并列或是前后排列的四合院组成的大宅院，通常还有私人花园。

北京人将两个四合院中间或宽或窄的通道称为胡同，胡同两端连着繁忙的街道。在老北京的地图上，人们会发现整座城市都被一个个胡同分割为整齐的街区，每一个街区都是一个居民区，北京正在日新月异地现代化，许多老四合院都被拆掉了，胡同也都被拓宽了。现在，坐三轮车在仅存的几条胡同里旅游越来越受欢迎，它可以使人们想起从前，在长短宽窄不一的胡同里，做小买卖的商人的叫卖声，卖的还有像"糖水"和二手衣服这样的东西。这些具有百年历史的胡同文化应该受到保护，我们希望会是这样。

---

illustrate 描述	play a role 起作用	mutual 相互
as recently as 一直到	go wrong 出问题	adapting 适应

 **Exercises** 练习

Answer these questions.
1. What does "bound feet security guards" mean?
2. Why did everyone know everyone else in the past?
3. Why are Chinese people happier?

Translate these sentences into Chinese.
1. Neighbors are an important part of community relationship in China.
2. These people played a key role in stabilizing social order during that time.
3. There was almost no population mobility.
4. People lived in one place for generations with no interaction with the outside world.
5. There was a lot of mutual understanding and interdependence.
6. Their neighbors thought something might have gone wrong.
7. You can imagine how embarrassed the young couple was.
8. The closeness that is typical in a traditional courtyard is gone.
9. People live behind closed doors and often do not even know the next-door neighbor.
10. The older people, in particular, have problems adapting to this change.

Complete this paragraph with suitable words.
In a __1__ agricultural society, there was almost no population mobility. People lived in one place __2__ generations with no interaction __3__ the outside world. Everyone knew everyone __4__. There was a lot of __5__ understanding and interdependence. Whenever someone needed __6__ help, the first __7__ was to ask the neighbors. This is where the expression "a neighbor is more dependable than a distant relative" came __8__.

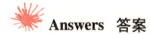 **Answers** 答案

Translate these sentences into Chinese.
1. 街坊邻居是中国社会人际关际中重要的一部分。
2. 他们在当时是治安力量的重要部分。
3. 几乎没有任何人口流动。
4. 人们世代居于一地，与外界甚少往来。
5. 人们互相了解，相互依存。
6. 邻居们以为出了意外。
7. 你能想像两个年轻人多么不好意思。
8. 大杂院中亲密的邻里关系已经不复存在。
9. 各家关门闭户，常常不知隔壁所住何人。
10. 老人尤其不适应这种变化。

Complete this paragraph with suitable words.
1. traditional 2. for 3. with 4. else 5. mutual 6. any 7. solution 8. from

22. Personal Privacy vs. Hospitality

隐私与亲密

Dialogue

A： I don't like my Chinese friends calling me *lao wai*. It makes me feel that I am not one of them.

B： Actually, Chinese people want to treat you as one of us. The word *lao* always implies respect and closeness, when used to **address** someone. For example, senior people are often addressed as *Lao Wang* or *Lao Li*.

A： I see. Many people are learning English nowadays because of the Olympics. But it's a bit weird to hear people say "hello" to me in the street. That's the word you use to answer a phone. So it feels like everybody in the street is **on the phone**.

B： Chinese people are friendly. We are also curious about people **from afar**. What you've just said is an example of such a feeling.

A： But occasionally, some people tend to be overly enthusiastic. I was riding the subway one hot summer day when a young man looked at my arm and asked, "Don't you feel hot with so much hair on your arm?" I have a five-year-old son and sometimes people like to touch his face or even hold him up in their arms. He doesn't like that so I have to explain to him that it's the Chinese way of showing **affection**. Another time, I was reading a newspaper in the subway and a person suddenly poked his head over my shoulder and helped himself to my paper.

B： That's just like what we read in "A neighbor is more dependable than a distant relative." Today's China has evolved from its agricultural origins where there was limited **mobility**. Those old traditions have **given rise to** a unique level of human relationship which doesn't accommodate personal privacy. People treat each other like one big family. The level of closeness is easily visible in everyday greetings, such as "have you eaten?" and "where are you going?" Even during first encounters, Chinese people may still ask such questions as "are you married?", "how old are you?" or other questions, which may be very personal to a Westerner.

A: But you should learn to appreciate it rather than feeling **offended**.

B: You've got it! This is Chinese hospitality, just like the person who shared your newspaper. I remember some of my Western friends telling me that sometimes they were either charged less or offered more, when doing their **grocery shopping**. Again, this is all about Chinese hospitality.

A: Well, it seems I'm an unlucky person because I've never been in a situation where people are willing to **charge** me less.

对 话

A: 我很不习惯中国朋友把我称为"老外",让我感觉自己像个外人。

B: 其实,这恰恰说明中国人不把你当外人。称呼某人"老"是表示尊重和亲密。比如年长的人被称作"老王"、"老李"。

A: 我明白了。中国正在准备奥运会,很多人在学英文。但听见别人在街上对我喊 hello,感觉有点儿怪怪的。通常打电话时才说 hello。他们这样一喊,搞得像满街人都在打电话。

B: 中国人很友好,对来自远方的人有一种好奇心。你所遇到的情况正是这种情感的表达。

A: 但偶尔有些人过于热情。夏天我坐地铁,旁边的小伙子看着我的胳膊问:"这么多毛,肯定热吧?"我有个 5 岁的儿子,总有人过来捏他的脸,甚至把他抱起来。我儿子十分不解。我只得告诉他,人们喜欢他才那样做。还有一次,我在地铁里看报纸,一个人突然把头凑到我的肩膀上,跟我一块儿看。

B: 正像"远亲不如近邻"这句话所说的,今天的中国以农业社会为基础,流动性小,在这种传统当中产生了独特的人际关系,相互之间没有隐私。人们彼此像家里人一样,见面时的问候语就透着亲密,比如"吃了吗?"、"去哪儿?"初次相见,中国人就会问"结婚了吗?"、"你多大了?"等等在西方人看来很私人的问题。

A: 但你得接受这些,而不是感到被冒犯。

B: 说对了!这就是中国人的热情,就像有人跟你同看一份报纸。有外国朋友告诉我,他们在买东西时,店主有时会少收他们的钱,或多给些份量。这也是友好的表示。

A: 看来我不走运,从来没有人向我少收钱。

Youth in Blended Culture 年轻人兼收中西文化

In this era of highly developed media culture, young people have more contact than ever with foreign culture. According to CNNIC statistics, by June 30, 2004, China had 87 million Internet users, most of them young people. Coupled with the openness and diversity of modern society, this means that young Chinese people now seek their cultural orientation within the ambit of Western culture.

In contrast to the youth that wholeheartedly allied themselves with the liberal trends of the 1980s, however, today's young Chinese have a more rational stance on Western culture. They do not unconditionally accept Western concepts, nor do they regard Western culture as the be all and end all of civilization; today's young Chinese people absorb elements of both the East and the West. In 2000 a sample survey carried out on 2,500 participants in Tianjin on the topic "Chinese youth, their values and outlook on life" showed the number of those that follow Western concepts of marriage and sex to be minimal. This is another sign that Chinese youth do not accept Western morals wholesale and that their attitude to traditional culture is influenced by informed and rational contemporary cultural theories—a sign of social progress.

On the surface, certain aspects of the Western/Eastern youth lifestyle have so blended as to make them indistinguishable.

在媒介文化高度发展的今天，年轻人接触外来文化的方式越来越多。据中国互联网信息中心统计，截止到2004年6月30日，中国上网用户总数达到8 700万人，其中多数是年轻人。现代社会的开放性、多样性，使年轻人不得不在西方文化的冲击中寻找自己的文化定位。

与20世纪80年代的自由倾向不同，现在的中国年轻人对待西方文化更加理性，对西方观念不再是盲目地相信和接受，更不是以西方文化为时尚。而是吸收中西文化中的精华。在2000年天津市范围内组织的一次"青年世界观、人生观、价值观"专题调研中的2 500个样本显示，在婚姻和性等问题上认同西方观念的人数比例降低。从调查中可以看出，年轻人并不全盘接受外来文化，对待中国传统文化也一样，他们选择合理的、先进的文化理念。这是社会进步的一种表现。

实际上，现在年轻人的很多生活方式已经很难分清它是来自西方还是东方。

---

address 称呼	on the phone 打电话	from afar 来自远方
affection 爱，喜欢	mobility 流动性	give rise to 引起，导致
offend 惹怒	grocery shopping 买菜，买日用品	charge 卖，索价

 **Exercises** 练习

Answer these questions.
1. Why doesn't the Westerner like to be called *lao wai*?
2. When do people usually use the word "hello"?
3. What do Chinese people usually say when greeting people every day?

Translate these sentences into Chinese.
1. It makes me feel that I am not one of them.
2. The word *lao* always implies respect and closeness.
3. We are also curious about people from afar.
4. It's weird to hear people in the street say "hello" to me.
5. Occasionally, some people tend to be overly enthusiastic.
6. Sometimes, people in the street like to hold him up in their arms.
7. One person suddenly poked his head over my shoulder.
8. The tradition has given rise to a unique level of human relationship.
9. You should learn to appreciate it rather than feeling offended.
10. Sometimes, they were charged less when doing their grocery shopping.

Complete this paragraph with suitable words.
Occasionally, some people tend to be __1__ enthusiastic. I have a five-year-old son and, sometimes, people in the street like to __2__ his face or even hold him __3__ in their arms. He doesn't like that so, I have to explain to him it's the Chinese __4__ to show __5__ . Another time, I was reading a newspaper in the __6__ and a person, suddenly, __7__ his head over my shoulder and __8__ himself to my paper.

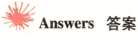 **Answers** 答案

Translate these sentences into Chinese.
1. 这让我感觉自己像个外人。
2. 称呼某人"老"是表示尊重和亲密。
3. 我们对来自远方的人有一种好奇心。
4. 听见别人在街上对我喊 hello，感觉有点儿怪怪的。
5. 偶尔有些人过于热情。
6. 时常会有过路人把他抱起来。
7. 一个人突然把头凑到我的肩膀上。
8. 在这种传统当中产生了独特的人际关系。
9. 但你得接受这些，而不是感到被冒犯。
10. 他们在买东西时，店主有时会少收他们的钱。

Complete this paragraph with suitable words.
1. overly   2. touch   3. up   4. way   5. affection   6. subway   7. poked   8. helped

23. The Exchange of Gifts

礼尚往来

Dialogue

A: When offered a gift, a Chinese person will usually say "No, no, I can't take it." Even after he takes it, he does not always open it. **On the contrary**, a Westerner will take the gift with appreciation and open it immediately.

B: You know why? We Chinese believe that only a valuable gift is **presentable** and can best convey our feelings. This is why Chinese people often use precious or expensive items as gifts. During the Mid Autumn Festival, or the Moon Festival, people will buy well-packaged, high quality moon cakes for gifts and keep the ordinary ones for their own consumption. Because gifts are usually valuable items, people are reluctant to receive them **out of consideration for** the person who offers them.

A: Really? I never thought of that!

B: Westerners are different. For them, gifts are an expression of appreciation and don't have to be very expensive. So, in receiving a souvenir, it is very appropriate to say "Thank you" in return. It will certainly make the person even happier if you open it in front of him or her.

A: Chinese people pay great attention to gifts. Some people spend a lot of time and effort buying gifts before **going abroad**.

B: This is very different from the West. Before each public holiday, you can find a large variety of gifts **on display** at supermarkets. They are very well wrapped and are inexpensive to buy. Most of the gifts are items for daily use. This saves people a lot of time looking for appropriate holiday gifts. On the other hand, a Chinese person seeks a gift which is decently priced, well wrapped and has some unique meaning. It is always a challenge to buy a gift for a Chinese person. When people buy gifts for their overseas trips, they usually choose items with Chinese features, such as Peking opera masks, fans, and knots.

A：As more and more Chinese people go abroad, an **oversupply** of Chinese gifts has occurred in many countries. Chinese gift items are not that unique any more. A friend of mine is a university professor in the United States. She told me that at the end of the semester she received three Peking opera masks from her Chinese students. I also heard that Chinese fans are all over the place in Mexico.

B：What is an appropriate gift for a Westerner?

A：Flowers, wine and chocolates are the three universal gifts that are suitable **for all purposes**. I sometimes wonder whether the Chinese saying "A gift may be insignificant, but it carries tremendous friendship" originated in the West.

对 话

A：中国人在接受礼品时总是先拒绝："不要，不要，怎么好意思。"就算他们接受了，也从不当场打开礼物。西方人相反，他们边道谢边收下礼物，并且马上打开来看。

B：这是有原因的。我们中国人总觉得贵重的礼品才拿得出手，才能表达心意，常常会把价格不菲的礼物送人。中秋节时，人们把包装精致、馅料讲究的月饼送礼，自己则吃很普通的月饼。正因为礼品珍贵，接受的人才会感到受之有愧，而不是欣然接受。

A：是这样啊？真没想到！

B：西方人不是这样。礼品只是一种心意的表示，并不一定要很贵重。接受礼物时表示感谢就再好不过，当面打开更是给足了送礼者面子。

A：中国人对礼物的确很重视，一些人出国之前总是花大量的时间和精力购买礼品。

B：西方人大不一样。过节前，超市会摆放很多种礼品供人选择。它们都是些日用品，包装漂亮，价钱不贵，送礼者不必花心思去寻找。中国人的礼品既要价格不低，又要包装不俗，还要意义不浅。选购礼品真是一个不小的挑战。中国人出国总要带些有中国特色的礼品，比如京剧脸谱、中国扇子、中国结等等。

A：随着越来越多的中国人走向世界，这种礼品在许多国家已经泛滥，因此不那么新鲜了。我有一个在美国大学教书的朋友，她说在一个学期结束时，三个中国学生一人送她一个京剧脸谱。我还听说，墨西哥满大街都是中国扇子。

B：你觉得送洋人什么更好呢？

A：鲜花、酒和巧克力这三种礼品能应对各种场合。我一直怀疑，"礼轻情义重"这句话最初是从西方传到中国的。

Background Reading 背景阅读

Greedy or Stingy 贪吃还是吝啬

Chinese customers have a curious characteristic unknown in Western countries—they order too much food. First of all, it is because the Chinese attach a lot of value to the concept of "keeping face." When inviting guests and friends out to dinner, the Chinese do not view it simply as "eating together." People come to restaurants (in many cases, expensive ones) to strengthen friendly ties and to do business. A big banquet is therefore considered a good investment. Impressive banquets in China are similar to lengthy business negotiations in the West, so Chinese hosts tend to splash out on these occasions. Western partners should not regard their Chinese hosts as greedy that would ruin both the friendship and the business deal. The reason behind the phenomenon is simple. The hosts feel that if all the food is gone at the end of the meal, their guests might think they were stingy.

中国的消费者有一些不为西方人所了解的特点——在餐馆，他们会点一大堆食物。这首先是因为中国人"好面子"的价值观。当请客人或朋友外出吃饭时，中国人并不简单地把这看作是"一起吃顿饭"。大家去餐馆吃饭（在许多情形下是去一些奢华的餐馆）是为了加强友好的关系和做生意。一次宴请因此被看作是一项大投资。在中国，一个隆重的宴会其作用就如同西方的商业洽谈一样，所以中国的主人倾向于在这样的场合中一掷千金。西方的合作伙伴们不应由此以为中国的主人们贪吃——这样会毁了双方的关系和生意。这种现象背后的原因很简单。主人觉得如果一餐结束时所有的菜被吃光了，客人会以为主人很吝啬。

Tea Drinking 喝茶

Tea drinking in China is a ritual, a demonstration of class and refined taste. Chatting over a pot of tea is very popular pastime among Chinese, and in the past, they would start the day with a visit to a well-known teahouse. Teahouses are the Chinese answer to French cafés and English pubs. People come here not just for tea, but also to discuss local news or to have furious political debates.

在中国喝茶是一种仪式，一种精致品味的展示。喝茶聊天是中国人中最流行的打发时间的方式，过去，他们是以进有名的茶馆而开始一天的生活的。中国的茶馆相当于法国的咖啡馆和英国的酒馆。人们到这里不仅为了喝茶，也是为了议论当地的新闻或对政治话题进行激烈的争论。

on the contrary 相反	presentable 拿得出手	out of consideration for 出于对…的考虑
go abroad 出国	on display 展示	oversupply 供应过剩
for all purposes 各种用途		

 **Exercises** 练习

Answer these questions.

1. What does a Westerner do when receiving a gift?
2. What are some typical Chinese gifts?
3. What is an appropriate gift for a Westerner?

Translate these sentences into Chinese.

1. On the contrary, a Westerner will take the gift with appreciation.
2. We Chinese believe that only a valuable gift is presentable.
3. People will keep ordinary moon cakes for their own consumption.
4. Gifts are an expression of appreciation and don't have to be very expensive.
5. It will certainly make him happy if you open it in front of him.
6. Some people spend a lot of time and effort to buy gifts before going abroad.
7. You can find a large variety of gifts on display at supermarkets.
8. It is always a challenge to buy a gift for a Chinese person.
9. There has been an oversupply of Chinese gifts in many countries.
10. Flowers, wine and chocolates are the three universal gifts that are suitable for all purposes.

Complete this paragraph with suitable words.

We Chinese believe that only a __1__ gift is presentable and can best __2__ our feelings. This is why Chinese people often use __3__, or expensive items, as gifts. Because gifts are usually valuable items, people are __4__ to receive them out of __5__ for the person who offers them. Westerners are __6__. For them, gifts are an __7__ of appreciation and don't have to be very __8__.

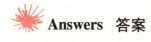 **Answers** 答案

Translate these sentences into Chinese.

1. 西方人相反，他们边道谢边收下礼物。
2. 我们中国人总觉得贵重的礼品才拿得出手。
3. 人们会把普通月饼留着自己吃。
4. 礼品只是一种心意的表示，并不一定要很贵重。
5. 当面打开会使他很高兴。
6. 一些人出国之前总是花大量的时间和精力购买礼品。
7. 超市会摆放很多种礼品供人选择。
8. 对中国人来说，选购礼品真是一个不小的挑战。
9. 中国礼品在许多国家泛滥成灾。
10. 鲜花、酒和巧克力这三种礼品能应对各种场合。

Complete this paragraph with suitable words.

1. valuable   2. convey   3. precious   4. reluctant   5. consideration   6. different
7. expression   8. expensive

24. Chinese Hospitality

中国人的待客之道

Dialogue

A： I was invited to a traditional Beijing household for dinner once. It was an **eye-opening** experience. The girl who invited me was my colleague. Her father was over 60 years old. He didn't eat much but was constantly **proposing a toast**. His wife was busy cooking in the kitchen all the time. I asked her to join us but her husband said "No, she doesn't." After dinner, I asked my colleague why her father didn't eat much and why her mother didn't join us. She said that was an old tradition. Her father was there to keep me company because I was a guest of honor and usually women did not eat with the guests.

B： I had a similar experience too. I always feel **spoiled** to be a guest in a Chinese household. The host usually prepares **a sumptuous meal**. The kids are sent to the neighbors so the guests can have a peaceful meal. Usually, they would start preparing for our visit days ahead. Even though there would be a lot of food on the table, the host would still say "We don't have much, so please **bear with** us." They keep putting food on my plate despite the fact I may not like certain food. I usually feel very embarrassed. Some hosts even force their children to perform a song or recite a poem for me.

A： That is Chinese hospitality. People want to bring out their best food to welcome the guests. Westerners are different. They don't stay in the kitchen when the guests have arrived. They want to socialize with the guests rather than simply showing hospitality.

B： Chinese people are very friendly and always ready to treat their guests with the best things they have. But this hospitality may cause inconvenience to both the guests and the hosts themselves. An American said in a book over 100 years ago that Chinese hospitality is meant to show the politeness of the host rather than keeping the guest happy. The host may **insist on** starting a fire so he can make tea for the guest, despite the fact that the guest may be irritated by the smoke. At least the host gives the impression that he is very hospitable.

A： That was over 100 years ago. Things are different now. More and more people prefer a relaxed atmosphere rather than showing hospitality just **for the sake of** it. But there are **exceptions**. I went to visit a fairly affluent village in southern China last year. The host was asked to make a special tea for us. She was very friendly, but when she finished making the tea she charged each of us 10 yuan for the treat. As a result of the economic growth people have become money conscious. Although you may not feel comfortable with the traditional hospitality, it could disappear any time.

B： Shall I feel lucky or sorry then?

对 话

A： 我曾到一个老北京家里做客，可真是开了眼了。请客的是这家的女儿，她是我的同事。她的父亲六十多岁，作为主人，他在饭桌上几乎没吃什么，只是隔一会儿就端起酒杯劝酒。他的太太一直在厨房里忙着。我们招呼她一起吃，同事的父亲说"她不上桌"。告辞出来，我问同事为什么她父亲几乎不吃东西，而她母亲一直不加入我们。她说这是老礼数。她父亲把我们当作贵客所以要陪酒，而女人一般是不和客人同桌的。

B： 我也有过同样的经历。到中国人家里做客总感觉他们招待得很隆重：上一大桌菜，小孩子被赶到邻居家，以便客人吃得尽兴。请一次客得提前几天做准备。既便做了一大桌菜，他们还是说："没什么东西，凑合吃吧。"还不停地为你布菜，不管你是不是爱吃。这让我觉得很尴尬。有些人家还逼着孩子给客人表演唱歌，或者背诗。

A： 这就是中国人的待客之道：把最好的东西拿出来招待客人。西方人并不如此。他们不会在客人到来后还在厨房中忙碌，他们的目的是交流而不是表现待客的热情。

B： 中国人非常友好，所以才会用最好的东西招待客人。但这样一来，家人跟着受累，客人也不自在。一百多年前，一位美国人在他的书中写道：中国人待人热情的目的通常是为了表现自己懂礼节，而并非想使客人满意。主人执意生火为客人沏茶，而不在乎客人是否被烟呛着，因为他至少树立了待客有礼的形象。

A： 这是一百年前的情形，现在有所不同。更多的人已经懂得，自在随意比过分礼貌要好得多。也有例外：去年，我到一个富裕的南方村庄去采访，请主人给我们一杯当地特有的茶。她热情地为我们上了茶，然后向我们每位收了 10 元钱作为服务的报偿。经济发展了，中国人也有了金钱意识。你不适应传统的待客之道，它也许很快就不复存在了。

B： 我该为此庆幸还是遗憾呢？

Background Reading 背景阅读

Whisky? Whisky! 威士忌? 威士忌!

Chinese poseurs happily purchasing expensive scotches might be the salvation of Western spirits makers but local whisky culture is still in gestation. Only an elite few Chinese drinkers are able to tell a blended whisky from single malt and are unprepared for the snobbery and connoisseurship that goes with fine whisky drinking.

Increasing numbers of Chinese tourists heading to Europe are bringing back new tastes. The most popular destinations for local tourists are the UK and Scotland, home of scotches such as Chivas Regal. More than half of the distilleries in Scotland are located in the relatively small Speyside region, and produce many brands that are highly recommended. Islay (pronounced "eye-la") is a small island off the western coast of Scotland, and is home to the heaviest, strongest-flavored, smokiest, and most challenging of the single malts. Across the narrow Irish sea from Scotland, Irish whiskey has a more smooth and natural flavor.

There's certainly plenty of acquired knowledge attached to whisky drinking. The more expensive malt whiskys have yet to find huge favor in China, with most of the market held by less challenging blended whiskies like Ballantine's, Cutty Sark and The Famous Grouse.

一些时髦的中国人对价格昂贵的苏格兰威士忌的追捧对于西方酿酒商们来说是值得庆贺的事，但是中国本土在威士忌文化上还存在很大的欠缺。在喝威士忌的中国人中，只有少数人能够区分混合型威士忌和单一型威士忌，也只有他们在喝一杯好的威士忌的时候不会评头品足、津津乐道。

越来越多的中国人从欧洲游历归来，他们对于威士忌口味有更真切的体验。中国人最喜欢的旅游目的地是英国和苏格兰，那里正是芝华士之类的苏格兰威士忌的产地。在苏格兰，超过半数的酿酒商集中在斯佩塞德地区，这里生产的很多品牌威士忌闻名遐迩。艾拉岛是位于苏格兰西海岸的一个小岛，此区的威士忌酒体最厚重、气味最浓郁，泥炭味道也最强，很容易辨识。这里酿造的单一型麦芽威士忌非常有名。从苏格兰跨过狭窄的爱尔兰海，这里酿造的爱尔兰威士忌口味更加平和而自然。

关于怎样喝威士忌确实有很多东西需要去了解。中国的威士忌市场充斥着普通的混合型威士忌，比如百龄坛威士忌、顺风威士忌和威雀苏格兰威士忌，因此需要更昂贵的麦芽威士忌来赢得中国人的喜爱。

---

eye-opening 开眼	propose a toast 敬酒，劝酒	spoil 受宠
a sumptuous meal 丰盛的大餐	bear with 包涵	insist on 执意
for the sake of 为了	exception 例外	

 **Exercises** 练习

Answer these questions.

1. How does a traditional Beijing household treat its guests of honor?
2. Why does a Westerner feel spoiled to be a guest in a Chinese household?
3. How does a Westerner treat his guest?

Translate these sentences into Chinese.

1. I was invited to a traditional Beijing household for dinner once.
2. His wife was busy cooking in the kitchen all the time.
3. I had a similar experience too.
4. Kids are sent to the neighbors so the guests can have a peaceful meal.
5. Usually, they would start preparing for our visit, days ahead.
6. Westerners don't stay in the kitchen when the guests have arrived.
7. Chinese people are always ready to treat their guests with the best things they have.
8. The host insisted on starting a fire so he could make tea for the guest.
9. That was over 100 years ago. Things are different now.
10. She charged each of us 10 yuan for the treat.

Complete this paragraph with suitable words.

I was ___1___ to a traditional Beijing household ___2___ dinner once. It was an ___3___ experience. The girl who invited me was my colleague and her father was ___4___ 60 years old. He didn't eat much but, was ___5___ proposing a toast. His wife was ___6___ cooking in the kitchen all the time. I asked her to ___7___ us but, her husband said, "No, she doesn't." After dinner, I asked my colleague ___8___ her father didn't eat much and why her mother didn't join us.

 Answers 答案

Translate these sentences into Chinese.

1. 我曾到一个老北京家里做客。
2. 他的太太一直在厨房里忙着。
3. 我也有过同样的经历。
4. 小孩子被赶到邻居家, 以便客人吃得尽兴。
5. 他们请一次客得提前几天做准备。
6. 西方人不会在客人到来后还在厨房中忙碌。
7. 中国人总是把最好的东西拿出来招待客人。
8. 主人执意生火为客人沏茶。
9. 这是一百年前的情形, 现在有所不同。
10. 她向我们每位收了10元钱作为服务的报偿。

Complete this paragraph with suitable words.

1. invited 2. for 3. eye-opening 4. over 5. constantly 6. busy 7. join 8. why

25. Table Manners

餐桌礼仪

Dialogue

A： A Westerner said to his Chinese friend, "Chinese people slurp when drinking soup. It's **disgusting**. " The Chinese friend replied, "Westerners make a lot of noise licking their fingers when eating. It's even worse. "

B： Everyone has his own habits, but these habits are not very good. The noise often **spoils** other people's appetite.

A： I attended a course on **table manners** while I was in the United States. Some of the things we learnt included how to place the napkin and utensils and how to pass the bread. Before each course, the teacher would ask if we wanted to learn the Continental European way or the American way. We always said "The American way. " It's **amazing** that everyone is so used to their own table manners. What is the Chinese way?

B： The Westerners use knives and forks to eat so it is complicated. The Chinese use a pair of chopsticks and eat out of the same plate. I assume it is less complicated, right?

A： Not really. I did some research about Chinese table manners. The important rule is to remain silent while eating. Of course, this **refers to** family meals only. Not talking over meals is supposed to be good for the health. It is impolite if people do not talk to each other during a social party. The **table arrangements** and serving order for a social party are equally complicated. Each dish should be placed in the correct position. When fish is served, the tail should be pointing at the guest because tail meat is supposed to be tasty. If it is in winter, the stomach should face the **right-hand side** of the guest because that portion of the fish is very rich in winter. Each dish should be commenced by the eldest person who is seated at the head of the table. The diners should sit close to the table so food won't drop on their clothes. No noise should be made when chewing. No one should move food back to the communal plate even if he doesn't like it. One should drink soup slowly and is not supposed to make a lot of noise. All these table manners are very similar to Western habits.

B： It seems that people share the same basic sense of etiquette regardless of their background. Apart from the different tools used for eating we seem to follow the same principles. We do not let inappropriate manners spoil other people's appetite. Westerners like to say, "bon appetite" before meals which is one way to suggest "mind your table manners." Is there such an expression in Chinese?

A： Yes. We say "eat well and drink well."

对 话

A： 有个外国人对他的中国朋友说："你们中国人喝汤的时候发出很大的声响，实在不雅。"中国朋友反驳道："你们外国人吃饭的时候吮手指头的响动也不小，更恶心。"

B： 各人有各人的习惯，不过这两种行为都不太好，至少噪音会影响别人的胃口。

A： 在美国时，我参加了一个餐桌礼仪课，学习如何摆放口布、如何使用刀叉、怎样递面包等。每教一个礼节之前，那位老师都会问："你们是学欧陆式的还是美式的？"我们总是回答："美式的。"每个人都如此习惯于自己的餐桌礼仪，真是不可思议。中国式的餐桌礼仪是什么呢？

B： 西洋人用刀叉吃饭，所以比较复杂。中国人只用一双筷子，在同一个盘子里取食，礼仪会简单许多吧？

A： 并不尽然，我对中国的餐桌礼仪作了些探究。重要的原则是："食不言。"当然，这是指在家中就餐时。吃饭不讲话被认为有益健康。但若是参加社交的宴饮，不语就失礼了。社交宴会上的座次和上菜次序同样很复杂，菜品的摆放也很讲究。比如上整条鱼时，一般鱼尾向着宾客，因为鲜鱼肉尾部的味道更好。但冬天时鱼的腹部肥美，摆放时鱼腹应向着主宾的右方。进餐时，每上一道菜要由尊者或长者先食，他一般坐于桌首位置。开饭后要尽量坐得靠前，以免掉落食物弄脏衣服。咀嚼时不可发出声响；不能把夹过来的食物再放回去。喝汤时不可过快、不能发出声响。这些礼仪是不是与西洋差不多？

B： 看起来，尽管背景不同，人类的基本礼仪却是共通的。除了餐具不同，我们似乎在遵循着相同的原则。不要让你不适当的行为倒了别人的胃口。西洋人吃饭前会说："祝你好胃口，"也许就是提醒"注意你的用餐礼节"的一种方式。中国有类似的的表达方式吗？

A： 有。叫作"吃好，喝好。"

Background Reading 背景阅读

Five Tastes and Four Natures of the Food 饮食的五味与四性

The recommended dietary regime comprises five tastes: sour, bitter, sweet, pungent and salty, and four natures: cold, hot, warm and cool. The five tastes determine how a food or drug affects the organism. For example, pungent food promotes circulation and evaporation of vital energy *qi*. Bitter tasting food opens blocked centers and promotes healthy bowel movement. Eating sour dishes accumulates and concentrates vital energy, and salty food alleviates all feelings of heaviness. The four natures are effective in treating diseases through being opposite in nature to them. According to ancient theory, the body is an organic whole. If any part of it does not work properly within the overall regime the body becomes unbalanced and the person falls sick. Medical remedies opposite in nature to the illness being treated should be prescribed in order to return the body to a balanced state. For example, medication considered hot by nature is used to treat diseases cold by nature.

There is a specific term in Chinese—*yaoshan* or medicinal food—for dishes with medicinal functions. In ancient times the Chinese believed that treatment of any disease consists of three stages. The first is *yaoshan*—medicinal food, the second *daoyin*—physical exercise. The third, drugs, were considered a last resort if the first two failed. As Traditional Chinese medicine (TCM) still follows these rules it may be assumed they are effective. Any TCM practitioner will tell you that medicine and food share the same origins, which is why an everyday meal can also be of medicinal value.

饮食有五味：酸、苦、甜、辣和咸；也有四种特性：寒、热、温和凉。五味决定着食物或药物对于机体的疗效。比如，辣味可以促进循环，使重要的能量"气"得以发挥。苦味能够通塞，促使肠胃的蠕动。酸性的食物能够积累能量，而咸味的食物能够缓解压力。食物的四种特性是通过对相反性态的抑制起到治疗的作用的。根据古代理论，身体是一个有机的整体。如果某一个部位出现问题，整个身体状况就会失去平衡，人就会生病。针对疾病的药物治疗，其目的就是使人体达到一种平衡。比如，药性为温热的药物常用于治疗寒症。

中文中有一个特别的词——药膳，是指有医疗作用的食物。在中国古代，人们相信治疗疾病有三个步骤。第一是药膳；第二是导引，即身体的运动；第三才是药剂，这是在前两种办法不奏效的情况下才会采用的最终方式。传统的中医依然沿用这一被认为有效的规则。每一位中医都会告诉你医药同源这个道理，这就是为什么日常的饮食中也有药用价值。

---

disgusting 恶心的	spoil 破坏，搅乱	table manner 餐桌上的礼仪，规矩
amazing 不可思议	refer to 指，属于	table arrangement 座次
right-hand side 右手边		

 **Exercises** 练习

Answer these questions.

1. What are some of the Chinese table manners?
2. How is fish served at a Chinese dinner?
3. What do Westerners like to say before meals?

Translate these sentences into Chinese.

1. I attended a course on table manners while I was in the United States.
2. It's amazing that everyone is so used to their own table manners.
3. I did some research about Chinese table manners.
4. Table arrangements and serving order for a social party are equally complicated.
5. Each dish should be placed in the correct position.
6. Each dish should be commenced by the eldest person.
7. No one should move food back to the communal plate.
8. One is not supposed to make a lot of noise when drinking soup.
9. People share the same basic sense of etiquette regardless of their background.
10. We seem to follow the same principles.

Complete this paragraph with suitable words.

It seems that people __1__ the same basic __2__ of etiquette, __3__ of their background. Apart from the different tools used for eating, we seem to __4__ the same principles. We do not __5__ inappropriate manners spoil other people's appetite. Westerners __6__ to say, "bon appetite" before meals which, is one way to __7__, "mind your table manners." Is there __8__ an expression in Chinese?

 Answers 答案

Translate these sentences into Chinese.

1. 在美国时，我参加了一个餐桌礼仪课。
2. 每个人都如此习惯于自己的餐桌礼仪，真是不可思议。
3. 我对中国的餐桌礼仪作了些探究。
4. 社交宴会上的座次和上菜次序同样很复杂。
5. 菜品的摆放有讲究。
6. 每上一道菜都要由尊者或长者先食。
7. 谁也不能把取出来的食物再放回去。
8. 喝汤时不能发出声响。
9. 尽管背景不同，人类的基本礼仪却是共通的。
10. 我们似乎在遵循着相同的原则。

Complete this paragraph with suitable words.

1. share 2. sense 3. regardless 4. follow 5. let 6. like 7. suggest 8. such

26. The Fashion of Tea-Drinking

喝茶的时尚

A: There are a lot of Chinese expressions that link tea with food. For example, "firewood, rice, oil, salt, soy sauce, vinegar and tea are the seven **daily necessities**."

B: The purpose of tea and food is totally different though. People eat to fill their stomach. But, tea-drinking can help a person achieve an elevated **state of mind**. Tea-drinking is said to have originated with the advent of Buddhism. Monks drank tea to **keep** themselves **awake** and help their concentration. Ordinary people were tempted by the tranquility of the monasteries and began to imitate the monks. So tea-drinking is considered an elegant pastime.

A: Has tea-drinking become fashionable?

B: A few years ago it was fashionable to drink Lipton tea with milk and sugar to emulate a Western lifestyle. Later it was green tea. Fruit tea was also popular for a while.

A: I heard that pu'er tea is very popular in Japan and Taiwan. People think it can help them **lose weight** and control their blood pressure.

B: It is also popular in China's mainland. Pu'er tea looks and smells more like French red wine than tea. Plus, its rumored function is to reduce weight. Pu'er tea-drinking has been very fashionable. Green tea is good for longevity and combating cancer. Red tea is good for keeping the stomach warm.

A: Many tea houses have been opened. Usually tea houses are where ordinary people like to **hang around**. But, some tea houses are destinations for high-brow **social life**.

B: Tea houses have even changed the way people do business. It used to be over meals. The saying now is "At a table of spirits, the more you talk, the more muddled things become. But at a table of tea, the more you talk, the clearer things become."

A： **Tea parties** also seem to have become popular.

B： Tea represents thriftiness and cleanliness. Government agencies like to host tea parties to celebrate public holidays. It serves the purposes of both socializing and saving money.

A： A cup of tea, not only serves social and economic purposes, but also political purposes as well. No wonder tea is always with food in Chinese culture.

对 话

A： 中国有不少茶饭相关联的俗语，比如，"开门七件事，柴米油盐酱醋茶。"

B： 但饮茶与吃饭的目的却大不相同。人们吃饭是为了裹腹，饮茶却能够提升精神境界。茶的流传据说与佛教有关。僧侣们喝茶为提神醒脑。世俗社会模仿这种清静脱俗的举动，所以品茶被看作是清雅之事。

A： 喝茶也有时尚吗？

B： 前些年，流行喝立顿红茶，配了奶和糖，与西洋的方式相仿；后来流行喝绿茶；还曾经流行过喝水果茶。

A： 我听说近些年日本和台湾流行喝普洱茶，人们认为它可以减肥和降血压。

B： 这在中国大陆也流行。普洱茶的色泽和气味更类似于法国红葡萄酒，加之传说中的减肥作用，就成了时尚。绿茶有延年益寿和抗癌的作用。红茶有暖胃的作用。

A： 这些年城市里开了许多茶馆，传统茶馆多是平民待的地方，而这些大城市的茶馆则成为高档的社交场所。

B： 茶馆甚至改变了商人做生意的方式。传统上，中国商人习惯于在酒桌上谈生意，现在有人说："在酒桌上说得越多，事情越糟；在茶桌上，说得越多，事情越清楚。"

A： 好像茶话会也很流行？

B： 茶是节俭和清廉的象征。官方和一些政府机构在节庆的日子会举办茶话会，既沟通了情感，也不会太破费。

A： 茶不但有社会功能、经济功能，还有政治功能。难怪中国文化中，茶总是与饭相提并论。

Background Reading　背景阅读

Selling Tea to China　把茶卖到中国去

Spare a thought for Loic Tardy, managing director of the Chinese division of Lipton. He's facing a challenge similar to opening a Starbucks outlet in Italy: How to sell Liptons British-style black tea, the world's most recognized brand, in the country where the story of tea began.

Tardy is reluctant to discuss market strategies and figures, but notes that while Chinese people usually don't drink black tea hot, the black-tea variety has a 60% share in the iced-tea market. "Young people are open to changes," says Tardy, pointing out the surging popularity of milk in China.

Indeed, tea with milk and sugar might just be catching on among young, urban Chinese. The fashion, however, does not come from Britain, but, as with the upmarket teahouse in Beijing, from Taiwan, where Zhenzhu naicha, sweet milk tea with small, chewy balls of taro flour, has been popular for several years.

China, the home of tea, is embracing its favorite brew as never before. Between 1980 and 2003, total tea production in China grew from 300 million tonnes to 760 million tonnes. China is the world's third-largest producer of tea, after India and Sri Lanka, and the third-largest exporter after Sri Lanka and Kenya.

　　站在立顿公司中国区的总经理谈奕文的角度想一想，他正面临着一个类似星巴克在意大利开咖啡店式的问题：即如何在一个茶的发源地销售世界上最为著名的立顿牌英式红茶。

　　谈奕文不愿意谈及市场战略和相关数字，但是他介绍说，尽管中国人通常不喝热红茶，但红茶占冰茶市场的份额达 60% 。谈奕文说："年轻人愿意尝试新的事物，"他以牛奶在中国变得极为流行为佐证。

　　事实上，茶搭配奶和糖的饮用方式在中国的城市年轻人中很流行。然而这一时尚就如同北京的高档茶馆一样，并不是源自英国，而是来自台湾。台湾的珍珠奶茶，即用甜牛奶配以芋头味的、耐嚼的小圆颗粒，在当地已经流行了若干年。

　　中国作为茶的故乡，对茶叶的热中是前所未有的。在 1980 至 2003 年间，茶叶总产量从 3 亿吨增加到 7. 6 亿吨。中国已成为继印度和斯里兰卡之后的第三大产茶国，也是继斯里兰卡和肯尼亚之后的第三大茶叶出口国。

---

daily necessities　日常必需品	state of mind　境界	keep...awake　使…清醒
lose weight　减肥	hang around　泡，待在	social life　社交生活
tea party　茶话会		

 **Exercises** 练习

Answer these questions.

1. What do people do in tea houses?
2. What are some of the functions of pu'er tea?
3. Why is tea party fashionable?

Translate these sentences into Chinese.

1. There are a lot of Chinese expressions that link tea with food.
2. Tea-drinking can help a person achieve an elevated state of mind.
3. Monks drank tea to keep themselves awake.
4. People think it can help lose weight and control blood pressure.
5. Pu'er tea looks and smells more like French red wine than tea.
6. Usually tea houses are where ordinary people like to hang around.
7. These tea houses are destinations for a high-brow social life.
8. Tea houses have even changed the way people do business.
9. It serves the purposes of both socializing and saving money.
10. No wonder tea is always mentioned together with food in Chinese.

Complete this paragraph with suitable words.

Many tea houses have been opened. __1__ tea houses are where ordinary people like to __2__ around. But these tea houses are __3__ for high-brow social life. Tea houses have __4__ changed the __5__ people do business. It used to be __6__ meals. The saying now is "At a table of spirits, the __7__ you talk, the more muddled things become. But at a table of tea, the more you talk, the more clear things __8__ ."

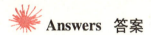 **Answers** 答案

Translate these sentences into Chinese.

1. 中国有不少茶饭相关联的俗语。
2. 饮茶能提升精神境界。
3. 僧侣们喝茶为提神醒脑。
4. 人们认为它可以减肥和降血压。
5. 普洱茶的色泽和气味更类似于法国红葡萄酒。
6. 传统茶馆多是平民待的地方。
7. 这些茶馆成为高档的社交场所。
8. 茶馆甚至改变了商人做生意的方式。
9. 这既沟通了情感，也不会太破费。
10. 难怪中国文化中，茶总是与饭相提并论。

Complete this paragraph with suitable words.

1. Usually 2. hang 3. destinations 4. even 5. way 6. over 7. more 8. become

27. Meanings in a Chinese Name

中国人姓名的含意

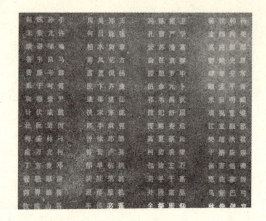

Dialogue

A: Unlike in a Western name, the family name in a Chinese name comes before the first name. There are also meanings in a Chinese name.

B: That's correct. The meanings in a Chinese name are reflected in the **combination** of the characters, which are influenced either by elements of culture or era. Usually the cultural influence is stronger in the characters for family names. Any character that has the particle that means "woman" suggests its traces back to the matriarchal society. Some family names originated either in official titles or **occupation**, or in animals of worship. A few others come from numbers.

A: I see. What about given names?

B: In comparison, meanings in given names are always chosen to reflect elements of the era. In the old days, characters meaning "wealth", "fortune", and "happiness" were very common in names. Characters with the meanings of "gifted", "handsome", and "clever" were often chosen by parents as well wishes for their children to be beautiful, capable, and intelligent. During the 1950s and 1960s, many boys were given the name with the meaning of "building the country", "celebrating the nation", "fighting the American imperialists", and "overtaking the British". The reform and opening policies also provided more choices of characters, such as "bo" meaning "strive", "si" meaning "thoughtful", and "yuhang" meaning "aeronautics". Parents would like their children to learn more knowledge, to be more thoughtful and to have great **aspirations**. Some people also like to use translated Western names such David, Richard, Lisa and Linda.

A: This is quite similar to English names. Some of the surnames also come from occupations, such as Sheppard, Smith and Baker. Some Western names also have meanings. "Laura" for example means "laureate" in Latin, and "Samson" means "Sun" in Hebrew.

B： I don't know much about Western names. When translated into Chinese，Westerns names are simply a phonetic combination of Chinese characters. In order for people to remember Western names，translators in the 1950s and 1960s tried to **localize** names in literature，such as Scarlett O'Hara and Rhett Butler in *Gone with the Wind*. Even a place like Atlanta was translated in such a way. Although it was easier to remember these names，they don't look Western any more. So when some of the literary works were retranslated in the 1990s，phonetic translation was used again.

A： A Western novel with each of its characters having a Chinese name is very similar to a Westerner having a typical Chinese name like Da Shan，meaning "Big Mountain". It sounds **weird**. **I'd rather** have something that can **remind** me of the original.

对 话

A： 中国人的姓名是姓在前，名在后，英美人则相反。另外，中国人的名字还有意义。

B： 对。中国人姓名中的意思包含在文字中，同时也受到文化和时代的影响。文化的影响通常在姓氏上更明显。带有"女"字旁的姓，暗示着与母系氏族社会的关联；还有一些姓氏来源于古代的官职称谓或职业的称谓以及对动物的崇拜；也有的源自数字。

A： 原来是这样。那么名字呢？

B： 相比较而言，名字与时代紧密相关。旧时以"富、发、禄"取名的多，因为它们有发财升官之意；以"杰、俊、才"为名的，是父母希望孩子能美丽、贤能、聪慧。五六十年代，男子叫"建国、国庆、抗美、超英"的多；改革开放后，取名字的范围更广，叫"博、思、宇航"的多，是父母希望孩子拥有现代化的知识，有思想和远大的志向。借用外国人名字的也不少，男孩叫"大卫、查理"，女孩叫"丽莎、琳达"等。

A： 这与英文名有相似之处。英文名中也有源自职业的，比如 Sheppard（牧羊人），Smith（铁匠），Baker（面包师）；英文名字也有意思，如 Laura 源自拉丁语，是"桂冠"之义；Samson 是希伯莱语，有"太阳"之义等。

B： 我对英文名了解得不多。翻译成中文，外国人名就是一些中文字音的集合。所以上世纪五六十年代中国翻译外国小说时有一个倾向，就是把外国人名完全中国化，以便中国人记住。最典型的要算小说《飘》，主人公 Scarlett O'Hara 和 Rhett Butler 被译成郝思嘉和白瑞德；连地名也译出中国特色：Atlanta（亚特兰大）译成"饿狼陀"。易懂，但失去了英文原有的感觉。到 90 年代重译时，又变成音译以符合原著的感觉。

A： 一本外国小说充满了中国式的人名，就像一个外国人叫"大山"，听起来很怪。我宁可要能使我想起原汁原味的东西来。

Is Your Name Your Fate? 姓名即是命运？

Social scientists say that what you're called can effect your life. Throughout history, names have not merely identified people but also described them. Webster's Dictionary includes the following definition of name: "a word or words expressing some quality considered characteristic or descriptive of a person or a thing, often expressing approval or disapproval." Note well "approval or disapproval": for better or worse, qualities such as friendliness or reserve, plainness or charm may be suggested by your name and conveyed to other people before they even meet you.

Of course, names with a positive sense can work for you—even encouraging new acquaintances. A recent survey showed that American men thought Susan to be the attractive female name, while women believed Richard and David were the most attractive for men.

In a study conducted by Herbert Harari of San Diego State University, and John McDavid of Georgia State University, teachers gave consistently lower grades on essays supposedly written by boys named Elmer and Hubert than they awarded to the same papers when the author's names were given as Michael and David. However, teacher prejudice isn't the only source of classroom difference; Dr. Thomas V. Busse and Louisa Seraydarian of Temple University found that girls with names such as Linda, Diane, Barbara, Carol, and Cindy performed better on objectively graded IQ and achievement tests than did girls with less appealing names.

社会学家说，你的称呼会影响你的生活。纵观历史，名字不仅仅是一个人的称号，也描述了一个人的特性。韦伯斯特大词典对名字的解释是："表现一个人或一件事具有代表性的特征或描述人或事物的一个或几个字，常常带有认可或不认可的态度。"请注意"认可与不认可"的意思即不管怎样，你的名字当中可能会包含一些诸如友善或矜持、庸常或魅力的品性，这些品性可能在未曾谋面之前就已经传达给对方了。

当然，有积极意义的名字有助于你的成功，甚至可以帮助你结识新朋友。最近的一项调查显示，美国人认为苏珊是具有魅力的女性名字，女人们则认为理查德和大卫是最有吸引力的男性名字。

由圣迭哥州立大学的赫伯特·哈里里和乔治亚州立大学的约翰·麦克大卫进行的一项研究表明，教师们一向把低分给予那些名字是艾尔默和休伯特的学生们所写的作文，而同样水平的作文，那些名字为麦克尔或大卫的学生们的得分则相对更高。然而，教师的偏见并不是这种学校差异的唯一原因；天普大学的托马斯·布瑟和路易斯·塞拉夫达理安博士发现，与那些名字并不吸引人的女孩相比，名叫琳达、戴安、芭芭拉、卡罗以及辛迪的女孩在独立进行的 IQ 测试中得分更高，而且考试成绩也更好。

---

combination 组合	occupation 职业	aspiration 抱负，志向
localize 本土化	weird 怪	I'd rather 我宁愿
remind 使…想起		

 **Exercises** 练习

Answer these questions.

1. What are some popular characters in a Chinese name in the past?
2. What can characters like "gifted" and "handsome" reflect in a name?
3. How did people translate Western names in the 1950s?

Translate these sentences into Chinese.

1. The family name in a Chinese name comes before the first name.
2. The meanings in a Chinese name are reflected in the combination of the characters.
3. Some family names are originated either in official titles or occupation.
4. Many boys were given names with the meaning of "building the country".
5. Parents would like their children to have great aspirations.
6. This is quite similar to English names.
7. Western names are simply a phonetic combination of Chinese characters.
8. Translators in the 1950s tried to localize names in literature.
9. It sounds weird.
10. I'd rather have something that can remind me of the original.

Complete this paragraph with suitable words.

When translated __1__ Chinese, Westerns names are __2__ a phonetic combination of Chinese characters. In __3__ for people to remember Western names, translators __4__ the 1950s and 1960s tried to __5__ names in literature. Although it was __6__ to remember these names, they don't look Western __7__ more. So when some of the literary __8__ were retranslated in the 1990s, phonetic translation was used again.

 Answers 答案

Translate these sentences into Chinese.

1. 中国人的姓名是姓在前，名在后。
2. 中国人姓名中的意思包含在文字中。
3. 有一些姓氏来源于官职或职业称谓。
4. 许多男孩取名"建国"。
5. 父母希望孩子有远大的志向。
6. 这与英文名有相似之处。
7. 外国人名就是一些中文字音的集合。
8. 上世纪50年代翻译外国小说时汉化外国名字。
9. 这听起来很怪。
10. 我宁可要能使我想起原汁原味的东西来。

Complete this paragraph with suitable words.

1. into 2. simply 3. order 4. in 5. localize 6. easier 7. any 8. works

28. Feng Shui

风水

Dialogue

A： Some Chinese people like to keep a bowl of gold fish in their office. They think this can bring good luck in dealing with **office politics** and in their career.

B： That's what we call Feng Shui, or geomancy. Some people think Feng Shui is superstition but, once you have a closer look, you'll find it's much more **sophisticated**. It is a juxtaposition of environmental, psychological and, hygienic studies. Elements, such as, structures, noise, smell and lighting, which are harmful to a living environment, are called, "evil". For instance, a room that is either, too bright or, too dark, can have an **adverse effect** on people's emotions. Feng Shui **is supposed to** help people adapt to that sort of harmful environment.

A： Are there any Chinese cultural elements in Feng Shui?

B： Of course, there are. It is heavily influenced by the theory of the five natural elements of metal, wood, water, fire and earth. The theory is all about how things **complement**, or check, each other, and, how people should **pursue** harmony to avoid harm. In other words, it's about balance. For example, if a person lives in a light colored house for too long, he, or she, is likely to lose patience and become restless. According to Feng Shui, the colors in the room are not harmonious and need to be adjusted to achieve balance. Feng Shui also has an influence over people's life and psyche. Chinese culture is developed around the belief of the golden mean. In other words, refrain from being excessive. If a small family occupies a large house, it is believed to bring bad fortune, sooner or later. The message here is, to maintain balance.

A： How does Feng Shui interpret the location of a house? If the location is not **desirable**, do people have to desert it?

B： Not really. Feng Shui emphasizes the pursuit of harmony to avoid harm. For example, if the door of a house opens in the wrong direction, the solution is not to seal it but to place something else near the door. That **diverts** the potential harm and makes people feel secure. It's quite similar to the fish bowl in the office. It gives people a psychological boost that helps them be more relaxed, and confident at work. Hopefully, it will help them earn promotions. Is this a benefit from the fish bowl, or a psychological boost, or neither? Whatever the answer, if Feng Shui can help people live a smoother and more successful life, why not?

对 话

A： 有些中国人喜欢在办公室里摆放鱼缸，目的是化解工作中的不利因素，使职场上的奋斗更加顺利。

B： 这就是风水。有些人认为风水是迷信，但深入了解后，你会发现并不这么简单。风水其实包含了环境学、心理学、卫生学等学科的知识。在风水学中，那些对居住环境构成不良影响的物体、声音、气味、光线等都被称为"煞"。比如，房间的光线过明或过暗，都会对人的情绪产生负面影响。风水可以帮助人们适应有害的环境。

A： 风水学中是否有中国传统文化的因素？

B： 当然。最主要的就是金、木、水、火、土五行之说的影响。五行说的本质是事物相生相克，人们应趋利避害，换句话说，就是达到平衡。比如，房屋内完全以浅色为主，时间长了就会使人失去耐性，心躁气浮。依据风水之说，这个房间的颜色失调，需要加以调整，达到平衡。风水学对人的生活观念和心理也有影响。中国文化基于中庸思想，凡事不可缺也不可过。所以风水学讲究人口少住大宅不吉利。意思是保持均衡。

A： 风水学对于房屋的坐落位置有哪些讲究？如果位置不佳，人们就弃房不住了吗？

B： 不是这样的。风水学强调趋利避害。比如这家人的大门朝向没有开对，并不是把门封死，办法是在门旁摆放一些东西化解。就像你提到的员工们认为在办公室摆鱼缸就吉利，有了这种心理暗示，他的情绪就会放松，工作中就更加自信，提职或加薪就有可能。这是鱼缸的作用还是心理暗示的作用？或者都不是？不管怎样，如果风水可以帮助人们生活得更加和顺，何乐而不为呢？

Background Reading 背景阅读

Feng Shui Becomes Popular 风水开始流行

In Europe and America, Feng Shui has become as popular as the martial arts and Shaolin Gongfu. More and more people talk about Feng Shui with great relish. Many universities and institutes have supplementary courses, using a modern scientific approach to research and calculate statistics, to rigorously test and examine the truth of Feng Shui.

The background of 5,000 years of Chinese culture includes Confucianism, Buddhism, Daoism, and the Yi Jing, along with the types of metaphysics derived from it. Of all of these, Feng Shui is the most able to coexist with the powerful current of history until today in East Asian culture.

Men put their own safety and wealth as the first priority, followed by the welfare of others, society, and then finally the country. To learn metaphysics is to seek methods of prediction. In this way, by choosing a suitable pace and time, one can change the variables to turn disaster into felicity, pursuing a good future and shunning the course of calamity. The ability to predict is the most highly desired knowledge for human beings.

True Feng Shui masters are few, whereas cheaters are everywhere. In a Chinese mall in San Gabirel, California, there was a large restaurant. On the instructions of a Feng Shui master, they put half-filled fish tanks on both sides of their escalator. The tanks were without fish. At the reception counter, they placed a picture of the Chinese ghost hunter, Zhong Kui. This so-called Feng Shui is ridiculous.

在欧洲和美国，风水已经像武术和少林功夫一样变得流行起来。越来越多的人饶有兴趣地谈论风水。许多大学和研究机构开设了有关风水的选修课，用现代科学的研究方法和统计学对风水的实质进行严格的测评和探究。

中国5000年的文化包含在儒学、佛教、道教和易经之中，由此产生出形而上学的方法。而风水则最能够与这些强有力的历史潮流相依存，直到今天在东亚文化中产生影响。

人们总是将其安全和财富放到优先考虑的位置，相伴随的是他人和社会的利益，最后才是国家。学习形而上学的方法就是探求预见的手段。通过选择适宜的空间和时间，人们能够将不幸转化为幸运，追求一个美好的未来，避开灾难，即所谓趋利避害。预见的能力是人类最为渴望的真知。

真正的风水大师不多，骗子倒是比比皆是。加州的圣加布里埃尔市有个中国城，里面有家很大的中餐馆。根据风水师的指示，他们在电动扶梯的两旁放了灌了半缸水的鱼缸，其中没有放鱼。在接待台，他们放着钟馗的画像，他是专门驱鬼的人。这种所谓的风水是荒谬的。

---

office politics 办公室里的勾心斗角	sophisticated 复杂的，老练的	adverse effect 反作用
is supposed to 被认为是	complement 弥补，补充	pursue 追求
desirable 理想的，渴望得到的	divert 使…转向	

 **Exercises** 练习

Answer these questions.
1. Why do some people keep a bowl of fish in their office?
2. What is the purpose of Fengshui?
3. Are there any Chinese cultural elements in Fengshui?

Translate these sentences into Chinese.
1. Some people like to keep a bowl of gold fish in their office.
2. Some people think Fengshui is superstition.
3. A room either too bright or too dark can have an adverse effect on people's emotions.
4. Fengshui is supposed to help people make adaptation to a harmful environment.
5. Fengshui also has an influence over people's life.
6. Chinese culture is developed around the belief of the golden mean.
7. The message is to maintain balance.
8. Fengshui emphasizes the pursuit of harmony to avoid harm.
9. The solution is to place something else near the door.
10. If Fengshui can help people live a smoother life, why not?

Complete this paragraph with suitable words.
Some people think Fengshui is superstition, but __1__ you have a __2__ look, you'll find that it's __3__ more sophisticated. Elements that are __4__ to a living environment, such __5__ structures, noise, smell, lighting, etc., are called "evil". For __6__, a room that is either too bright or too dark can have an adverse effect __7__ people's emotions. Fengshui is __8__ to help people make adaptation to such a harmful environment.

 **Answers** 答案

Translate these sentences into Chinese.
1. 有些人喜欢在办公室里摆放鱼缸。
2. 有些人认为风水是迷信。
3. 房间的光线过明或过暗，都会对人的情绪产生负面影响。
4. 风水可以帮助人们适应有害的环境。
5. 风水对人的生活也有影响。
6. 中国文化基于中庸思想。
7. 意思是保持均衡。
8. 风水讲求趋利避害。
9. 解决方法是在门旁摆放一些东西。
10. 如果风水可以帮助人们生活得更加和顺，何乐而不为呢？

Complete this paragraph with suitable words.
1. once 2. closer 3. much 4. harmful 5. as 6. instance 7. on 8. supposed

29. The Secret of Numbers

数字的秘密

Dialogue

A： I noticed that some people like to use 001 for their personalized licence plates, such as BTV 001 and CRC 001. Why does everybody like 001?

B： Because, in Chinese, the number one represents "the first" or "the most original". It's a differentiator. The 001 in the licence plate, is an expression of the car owner's aspirations.

A： At an auction in Shanghai last year, one particular licence plate, with a **combination** of four 8's, was sold for, well over, 100,000 yuan. That made me think, whether there is any special meaning behind the numbers and, how people are influenced by them.

B： In Cantonese, the number "8" has a similar pronunciation to, the word "prosper". Guangdong is one of the first provinces to benefit from China's **open policy**. There is a lot of **temptation** to become wealthy so, "8" is a lucky number for people in Guangdong. Similarly, "6" is often **associated with** smoothness. Many people like to choose a date for their weddings which includes the number "6". Lots of people got married on June 6, 2006. **In contrast**, "4" is the least favorable number because, it sounds very similar to the word, "death". Many buildings do not, even, use the number for their elevator programming. Now, **as a result of** Western influence, more and more Chinese people started to dislike the number "13".

A： Does the number, "3" have a special meaning too?

B： Number "3" is, always, associated with abundance or, the ultimate limit. There are a lot of proverbs with the number "3." "Shi bu guo san" is one which, literally, means, "You are only allowed three chances". Another proverb is "San si er xing", meaning, "Think three times before you act".

A： Does this have any effect on people's lives?

B： It depends. Some time ago, a man received **a blackmail message** on his cell phone. It told him to deposit 3,000 yuan in a designated bank account by a certain time or, his family would face danger. Similar blackmail threats have happened to a number of other people. The police found that there was, at least, an "8" in the cell phone numbers of the victims. The robbers thought that only wealthy people could afford to choose the number "8". So, instead of bringing the victims prosperity and wealth, the number nearly got them in trouble.

A： That reminds me of a saying："Things will have an **adverse effect** if pushed to the limit."

对 话

A： 我发现一些人喜欢在个性化的车牌后使用 001 的数字。比如 BTV-001，CRC-001 等等。为什么呢？

B： 因为中国人认为"1"有"第一"、"最先"的意思。这个数字使人感到自己与众不同。所以汽车牌照里的 001 表现了车主的愿望。

A： 去年上海市拍卖车牌号，一个四个"8"连在一起的牌照卖出了十几万元的价格。由此我想，是不是中国的数字有一些特别的含义，它对人们的生活有着怎样的影响？

B： 广东话里"8"与"发"同音，有发财的意思。广东是中国最先受益于改革开放政策的省份之一，金钱的诱惑力很大，人人都做着发财的梦，因此"8"成为人们偏爱的数字。"6"有顺利之意，许多人爱选带"6"的日子作为结婚日。许多人在 2006 年 6 月 6 日结婚。相比之下，"4"与"死"同音，是最不讨人喜欢的数字。不少建筑物甚至没有"4"层。现在，受西洋文化的影响，许多中国人开始讨厌数字"13"了。

A： "3"有什么讲究吗？

B： "3"是言之多也的意思，也有极限的意思。比如"事不过三"、"三思而行"等等。

A： 数字的寓意真的很灵验吗？

B： 那要看情形而定。不久前，某人的手机上收到了一条敲诈短信，让他在指定时间向一个银行帐户内存入 3000 元钱，否则他家人就会危险。有十多个人遇到了同样的遭遇。警察发现，被勒索者的手机号码的后四位数都有"8"，勒索者认为能够得到带有一个甚至三四个"8"的手机号码，机主一定花了大价钱，必定是有钱人。"8"这个数字不但没有给他带来财富，反而差点儿给他找了麻烦。

A： 这让我想起一句老话：物极必反。

A license Plate—Status Symbol 车牌——地位的象征

At a government auction inside a dingy gymnasium, a young businessman named Ding walked away a happy winner the other day. Like everyone else, he was bidding on license plates and did not seem to mind that his cost $6,750.

For the same money, Mr. Ding could almost have afforded two of the Chinese-made roadsters popular in the domestic car market. His bid was almost 20 times what a Chinese farmer earns in a year, and almost 7 times the country's per capita annual income.

And yet, in the auction in this manufacturing capital in southern China, Mr. Ding, who gave only his last name, could not even claim top price. The most expensive plate—AC6688—fetched $10,000 on a day when officials sold hundreds of plates for a total of $366,500.

No country is more bonkers over cars than China, where achieving the new middle-class dream means owning a shiny new vehicle. But the car is not always enough for those who aspire beyond the middle class. A license plate has become almost as much of a status symbol as the car.

License plates are usually issued randomly. But in a country where 100,000 people die annually in traffic accidents, a plate that ends in 4 is considered a very bad omen for a superstitious motorist; it might as well read DEATH. Yet a plate overflowing with 8's portends good fortune.

在一座简陋的体育馆内，政府部门正在拍卖车牌照，年轻的商人丁某走过一位高兴的获胜者身旁，他是在另一天拍得了一个理想的牌照。像所有的人一样，丁某正在为汽车牌照竞标，而且似乎并不在意这要花掉他6 750美元。

以同样的价格，丁先生几乎可以买下两辆中国国内汽车市场上流行的国产跑车。他为牌照所出的资金几乎是中国一个农民一年收入的20倍，大约7倍于中国的人均年收入。

然而，在中国南部的这个制造业之都，丁先生——他只说出自己的姓氏——并没有报出顶尖的价位。最贵的车牌照号是AC6688，价值10 000美元，当时官方卖出了几百个牌照号，总价值为366 500美元。

没有哪个国家比中国对汽车更痴狂了，这里新到达中产阶层的人们的梦想就是一辆闪闪发光的新汽车。但是仅仅有汽车对这些渴望超越中产阶层的人们是不够的，牌照号就成为与汽车一样最能够象征身份和地位的东西。

车牌号的发放通常是随机的。但是在这个国家，每年死于交通事故的人达到10万人，对于迷信的常乘车的人来说，以4结尾的牌照号就被认为是不吉利的象征；它的读音与"死"相同。而带8的车牌号则预示着好运和发财。

---

combination 组合	open policy 开放政策	temptation 诱惑
associate with 与…相关	in contrast 相比之下，反之	as a result of 由于
a blackmail message 一封敲诈短信		adverse effect 相反的效果

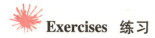 **Exercises** 练习

Answer these questions.

1. Why do many people like 001 in their license plates?
2. Why do Guangdong people like the number "8"?
3. Why is number "4" an unlucky number?

Translate these sentences into Chinese.

1. The 001 in the license plate is an expression of the car owner's aspirations.
2. One license plate with a combination of four 8's was sold for well over 100, 000 yuan.
3. Guangdong is one of first provinces to benefit from China's open policy.
4. The number "6" is often associated with smoothness.
5. Many Chinese people have started to dislike number "13".
6. June 6, 2006 happened to be a Saturday.
7. You are only allowed three chances.
8. A man received a blackmail message on his cell phone.
9. Instead of bringing him wealth, the number nearly got him in trouble.
10. Things will have an adverse effect if pushed to the limit.

Complete this paragraph with suitable words.

In Cantonese, the number "8" has a ___1___ pronunciation to "prosper". Guangdong is one of ___2___ provinces to ___3___ from China's open policy. There is a lot of temptation to become wealthy, so "8" is a ___4___ number for people in Guangdong. Similarly, "6" is often associated ___5___ smoothness. Many people like to choose a date for their ___6___ which includes the number "6". June 6, 2006 ___7___ to be a Saturday and lots of people ___8___ married that day.

 Answers 答案

Translate these sentences into Chinese.

1. 汽车牌照里的 001 表现了车主的愿望。
2. 一个四个 "8" 连在一起的牌照卖出了十几万元的价格。
3. 广东是中国最先受益于改革开放政策的省份之一。
4. 数字 "6" 有顺利之意。
5. 许多中国人开始讨厌数字 "13" 了。
6. 2006 年 6 月 6 日恰好是个星期六。
7. 你只有 3 次机会。
8. 某人的手机上收到了一条敲诈短信。
9. 这个数字不但没有给他带来财富，反而差点儿给他找了麻烦。
10. 物极必反。

Complete this paragraph with suitable words.

1. similar 2. first 3. benefit 4. lucky 5. with 6. weddings 7. happened 8. got

30. Paintings，Calendars and Christmas Trees

年画、挂历、圣诞树

Dialogue

A： I bought a few old Chinese New Year paintings at the Pan Jia Yuan Market. The person told me that they were block-printed Tao Hua Wu paintings.

B： It's almost impossible to buy **authentic** Tao Hua Wu paintings on the market now. This type of painting was originally produced in Tao Hua Wu near Suzhou. The place became well-known during the Qing Dynasty. Its paintings were sold across China, **as well as** in Japan and Southeast Asia. During the Taiping rebellion between 1851 and 1864, the imperial court sent troops and set Tao Hua Wu ablaze. Most of its paintings, wood types, shops and books were destroyed.

A： What a shame！Do Chinese people still hang up New Year paintings now?

B： New Year paintings were an important part of the annual celebrations. The contents of the paintings were well-wishing stories that could add to the **festive** atmosphere. Some of them also carried a moral message. At a time when education was not accessible to everyone, these paintings **served as** useful teaching tools. Some of the typical messages were loyalty, benevolence, kindness and retribution. For example, one painting was about a woman **abusing** her daughter-in-law but was later turned into a child bride herself as punishment. Beautiful lady figurines were another favorite topic for these paintings.

A： Sounds lovely！Are there any others?

B： During the 1950s, portraits of Mao Zedong and other leaders were popular. During the Cultural Revolution, the eight Peking Operas were the main theme. After the open-door policy in the 1980s, these paintings were replaced by 12-page calendars. These calendars were a favorite New Year gift for quite some time. They were well printed and were quite expensive to buy. Because they used quality paper, many students would use **out-of-date** calendars to cover their textbooks as protection.

A： That's odd！What kind of pictures did they have?

B： Movie stars were the main contents, a reaction to the cultural Puritanism during the

Cultural Revolution. **As a result of** improved living standards, calendar contents later evolved to include calligraphy, traditional paintings, as well as landscape pictures. In order to make these calendars worthy New Year gifts, silk, gilded sheets and other materials rather than paper were used. Calendars went out of fashion around the end of the 1990s. No one used a calendar for gifts any more.

A： What do people put up during the Spring Festival now?

B： Paper cuts in some townships, but in big cities, no one puts up anything. Instead, Christmas trees have become fashionable. Imagine, the whole family are enjoying *jiaozi* or playing *mahjong*, while Christmas lights are **blinking** in the background. That's a pretty happy atmosphere.

对 话

A： 我在潘家园旧货市场买了几张旧版年画。摊主说是桃花坞的木版年画。

B： 现在市场上买到真正旧版桃花坞年画的可能性不大了。这种画最初产自苏州的桃花坞，到了清代，这里已很著名，产品不但遍及中国，而且传到东南亚和日本。在1851到1864年太平天国运动时，朝廷派军队将桃花坞付之一炬。其大部分年画、模板、店铺以及画本都被毁了。

A： 太可惜了！中国人现在还贴年画吗？

B： 春节贴年画是节庆活动的重要内容之一。年画多为祈福内容，以增添节日氛围。其中一些含有道德寓意，在教育不普及的旧时代，这些画起到了教育作用。一些年画以忠孝仁义、善恶有报等为内容。比如，有一张年画是婆婆打儿媳，后世遭报应作了童养媳的故事。仕女图是另一个受欢迎的题材。

A： 那一定很可爱了！还有其他形式的年画吗？

B： 上世纪50年代，年画的内容多为领袖的画像，比如毛泽东等。六七十年代文化大革命时，八个样板戏成为流行的年画内容。20世纪80年代改革开放后，单张的年画被挂历取代，成为春节时的重要礼品。它们用非常精美的纸印制，价格昂贵。由于纸张质量很好，挂历还有另一个用途：学生们用旧挂历包书皮，以免新书磨损。

A： 太有意思了！上面印些什么？

B： 挂历的内容多是中外影视明星，这正是对文化大革命禁欲主义的一种反响。随着人们物质生活水平的提高，挂历的内容又增加了书法、绘画以及名胜古迹等内容。为了使挂历成为有价值的新年礼品，丝绸、金箔等材料代替了纸张。90年代末以后，挂历渐渐过时，没有人再把它当礼物赠送。

A： 现在春节挂什么呢？

B： 剪纸在一些小城镇流行，但大城市几乎没什么可张贴的了。圣诞树开始时髦了。想像一下，圣诞树的灯光在背景中闪烁，一家人吃着饺子、搓着麻将，那是怎样一种欢乐的氛围呵。

In Pursuit of Happiness and Good Luck 追求幸福与好运

The Chinese have always been family conscious. In old times, families of several generations living in complete harmony under one roof represented their highest pursuit, hence the saying "more children, more happiness". Traditional weddings invariably center on blessings on the couple to live in conjugal bliss to a ripe old age and to produce many children. Such blessings, so to speak, are "materialized" in those wedding rituals and articles special for the occasion.

When stepping into the nuptial chamber, the bridegroom and bride hold either end of a red silk ribbon with a heart-shaped bundle hanging from the middle, suggesting that the couple are resolved to share each other's weal and woe forever. The bridegroom and bride then will each cut off a tuft of hair and weave the two tufts into a bundle, suggesting that from now on they will be chained together as an officially married couple. Peony flowers are often embroidered on the pillows and sheets on the nuptial bed along with a white-crested bird. The peony flowers, symbolize riches and honor and the white-crested bird, the hope that the couple will love each other until their hair turns white. On the wall facing south in the nuptial chamber there is a colorful painting depicting two boy deities, one holding a lotus flower and the other, a round box. In the Chinese language, the characters 荷 (lotus flower), 盒 (box) and 和 (harmony) have the same pronunciation. So the painting embodies a hope that the couple will live in "double" or even "triple" harmony.

中国人的家庭观念很强。过去,几代人和和美美地同住一个屋檐下是人们的最高追求,故称"多子多福"。传统婚礼无一不祝福夫妻俩白头偕老、子孙满堂。这样的祝福还通过婚礼的仪式以及各种饰物表现出来。

步入洞房时,新郎新娘各拉着一条红绸带的两端,绸带中间是一个心形饰物,预示着两个人要同甘共苦。然后,新郎新娘各自剪下一撮头发,并将头发编入同心结,象征两人从此正式结为连理。洞房里的枕头和被子一般都绣有牡丹花和一只白色的鸟,牡丹花代表富贵和节操,白鸟则表示两人要相依相爱、白头偕老。洞房朝南的墙上挂一幅画,画的内容是两个童子,其中一个手拿荷花,另一个手捧圆盒子。中文里面,荷花的"荷"和盒子的"盒"与和睦的"和"谐音,因此,画的意思是祝福夫妻俩"双和睦",甚至"三和睦"。

authentic 正版	as well as 以及	festive 节日的	serve as 用于
abuse 欺负	out-of-date 过时的	as a result of 由于	blink 闪烁

 **Exercises** 练习

Answer these questions.
1. When did Tao Hua Wu paintings become well-known?
2. What paintings do people hang up during the Chinese New Year?
3. What are some of the contents of the calendars?

Translate these sentences into Chinese.
1. It's almost impossible to buy authentic Tao Hua Wu paintings on the market now.
2. The imperial court sent troops and set Tao Hua Wu ablaze.
3. Most of its paintings, wood types, shops and books were destroyed.
4. Some of them also carried a moral message.
5. These paintings served as useful teaching tools.
6. Beautiful lady figurines were another favorite topic for these paintings.
7. Students would use out-of-date calendars to cover their textbooks as protection.
8. Calendars went out of fashion around the end of 1990s.
9. Christmas trees have become fashionable.
10. Christmas lights are blinking in the background.

Complete this paragraph with suitable words.
These calendars were a __1__ New Year gift for quite some time. They were __2__ printed and were quite expensive to buy. Because they used __3__ paper, many students would use out-of-date calendars to __4__ their textbooks __5__ protection. Movie stars were the main contents, a __6__ to the cultural Puritanism during the Cultural Revolution. As a result of __7__ living standards, calendar contents later __8__ to include calligraphy, traditional paintings, as well as landscape pictures.

 Answers 答案

Translate these sentences into Chinese.
1. 现在市场上买到真正旧版桃花坞年画的可能性不大了。
2. 朝廷派军队将桃花坞付之一炬。
3. 其大部分年画、模板、店铺以及画本都被毁了。
4. 其中一些含有道德寓意。
5. 这些画起到了教育作用。
6. 仕女图是另一个受欢迎的题材。
7. 学生们用旧挂历包书皮，以免新书磨损。
8. 20 世纪 90 年代末以后，挂历渐渐过时。
9. 圣诞树开始时髦了。
10. 圣诞树的灯光在背景中闪烁。

Complete this paragraph with suitable words.
1. favorite 2. well 3. quality 4. cover 5. as 6. reaction 7. improved 8. evolved

31. Tea or Coffee?

茶还是咖啡？

Dialogue

A: Did you pay any attention to President Hu Jintao's visit to the United States in April 2006?

B: Of course, I did. His first stop was in Seattle. He was invited to Bill Gates' luxurious home as the **guest of honor**. He visited Boeing and met with a lot of Boeing workers. One Boeing employee presented President Hu with a baseball cap and he put it on his head, right on the stage. He impressed the local media as a very approachable leader.

A: But, do you know who the biggest winner was during his visit to Seattle?

B: Who?

A: I think Starbucks was the winner.

B: That's an interesting **insight**. Why?

A: According to media reports, Hu Jintao said that, if he had time, he'd love to visit a Starbucks in Beijing. That was a great compliment made by the President and **free publicity** for Starbucks. I'm sure it will see a significant boost to their brand recognition in China.

B: As a matter of fact, Starbucks is, already, doing very well in China. For a lot of young people, coffee drinking is a desirable part of their lifestyle. That's why Starbucks has become a favorite destination. Although, traditionally, Chinese people prefer tea, coffee is becoming very popular as more and more young people adopt a Western lifestyle.

A: What about you? Do you like coffee?

B: I used to drink a lot of coffee but, have **switched to** tea. I do not like the association of coffee with social status and lifestyle. I try to be different... **I'm teasing you!** It's a lot more sophisticated to drink tea. There's a ritual about how tea is made and how it should be enjoyed. Once you are **immersed** in the traditions, you can reach a state of tranquility and harmony. That's why scholars in ancient China liked to drink tea.

A: I'm also a tea drinker. I started last year. I much prefer green tea, though. **Apart from** the smell I, especially, like the green tea leaves dancing in the glass. It's very poetic. Sitting in a tea house with a cup of tea in one hand and a bamboo fan in the other. I feel like an ancient, Chinese, wise man.

B： How interesting... Chinese drinking coffee and Americans drinking tea.

A： Well, we are all living in a global village. It's only natural that people are going to influence each other. But, for people at Starbucks, they'd certainly like every Chinese, and American, to drink coffee rather than tea.

B： I heard that Starbucks, in Taiwan, is also selling Chinese drinks, such as, soy bean milk, in order to attract more customers.

A： This is why localization is important in the age of globalization.

对 话

A： 你关注胡锦涛主席 2006 年 4 月访美了吗?

B： 当然。他的第一站是西雅图。在那里，他到比尔·盖茨的豪宅做客，还到波音公司的总部与员工们见面。员工们送了他一顶波音的棒球帽，胡主席当即戴上。他给当地媒体留下了一个非常平易近人的领导人形象。

A： 但是你知道这一站最大的赢家是谁吗?

B： 是谁?

A： 我认为是星巴克咖啡。

B： 这倒是个有趣的看法。为什么?

A： 有媒体报道，胡锦涛说：如果我有时间，也想到北京的星巴克咖啡店去坐一坐。这是一个国家主席所给予的最好的褒奖。一个不小的免费广告。星巴克在中国的名声会因此而大增。

B： 事实上星巴克在中国已经有了相当大的市场。因为对于许多年轻人来说，喝咖啡成了一种生活方式。星巴克正迎合了这样的需求。传统上，中国人喜欢喝茶，但是，不少年轻人追求西方的生活方式，喝咖啡就是其中之一。

A： 你怎么样，也喜欢喝咖啡吗?

B： 我以前喝咖啡，后来改喝茶了，因为这么多中国人把喝咖啡当成一种身份和品味的象征，我追求与众不同——这是开玩笑。但是喝茶比喝咖啡有着更多的讲究，通过泡茶、品茶的过程，可以达到一种清静、超然的境界。这也是为什么中国古代文人都喜欢喝茶。

A： 从去年起我也开始喝茶。我喜欢喝绿茶，除了味道清香，我尤其喜欢漂在茶杯里的茶叶，很有诗意。坐在茶馆里，一只手捧着茶杯，一只手拿着竹扇，我感觉自己像个中国文人了。

B： 中国人喝咖啡，美国人喝茶，多么有趣的景象。

A： 我们都生活在同一个地球上。很自然，人们相互影响。当然，无论在美国还是中国，星巴克的老板总是希望人们都喝咖啡而不是茶。

B： 不过我听说在台湾的星巴克增加了中式的饮料，像豆奶之类，以吸引更多的消费者。

A： 全球化离不开本土化。

Background Reading 背景阅读

Producing Coffee in China 咖啡在中国

It's not well known that China grows coffee. That it should is logical, considering the temperate climate this vast land enjoys in its southern and eastern regions. Neighboring Vietnam has become the second largest coffee producer in the world after Brazil, and many have blamed the southeastern nation for flooding the market and dragging down prices. Most of China's coffee fields are in Yunnan Province, on Vietnam's border.

The first Chinese coffee processing factory opened in Shanghai in 1935, but it wasn't until the mid-1980s that the Chinese could taste packaged coffee, produced then by Kraft Foods' Maxwell House label. Today Maxwell House has lost its monopoly and its dominance of the Chinese market to Nestle's Nescafe brand. Both of these industry giants cultivate their coffee in Yunnan. According to statistics from the China Market Database (CMDB) Chinese people with higher education are most likely to drink coffee. Almost thirty six percent of China's coffee drinkers are university educated while only eight percent of people with only a primary education drink coffee.

中国生产咖啡并不著名。从适宜的气温方面考虑，中国南部和东部地区最为合适。邻国越南已经成为继巴西之后世界第二大咖啡生产国，许多人抱怨它冲击了市场，并降低了价格。中国的许多咖啡生产地就在与越南相邻的云南省。

中国第一个咖啡加工厂1935年在上海开办，但是直到20世纪80年代中期，中国人才品尝到了袋装咖啡，它是由卡夫食品公司生产的麦斯威尔牌咖啡。如今，这个品牌已经失去了它的垄断地位，在中国市场占优势的咖啡品牌是雀巢。这些咖啡生产的巨头产业的原料都产自云南省。据中国市场数据调查显示，在中国，受教育程度越高者越喜欢喝咖啡。差不多36%的中国咖啡饮用者都受过大学教育，在饮用咖啡的人群中，只有8%的人是初等教育者。

The Tastes of Coffee 咖啡的味道

Many people think that all coffees are alike—and that couldn't be more untrue! Each blend of freshly roasted coffee offers its own unique tastes and sensations. Roast, Acidity and Body are the varying characteristics that lend a coffee its special and complex qualities. Coffee roasts range from light to medium to heavy. Acidity refers to a coffee's brightness and sparkle. Body can be described as the weight or thickness of the coffee on your tongue. A coffee's body can be light and thin, medium, or heavy enough to remind you of syrup.

很多人认为所有咖啡都一个样，这真是大错特错！每种新焙的咖啡都有它独特的味道和口感。因焙烤度、酸度和醇度的不同，每种咖啡都具有特别的品质。咖啡的烘焙有轻度、中度、重度之分。酸度指咖啡的亮度和泡沫。醇度则是你品尝到的口味的轻重。按醇度分，咖啡有清淡、中度和浓厚之分，可以通过焦糖的多少来调制。

---

guest of honor 嘉宾，座上客	insight 看法，眼光	free publicity 免费宣传
switch to 转换，转变	I'm teasing you. 我在逗你玩。	immerse 沉浸，陷入
apart from 除了		

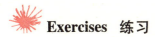 **Exercises 练习**

Answer these questions.

1. Why is Starbucks the winner?
2. Why do young people like to drink coffee?
3. Why do some people like to drink tea?

Translate these sentences into Chinese.

1. Did you pay any attention to President Hu Jintao's visit to the United States?
2. He impressed the local media as a very approachable leader.
3. That's an interesting insight.
4. This is a great compliment made by a President.
5. For a lot of young people, coffee drinking is a part of their lifestyle.
6. I used to drink a lot of coffee but, have switched to tea.
7. That's why scholars in ancient China liked to drink tea.
8. I, especially, like the green tea leaves dancing in the glass.
9. We are all living in a global village.
10. It's only natural that people influence each other.

Complete this paragraph with suitable words.

I __1__ to drink a lot of coffee but, have __2__ to tea. I do not like the association of coffee __3__ social status and lifestyle. I try to be __4__ —I'm teasing you! It is a lot __5__ sophisticated to drink tea. There's a ritual about __6__ tea is made and how it should be drunk. Once you are immersed in the traditions, you can __7__ a state of tranquility and harmony. That's why scholars, in __8__ China, liked to drink tea.

 **Answers 答案**

Translate these sentences into Chinese.

1. 你关注胡锦涛主席的访美了吗？
2. 他给当地媒体留下了一个非常平易近人的领导人形象。
3. 这倒是一个有趣的想法。
4. 这是一个国家主席所给予的最好的褒奖。
5. 对于许多年轻人来说，喝咖啡成了一种生活方式。
6. 我以前喝咖啡，后来改喝茶了。
7. 这也是为什么中国古代文人都喜欢喝茶。
8. 我尤其喜欢漂在茶杯里的茶叶。
9. 我们都生活在同一个地球上。
10. 很自然，人们相互影响。

Complete this paragraph with suitable words.

1. used 2. switched 3. with 4. different 5. more 6. how 7. reach 8. ancient

32. The Color of Food

美食的色相

Dialogue

A: Chinese food stresses color, smell and taste. Is this correct?

B: Correct. This is why people also refer to food as *mei shi*, meaning beautiful food. The primary element is color because only a good color combination can arouse people's appetite. Color is emphasized in home cooking as well. Color combination is at its best with some of the traditional household dishes, such as tomatoes with eggs or baby onions with tofu.

A: I assume color combination is stressed even more with major culinary styles.

B: Yes. There are eight major culinary styles in China. Color combinations reflect the **local features** of each style. Take Guangdong food for example. Because it is hot and humid there, people are **mindful** of the heat on their internal organs. Therefore Guangdong food is mild in both taste and color combinations. You don't find a lot of hot and spicy food in Guangdong dishes because warm colors in the hot summer can be repulsive to people's appetite. Sichuan food is **just the opposite**. Sichuan is also very humid but unlike Guangdong, Sichuan people choose to use extremely hot peppers to open their stomach.

A: Absolutely right! It is very strong and uses a lot of red color. Shanghai food, on the other hand, uses a lot of oil and soy sauce. **On the surface**, this style doesn't seem to go along with Shanghai people's preference for delicacy and tenderness. But if you take a closer look at the lifestyle in Shanghai, you will be able to appreciate why this is so. Once I was invited to dinner with a Shanghai family and they cut the fish into two portions, saving one portion for another meal. So the four of us **ended up** sharing half a fish, together with a few other dishes, none of which were very big. This is when I came to understand the role of thick oil and soy sauce.

B: You seem to suggest that milder dishes are **short on** the rich taste while dark color dishes are short on fun. Are there any culinary styles that combine the best of everything?

A： I would say Shandong food. Shandong food tends to highlight taste and color in order to satisfy the appetite for both.

B： That's an interesting observation.

A： This is similar to knowing a person from Shandong. **At first sight** that person may look tough and unrestrained, but once you get to know him better, you will find he is in fact very refined and sensitive. Only people with such qualities can develop a culinary style that is at once neutral and balanced, and able to appeal to all appetites.

对 话

A： 中国菜讲究色、香、味俱全，对吗？

B： 对，所以称为美食，食物有了色泽才能引起食欲。即使在家庭烹调中也强调色泽。因此就有了一些传统的讲究色相的家常菜，比如西红柿炒鸡蛋、韭菜炒鸡蛋、小葱拌豆腐。

A： 各大菜系是不是更看重菜品的色泽。

B： 对。中国有八大菜系，在色相上体现出地域的特点。比如粤菜，出自广东，那里气候炎热而潮湿，人们特别在意五脏燥热，所以广东菜的色泽和味道均以清淡为主，辛辣的食物在粤菜中不多见。因为炎热的天气，暖色调的食物会让人没有食欲。川菜就不同，四川气候也湿热，但与广东不同，四川人选择用极辣的辣椒来对付食欲低下。

A： 是这样。川菜很辣，呈红色。上海菜以浓油赤酱为特征，从表面上看，这似乎与上海人生活精细的特点不一致。不过当你了解了上海人的生活方式后，就会理解"浓油赤酱"为什么出自上海菜。我曾到一位上海人家中做客，一条鱼他们分成两半，上顿烧一半，下顿烧一半。我们四个人最后就吃这半条鱼，其他的菜也是份量少些。这时我理解了浓油和赤酱的作用。

B： 听你说来，这几种菜系中，色淡的少滋味，色浓的少品味，有没有两者相平衡的呢？

A： 大概要算山东菜了。鲁菜既强调味也强调色。能满足品味和口味两方面的要求。

B： 一个有趣的发现。

A： 就像山东人，乍看上去，豪放粗犷，相处久了，你就会发现他们其实精明而细致。只有这种风格的人才创得出相同风格的菜系——中庸又平衡，合乎所有人的口味。

Background Reading 背景阅读

Soup and Harmony 汤与和谐

Soup made from a variety of ingredients has taste because it is an organic mixture of the five flavors, each distinct, but which blend to give an altogether richer and more appetizing piquancy. It is hence advantageous to bring in more ingredients as they produce better results when functioning under the principle of harmony. Harmony is an essential concept:

First, it embodies a complementary relationship within which all the components are interactive and mutually beneficial. This is not only applicable to making soup; it also works when handling state affairs, as in the cooperation between ruler and courtier. In governance it serves to eliminate the wrong and emphasize that which is right. In China, therefore, harmony is regarded as a crucial facet of leadership or political philosophy.

Second, harmony as a strategy connotes a dynamic process of creative transformation during which all the elements involved undergo a transformational synthesis, changing and collaborating but maintaining individual identity. Something entirely new is thus created.

Last but not least, harmony suggests a dialectic state in which opposites are united. This makes possible further growth on top of all the other positive aspects already mentioned.

五味各具其味，但是融合到一起味道更足，引人食欲。所以用多种原料炖出的汤因混合了五味才颇具滋味。在和谐的原则之下，多种因素的混合更具功力。和谐是一个重要的概念：

首先，它可使各个不同的组成部分相互作用、相互补益，达到互补的关系。这不仅仅在炖汤中体现，也在治理国家中显示了其作用，如同统治者与臣子的关系。在管理中，它有助于消除错误，增强正确的因素。在中国，和谐也是领导和政治哲学中所认同的重要方面。

第二，和谐作为一种战略，意味着一个能动的转化过程，在这个过程中，所有的因素因共同的作用而改变和融合，同时也保持了自身的特性。但一个全新的东西已创造出来。

第三，和谐是对立统一的辩证表述。它使得正面因素的进一步发展成为可能。

---

local features 当地特点	mindful 在意，注意	just the opposite 正好相反
on the surface 表面上	end up doing something 最终只能做…	
short on 缺少	at first sight 第一眼	

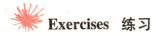 **Exercises 练习**

Answer these questions.

1. Why is color combination important in Chinese food?
2. What is typical of Sichuan food?
3. What is the author's impression of a Shandong person?

Translate these sentences into Chinese.

1. Only a good color combination can arouse people's appetite.
2. There are eight major culinary styles in China.
3. Guangdong food is mild in both taste and color combinations.
4. People are mindful of the heat on their internal organs.
5. Warm colors in the hot summer can be repulsive to people's appetite.
6. Sichuan people choose to use extremely hot peppers to open their stomach.
7. This style doesn't seem to go along with Shanghai people's preference for delicacy.
8. The four of us ended up sharing half a fish.
9. Shandong food tends to highlight both taste and color.
10. At first sight that person may look tough and unrestrained.

Complete this paragraph with suitable words.

Because it is hot and ___1___ there, people are mindful ___2___ the heat on their internal organs. Therefore Guangdong food is ___3___ in both taste and color combinations. You don't find a lot of ___4___ and ___5___ food in Guangdong dishes because, warm colors in the hot summer can be repulsive to people's appetite. Sichuan food is ___6___ the opposite. It is very strong and uses a lot of red color. Sichuan is also very humid, but ___7___ Guangdong, Sichuan people ___8___ to use extremely hot peppers to open their stomach.

 **Answers 答案**

Translate these sentences into Chinese.

1. 食物有了色相才能引起食欲。
2. 中国有八大菜系。
3. 广东菜的色相和味道均以清淡为主。
4. 人们特别在意五脏燥热。
5. 炎热的天气，暖色调的食物会让人没有食欲。
6. 四川人选择用极辣的辣椒来对付食欲低下。
7. 这似乎与上海人生活精细的特点不一致。
8. 我们四个人最后就吃了半条鱼。
9. 鲁菜既强调味也强调色。
10. 乍看上去，这个人豪放粗犷。

Complete this paragraph with suitable words.

1. humid   2. of   3. mild   4. hot   5. spicy   6. just   7. unlike   8. choose

33. The Ultimate Luxury Products

顶级奢侈品

A: Shanghai hosted its first **trade show** of luxury goods in 2005. In the 2006 show, the line of exhibits was expanded to include Chinese tea, porcelain, herbs, as well as Western cars and watches. You can see the differences between the Chinese and Western cultures from these exhibits.

B: I think we need to have **a second look** at the definition of luxury products. Usually, luxury items only refer to **high-end** or high-tech Western consumable products. Chinese luxury items, on the other hand, are related to nature in **one way or the other**. There was a sculpture at the 2006 show, carved out of a precious piece of mahogany, depicting Confucius with his students. It took a dozen or so master sculptors more than 80,000 hours to finish. While visitors **marveled at** the superb craftsmanship of the sculpture, many of them also said it wasn't useful. They'd rather have a sports car.

A: In general, Western luxury items with a **price tag** of over 800,000 yuan, be it a sports car, a watch, or a mattress, are products with practical values. They are either processed or manufactured, using high-tech tools. They represent the perfection of an object. Chinese luxury products emphasize the convergence of man and nature and, therefore, are based on a product of nature, such as tea or liquor. Usually, Chinese luxury items are for collection by connoisseurs rather than their practical usage. The mahogany sculpture is a good example.

B: The value of luxury goods **goes well beyond** their practical usage. From a practical point of view, we wear clothes to keep our bodies covered. If we choose brand names like Chanel, then we are indulging in luxury. From that standpoint, the Chinese items you've just mentioned are indeed luxury products.

130

A： When Western merchants came to China more than 200 years ago，they brought along clocks and other manufactured products. In return，they took home tea and other agricultural products. In today's world，a sports car is certainly more fashionable than tea or wood sculptures. Chinese culture is more inward-looking while Western culture is more out-going and ostentatious. That is why traditional Chinese objects can hardly be seen as luxurious because they are precious **in their own right** and there's no need for them to be viewed as luxury items.

B： No one knows what's going to happen decades or even centuries **down the road**. If，some day natural resources are **exhausted**，a box of tea leaves could probably sell for the price of several sports cars. For someone stranded on a deserted island，an apple is more precious than a bucket of gold.

对 话

A： 2005 年，上海首次举办了奢侈品博览会。2006 年这一届不但有西洋的名车、名表，还包括了中国的茶叶、瓷器和药材等。从展示的这些奢侈品中可以看出一些东西方文化的差异。

B： 我觉得我们需要重新思考对奢侈品的定义。通常奢侈品是指那些高端的或高科技的西洋消费产品；而中国的奢侈品总是与纯天然相关。2006 年参展的一幅立体木雕，用红木中的极品雕刻而成，内容是描述孔子和他的学生。这件作品是十多位雕刻大师耗费 8 万多个工时打造而成的。尽管参观者非常欣赏这件木雕的精致手法，但多数人认为它没有实用价值。他们宁可要一辆跑车。

A： 一般而言，标价八十多万元的跑车、名表、床垫等西洋的奢侈品都具有实用价值。这些产品用高科技的工具加工制造而成，是完美的体现。中国的奢侈品强调人与自然的融合，因此，其产品多是自然物品，比如茶叶或酒；通常中国的奢侈品是被鉴赏家收藏而不是为了实用。那件红木雕刻就是一个例证。

B： 奢侈品的价值远远超过其使用价值。从实用的角度看，我们穿衣是为了蔽体。但如果选择穿 Channel 等名牌，这就是奢侈了。从这个意义上看，中国的这些物品确实是奢侈品。

A： 大概在两百多年前，西洋的商人来到中国，带来的是钟表等手工业产品，带走的则是茶叶等农产品。当今世界，跑车确实比茶叶或木雕更时尚。中国文化更内敛，西洋文化更外化。中国传统的物品本身就是非常宝贵的，不必一定进入奢侈品的名目中。

B： 没有人知道几百年之后会发生什么。到那时，自然资源已被消耗得差不多了，一盒取自天然的茶叶也许能卖出几辆跑车的价格。就好比人在孤岛上，一只苹果比一桶黄金宝贵得多。

Background Reading 背景阅读

The Best Customers 最好的消费者

Department stores in China's largest cities are stuffed with the counters of the world's most famous cosmetics makers. China is the world's eighth largest consumer of cosmetics and the second largest in Asia, after Japan.

Young professionals are the best customers of mid-range cosmetics in China. University educated, this high-earning strata of Chinese society identifies more with the *Sex and the City* TV series ubiquitously available locally on pirated DVDs than they do with Confucian notions of beauty and modesty. "I only use skin care products and lipsticks, given that I don't need make-up for work" says financial analyst Amy Chen. The 25 year old Beijinger buys facial products by top-dollar brands like Clinique, Estee Lauder and Lancome. "I buy Lancome for my mom too because their aging products are pretty good." Chen spends "About 800 yuan a month" on cosmetics, "Counting in expenses for beauty salons." "I find the basic products from Clinique are the most suitable for me. I use their scrubs. I use body washes by Nivea, Vaseline, Waterson and Olay. I also use Adidas after sports. They're all pretty good." Chen chooses Lancome and Mentholaton lipcare products.

世界顶尖化妆品公司的产品充斥着遍布中国大城市的百货公司。中国消费化妆品的份额在全世界排第 8 位，在亚洲排第 2 位，仅次于日本。

在中国，年轻的白领是中档化妆品最好的客户。这个受过高等教育的有着丰厚收入的阶层对于到处都可以买到的 DVD 版电视剧《欲望都市》的认识远远超过他们对于儒家学说中关于美和优雅的理解。金融分析师艾米·陈说："因为上班不要求化妆，所以我只用护肤品和唇膏。"这个 25 岁的北京女孩平时都是购买一些比较昂贵的品牌，比如倩碧、雅诗兰黛和兰蔻。她说："我也给我妈妈买兰蔻，因为他们的抗衰老化妆品相当棒。"算上去美容院的支出，陈小姐每月花在化妆品上的钱大概是 800 元。"我发现，倩碧的一些基础产品非常适合我，按摩霜我用他们的，沐浴露我用妮维雅和凡士林，还有屈臣氏和玉兰油。运动过后，我会选择阿迪达斯。他们都很不错。"陈小姐用的护唇产品是兰蔻和曼秀雷敦。

---

trade show 行业展览	second look 重新审视	high-end 高端
one way or the other 无论如何，不管怎样		marvel at 欣赏，把玩
price tag 商品价签	go well beyond 远远超过	in their own right 本身
down the road 以后	exhausted 枯竭	

 **Exercises** 练习

Answer these questions.
1. What was included in the 2006 trade show of luxury goods?
2. What are some special features of Western luxury products?
3. Do you prefer a sports car or a wood sculpture? Why?

Translate these sentences into Chinese.
1. Shanghai hosted its first trade show of luxury goods in 2005.
2. We need to have a second look at the definition of luxury products.
3. It took a dozen or so master sculptors more than 80,000 hours to finish.
4. Visitors marveled at the superb craftsmanship of the sculpture.
5. They'd rather have a sports car.
6. The value of luxury goods goes well beyond their practical usage.
7. They are precious in their own right.
8. From a practical point of view, we wear clothes to keep our bodies covered.
9. No one knows what's going to happen centuries down the road.
10. An apple is more precious than a bucket of gold.

Complete this paragraph with suitable words.
We need to have a __1__ look at the definition of luxury products. Usually, luxury items only __2__ to high-end or high-tech Western consumable products. Chinese luxury items, on the __3__ hand, are related to nature in one __4__ or the other. One exhibit at the 2006 show was a wood sculpture. It took a __5__ or so master sculptors more than 80,000 hours to __6__. While visitors marveled at the superb __7__ of the sculpture, many of them also said that it was not __8__.

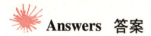 **Answers** 答案

Translate these sentences into Chinese.
1. 2005 年，上海首次举办了奢侈品博览会。
2. 我们应该重新思考对奢侈品的定义。
3. 十多位雕刻大师耗费 8 万多个工时打造而成。
4. 参观者非常欣赏这件木雕的精致手法。
5. 他们宁可要一辆跑车。
6. 奢侈品的价值远远超过其使用价值。
7. 它们本身就是非常宝贵的。
8. 从实用意义上讲，我们穿衣是为了蔽体。
9. 没有人知道几百年之后会发生什么。
10. 一个苹果比一桶黄金还宝贵。

Complete this paragraph with suitable words.
1. second   2. refer   3. other   4. way   5. dozen   6. finish   7. craftsmanship   8. useful

34. Driving on the Horse Road

开车上路

Dialogue

A： Last year's auto show in Beijing was very popular. Car parking alone generated a revenue of more than 1 million yuan. Business at nearby restaurants increased by 300%.

B： Cars are a symbol of accomplishment, status and wealth. **Thanks to** the economic reforms since the 1980s, a small number of people have become extremely wealthy. Many years ago, a person **made a fortune** and bought a car. He parked it in the hutong for the night but the car was burned to ashes by the following morning.

A： Someone got jealous?

B： Jealousy is no longer an issue as more people begin to buy cars. Instead, car theft has become a problem. My neighbor had a car and, in fear of it being stolen or damaged, he would ask his mother to sit next to the car over the weekend if it was not being used.

A： I heard there are organized car thefts too.

B： When family cars first appeared, the Santana 2000 was the target. It looked **showy** and spacious and therefore was seen at that time as a good indication of wealth. No one would steal a modest-looking Citroen ZX. Now their targets are Mercedes or BMWs.

A： For a foreigner, driving in China is quite a challenge. Too many people do not follow the rules.

B： That is why traffic rules are becoming stricter. Some people like to **be smart** and they come up with various ways to cheat the traffic cameras. They cover the license plates so they can escape punishment when **rushing a red light** or **speeding**. Sometimes they use a clipper to keep the seat belt in a certain position in order to cheat the police officer.

A： Two things I don't quite understand. Why do people try everything to violate traffic rules?   The rules are meant for the safety of the drivers anyway. Second, why do police officers hide themselves when checking for drivers breaking the law?

B: Good questions but I don't have good answers. Some people say that mentally we are still in the age of the horse and cart. Although there are a lot of cars on the streets, neither the drivers nor the police officers are ready yet. You know what? The Chinese word we use for road is "malu" which literally means "horse road."

对 话

A: 去年举办的北京国际汽车展览会非常火爆。仅停车费就收了上百万元。附近餐馆的收入上涨了300%。

B: 汽车是身份、地位和财富的象征。自20世纪80年代以来，拜中国的改革开放政策之赐，一部分人先富起来。多年前，一个人做生意赚到钱，买了一辆汽车，晚上停在胡同里。第二天早晨起来发现车被烧掉了。

A: 有人有嫉妒心理？

B: 买车的人多起来后，嫉妒不再是问题，然而，偷车却成了一个问题。我的邻居买了一辆汽车，因为怕被偷或被毁坏，每个周末不用车时，都要让他母亲到车旁坐着。

A: 好像还出现了偷车的团伙。

B: 刚刚开始有私家车时，桑塔纳2000是被偷的目标，因为它宽大、很气派，当时被看作财富的象征。没人会偷一辆不显山不露水的富康ZX。现在奔驰、宝马成为偷盗的目标。

A: 不少外国人觉得在中国开车是个挑战，因为太多的人不遵守交通规则了。

B: 所以交通法规越来越严格。不过，有些人喜欢耍小聪明，他们想出了各种办法逃避摄像监控。他们会遮挡牌号，好让自己在闯红灯和超速行驶时不会受罚。有时把安全带的一端用夹子固定住，以骗过警察。

A: 有两件事我不明白，司机们为什么要想尽办法违反交通规则呢？交规毕竟是为了保证驾车者的安全嘛。第二，警察为什么要在暗处突查驾车者呢？

B: 这两个问题很好，我也不知道答案。有人说，中国的驾车人和警察的意识还停留在马车的时代，虽然汽车出现在路上了，但无论是司机还是警察，都还没有准备好。你知道吗，至今人们还称路为"马路"——走马和马车的路。

Background Reading　背景阅读

China on a Roll　车轮上的中国

China's booming car sales are being driven by a growing middle class. Incomes are rising most rapidly in China's coastal urban areas and in developing markets like China, demand for cars soars when per-capita income reaches $ 4,000. Four cities—Shanghai, Guangzhou, Shenzhen and Xiamen—have already hit that level. Loans will help more of the new middle class become car owners.

Shanghai Pudong Development Bank saw car loans grow 40% last year（2002）to 1 billion renminbi and expects to see the same growth rate this year. Car loans will become more and more important.

日益增长的中产阶层，将中国的汽车销售热潮刺激起来。中国沿海城市居民的收入迅速提高，加之市场的不断开发，当人均收入达到 4 000 美元时，对汽车的需求就会攀升。四个城市——上海、广州、深圳和厦门——已经达到这一水平。汽车贷款将有助于更多新的中产阶层的人们成为有车族。

上海浦东发展银行已经看到汽车贷款在去年增长了 40%，达到 10 亿人民币，并且预计将在今年看到同样的增长速度。对于银行来说，汽车贷款将变得越来越重要。

Car Loans—A Sound Business　车贷火爆

Car loans are a growth business for China's banks. In the first three months of the year （2003）, Chinese banks gave out 20 billion renminbi in new loans. Since 1998—the year such financing was permitted—cumulative car loans have reached 110 billion renminbi. Shanghai is especially good—banks here gave out 5.05 billion renminbi in new car loans in the first four months of this year.

To be sure, China's consumer-lending regulations lack some key features. Most cities lack a personal credit-rating system and the government controls interest rates. But with pressure to reduce their bad-loan ratios, and car sales projected to grow by 20% annually for at least the next five years, China's banks are eager to do more vehicle financing.

中国的银行业中，车贷成为正在增长的业务。在这一年的前 3 个月（2003 年），中国的银行发放了超过 200 亿元人民币的汽车贷款。从车贷允许发放的 1998 年以来，总贷款额达到 1 000 亿元人民币。上海尤为突出——今年的头 4 个月，银行已发放新车贷款达 50.5 亿元人民币。

可以肯定的是，中国消费借贷规则缺乏一些关键性的特点。多数城市没有个人信用系统，政府控制着利率水平。但是，由于迫于降低其坏帐率的压力，以及至少在今后 5 年内，汽车销售将以每年 20% 增长的这一计划，中国的银行将热中于做更多的汽车金融项目。

---

thanks to　由于，亏了	make a fortune　发财	showy　炫耀，招摇
be smart　要小聪明	rush red light　闯红灯	speeding　超速

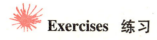 **Exercises** 练习

Answer these questions.

1. Why was the Beijing auto show successfull?
2. Why do foreigners find it difficult to drive in China?
3. How do people cheat traffic cameras?

Translate these sentences into Chinese.

1. Business at nearby restaurants increased by 30%.
2. Cars are a symbol of accomplishment, status and wealth.
3. Instead, car theft has become a problem.
4. No one would steal a modest-looking Citroen ZX.
5. Too many people do not follow the rules.
6. Some people like to be smart.
7. They come up with various ways to cheat the traffic cameras.
8. They would cover the license plates to escape punishment when rushing a red light.
9. The rules are meant for the safety of the drivers anyway.
10. Neither the drivers nor the police officers are ready yet.

Complete this paragraph with suitable words.

Jealousy is no __1__ an issue as more people begin to buy cars. Instead car __2__ has become a problem. My neighbor had a car. For __3__ of,it being stolen, or damaged, he would ask his mother to sit __4__ to the car when he was not using it __5__ the weekend. When family cars __6__ appeared, the Santana 2000 was the target. It looked showy and spacious and, __7__, was a good indication of wealth. No one __8__ steal a modest-looking Citroen ZX. Now their targets are Mercedes or BMW's.

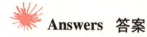 **Answers** 答案

Translate these sentences into Chinese.

1. 附近餐馆的收入上涨了300%。
2. 汽车是身份、地位和财富的象征。
3. 然而，偷车却成了一个问题。
4. 没人会偷一辆不显山不露水的富康 **ZX**。
5. 太多的人不遵守规则。
6. 有些人喜欢耍小聪明。
7. 他们想出了各种办法逃避摄像监控。
8. 他们会遮挡牌号，好让自己在闯红灯时不会受罚。
9. 交规毕竟为了保证驾车者的安全嘛。
10. 无论是司机还是警察，都还没有准备好。

Complete this paragraph with suitable words.

1. longer 2. theft 3. fear 4. next 5. during 6. first 7. therefore 8. would

35. A Hectic Long Holiday

忙碌的长假

Dialogue

A： Since 1999, China has been having three separate holidays, each extending over a week. These are the Labor Day holidays from May 1, the National Day holidays from October 1 and the Spring Festival. These holidays are also known as the **golden week holidays**. But the longer the holidays, the busier the people are.

B： People who have to work during these holidays are even busier, especially those in traffic management, tourism and the **service industries**. Going home is almost an obligation during the long holidays, particularly during the traditional Chinese Spring Festivals. Every family wants to have a **reunion**. A married woman **is supposed to** spend the holiday with her husband's family because she is no longer considered part of her own family. The good news is that young people today no longer feel **obligated** by these traditions. In fact, many young couples who are the only child of their **respective** families will argue about whose parents they should spend the holiday with. **More often than not**, they would reach a compromise by spending a few days with each family. It can be another challenge if both sets of parents do not live in the same city. In that case, the young couples may have to spend a lot of time on the road.

A： Some critics say that during the non-competitive "iron rice bowl" period, many people who were at work acted as if they were on a holiday and, for those who were on a holiday, they acted as if they were at work. This is still more or less the case during the golden week holidays. Many people still do not know how to spend a holiday.

B： I remember reading an article on the internet. The writer said the Tibetans are the best at living a relaxed life. Once, on a business trip to Tibet, the writer's boss noticed that although people there were less affluent, they were much happier and enjoying life much more than people in other cities. For example, when some farmers went to harvest crops, the first thing they did after they got to the fields was to eat, drink and dance, and then fall asleep when they got tired. No one worried about the crops. In the end, they all came back empty handed. He was very impressed by the lifestyle, which revolved around working, singing, and sleeping as they pleased and at a pace to suit themselves. Although the writer was a bit **tongue-in-cheek** when he said this, I can appreciate his admiration for a relaxed life.

A： My understanding is that Chinese people like to "steal" some leisure out of a busy schedule which makes it sound like leisure is not something people deserve. Honestly I admire the free spirit of the Tibetan farmers mentioned in the article.

B： Now that the Qinghai-Tibet Railway has opened to traffic, you can go to Tibet and enjoy a taste of their lifestyle.

对 话

A： 从1999年开始，中国人每年有3次长假，五一、十一和春节，每次假期7天。这些假日被称为黄金周。但越是长假，人们就越忙碌。

B： 不得不上班的人们就更忙碌，特别是交通部门、旅游和服务行业。回家几乎是长假的又一个任务，尤其是春节。每个家庭都想团聚。结了婚的女人不再被当作娘家人，只好到男方家中过节。现在的年轻人不再认同这些传统，这是个好消息。事实上，独生子女们在长假时还要为去谁的父母家过节发生争执。他们往往达成妥协，在双方家里各待几天。如果双方的家长不住在一个城市，这又是一个难题，他们不得不花很多时间在路上奔波。

A： 在"大锅饭"的年代，曾经有人说，中国人工作时像玩，玩时像工作。黄金周期间基本上还是这种情况。许多人仍然不知道如何休假。

B： 我看过一篇网上的文章。作者说西藏人最懂得休闲。在一次去西藏的商务旅行中，他的老板发现这里的人们不富足，但他们更快乐，比其它城市的人更能享受生活。比如，藏民们下地收割，到了地里，所有的人先喝酒，然后就跳舞、唱歌；累了就倒在地头睡觉，没有人担心收割之事。结果都空手而归。他的老板对这种生活方式印象深刻，想干活就干活、想唱歌就唱歌、想睡觉就睡觉。尽管作者的说法有些夸张，但能够感觉到他对这种轻松生活的羡慕。

A： 我的理解，中国人喜欢"忙里偷闲"，休闲是偷来的，而不是应该的。说实话，那几位西藏人心态放松，着实令人羡慕。

B： 青藏铁路已经通车了，你可以去西藏享受他们的生活方式了。

Background Reading　背景阅读

Well Fitness　健身产业

In May 2004, Chicago-based Bally celebrated its second anniversary of operations in China. Bally, the world's biggest operator in fitness clubs, is partnered with China Sports Industry, or CSI, a state-owned firm. CSI-Bally has calculated that Beijingers on average spend more than US $ 100 a year on fitness. If 10 million capital residents were to spend that figure the annual revenue of Beijing's fitness market would exceed US $ 10 billion. The company concedes, however, that reality is probably slightly different. "There are Chinese people who really want to get fit, because they have more consumer spending power, more time, more leisure. Fitness is becoming more important to Chinese people. At the same time we have the big 2008 Olympic wave. For all those reasons, China is really a market for Bally," says Rothschild.

Not all are so optimistic about China's fitness fanaticism. Pure Tsai, president of Taiwan's Youth Camp Health Group, urges caution. "I don't think the Chinese market is ready for the fitness industry. China is a developing country, so people here are concentrating more on making money. They generally put finance ahead of health fitness issues," says Tsai, whose chain, founded in 1977, was the first of its kind in Taiwan. "I figured out that although there are a large number of people joining fitness clubs, they only use their memberships to show off... I think it will take a lot longer for China to turn into a mature consumer market."

2004 年 5 月，本部在芝加哥的倍力健身俱乐部举行了其进军中国的两周年庆典。倍力健身俱乐部是全球最大的健身公司，它在中国的合作伙伴是中体产业，中体产业是一家国有企业，英文简称是 CSI。据中体倍力健身俱乐部估算，有健身习惯的北京人平均每人每年花在健身上的费用超过 100 美元。如果千万首都居民都照这个数字消费，北京健身市场的收入将超过 100 亿美元。该公司也承认调查情况与现实情况可能有些出入。卢正树说："有的中国人真的愿意去健身，因为他们有更强的消费能力、更多时间、更多空闲。对于中国人来说，健身越来越重要了。同时，2008 年奥运会的冲击波也对我们有利。因为这些原因，中国确实不失为倍力的市场。"

中国的健身产业也有不乐观的因素存在。台湾青年营健身集团的总裁普里·蔡警告说："我认为中国的健身行业市场尚未成熟，中国人所热中的是赚钱。他们普遍将金钱摆在更为重要的位置。我发现，哪怕有大量的人们加入健身俱乐部，他们的目的也只是为了炫耀身份而不是真正的健身。我认为中国要建成一个成熟的健身行业市场还需要较长的时间。"台湾青年营健身集团成立于 1977 年，为同行业之先。

---

golden week holidays 黄金周	service industries 服务行业	reunion 团聚
is supposed to 应该	obligate 受…约束	respective 各自的
more often than not 往往是，一般情况下		tongue-in-cheek 不可当真的

 **Exercises** 练习

Answer these questions.

1. When are the three golden week holidays?
2. Where do young couples usually spend their holidays?
3. Why do critics say some Chinese people do not know how to spend their holidays?

Translate these sentences into Chinese.

1. These holidays are also known as the golden week holidays.
2. The longer the holidays, the busier the people are.
3. Every family wants to have a reunion.
4. More often than not, they would reach a compromise.
5. They have to spend a lot of time on the road.
6. This is still more or less the case during the golden week holidays.
7. They are much happier and are enjoying life much more than people in other cities.
8. In the end, they all came back empty handed.
9. Chinese people like to "steal" some leisure out of a busy schedule.
10. It sounds like leisure is not something people deserve.

Complete this paragraph with suitable words.

In the past, a married woman was __1__ to spend the Spring Festival __2__ her husband's family. However, young people today are no __3__ feel obligated by this tradition. In fact, many young couples, who are the __4__ child of their respective families, will __5__ about whose parents they should __6__ the holiday with. More often __7__ not, they would __8__ a compromise by spending a few days with each family.

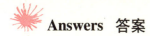 **Answers** 答案

Translate these sentences into Chinese.

1. 这些假日被称为黄金周。
2. 越是长假，人们越忙碌。
3. 每个家庭都想团聚。
4. 他们往往是达成妥协。
5. 他们不得不花很多时间在路上奔波。
6. 黄金周期间基本上还是这种情况。
7. 他们更高兴，比其它城市的人更能享受生活。
8. 结果他们都空手而归。
9. 中国人喜欢忙里偷闲。
10. 听起来似乎人们不应该有空闲。

Complete this paragraph with suitable words.

1. supposed 2. with 3. longer 4. only 5. argue 6. spend 7. than 8. reach

36. Chinese Tourists Abroad

出境旅游热

Dialogue

A: When I was on my holidays in the UK last summer, I saw a lot of visitors at the British Museum. Do you want to **take a guess** which country most of the visitors came from?

B: That's easy. China. In fact, that doesn't just happen in the UK. You'll see lots of Chinese tourists almost everywhere, even in Mexico. You can tell this from the fact that many local **peddlers** speak Chinese to promote their souvenirs.

A: You're right. Obviously this is something new. **Thanks to** your economic reforms, Chinese people have more **disposable income** now. It's like the Americans in the 19th century or the Japanese during the 1970s. As soon as people have more money to spend, they like to go sightseeing overseas. When American tourists first came to Europe, the Europeans didn't quite like them because they behaved differently.

B: That's similar to how the Chinese tourists are received in Europe today. A lot of the foreign media are very **critical of** Chinese tourists.

A: There was a recent article in the *New York Times* about the differences between American, Japanese and Chinese tourists. Unlike American and Japanese tourists, who usually spend their holidays at a resort, Chinese tourists prefer shopping and taking pictures of the well-known scenic spots. The journalist even used the word "pandemonium" to describe Chinese tourists at an L'Oreal shop. You can imagine how crowded it must be. I wonder why Chinese tourists like shopping and taking pictures rather than enjoying a relaxed holiday.

B: Well, as you've just said, American and Japanese tourists came through similar experiences themselves. Chinese tourists are indeed different. Take shopping for example. Many people buy a lot of things to give away as souvenirs rather than buying

142

for themselves. Chinese people like to share the joy of overseas travel with friends, family members and colleagues. That's why Chinese tourists usually spend more time in the shops. They need to find the right souvenirs at **affordable** prices. The same is true with taking pictures. Photographs are proof to show others that they have been to many places, especially when it costs a lot of money to travel to overseas countries. The photographs also give people the opportunity to **brag**.

A： I didn't realize there were so many obligations on Chinese tourists. Now I understand them better.

对 话

A： 这个暑假我回英国，在大英博物馆看到最多的旅游者是哪国人，你能猜出来吗？

B： 不用猜，一定是中国人。不仅仅在英国，几乎所有地方都能看到许多中国游客，甚至在墨西哥。从那些小商贩用中文来推销他们的旅游纪念品便可见一斑。

A： 对。显然这是一种新事物。拜经济改革之赐，中国人现在有钱了。就像 19 世纪的美国人和 20 世纪 70 年代时的日本人一样，国民们有了钱，就纷纷到海外旅游。那时，欧洲人不喜欢美国游客，因为他们的举止不能入乡随俗。

B： 有点儿像今天的中国人在欧洲。一些国外媒体也对中国旅游者的行为颇有微词。

A： 《纽约时报》最近有过一篇文章，谈及美国、日本和中国旅游者的差异，美国和日本的旅游者往往是在一些度假胜地住上几天，而中国游客则喜欢购物以及在旅游景点照相留影。在描述中国游客在欧莱雅柜台前买东西的场面时，作者用了 pandemonium（混乱）这个词。你可以想象的出来当时有多么乱。但是我不知道中国游客为什么喜欢购物拍照而不是轻松度假。

B： 正像你说的，美国和日本游客当年也是这样过来的。中国的游客确有不同。以购物为例，多数旅游者并不是为他们自己买东西，而是为那些不能出国旅游的亲戚、家人和同事买纪念品。中国游客喜欢与朋友分享海外旅游的喜悦。这也是为什么中国的游客花更多的时间在购物上，他们既要找到合适的礼物，价格还要便宜。至于拍照吗，也是同样道理，照片是向人们显示自己去过很多地方的依据。花了大把的钱出国，总要以照片为证，告诉人家到了哪里。照片成了向人们炫耀的依据。

A： 简直不能相信旅游者还担负着这么重的任务。我开始理解他们了。

Background Reading 背景阅读

Tourist Boom 旅游热潮

China's rapid economic growth has fostered a tourist boom among the mainland Chinese, with Southeast Asia the favorite destination, at least for now. The surge in package tour groups from China, an important source of income for the region, is also giving rise to an unflattering stereotype: the loud, rude and culturally naive Chinese tourist.

Sound familiar? The tide of travelers from China mirrors the emergence of virtually every group of overseas tourists since the Romans, from Britons behaving badly in the Victorian era and ugly Americans in postwar Europe to the Snapshot-happy Japanese of the 1980s.

For the first time in history, large numbers of Chinese are leaving their country as tourists, resulting in an unparalleled explosion in Chinese travel. If current projections are met, the global tourism industry will be undergoing a crash course in everything Chinese to accommodate the needs of what promises to be the greatest wave of international travelers ever.

As usual when something goes over big in China, the numbers are staggering. In 1995, only 4.5 million Chinese traveled overseas. By 2005 that figure had increased to 31 million, and if expectations for future growth are met or approached, even that gargantuan growth will be quickly dwarfed. Chinese and international travel industry experts forecast that at least 50 million Chinese tourists will travel overseas annually by 2010, and 100 million by 2020.

飞速发展的经济引发了中国的旅游热潮，目前看来，东南亚是最受欢迎的目的地。中国团队游的激增，成为这一地区重要的收入来源，同时也造成了对中国人不利的看法：大声喧哗、缺乏礼貌，还有对当地文化无知。

这听上去似曾相识是吗？一批批来自中国的游客折射出自古罗马以来的几乎每一次出国游热潮，无论是维多利亚时代英国人的粗鲁，还是二战之后美国人在欧洲的无礼，抑或还是20世纪80年代寻欢作乐的日本人。

有史以来，大批大批的中国人第一次作为旅游者走出国门，从而引发了前所未有的旅游热潮。如果目前的预测准确，全球的旅游业需要马上接受有关中国的各种培训，以满足很有可能成为最大的一次国际旅游热潮的需求。

像其他情况一样，在中国，什么事情一旦变大，其数字往往是惊人的。1995年，中国只有450万人出国。到了2005年，这个数字已经增加至3 100万。如果对于未来增长的预测能够实现，或者哪怕是接近的话，这个庞大的增长幅度也会骤然变得渺小。中国和国际旅游产业专家预计，到2010年，每年至少会有5 000万中国游客赴海外旅游，到2020年，这一数字将达到每年一亿人次。

---

take a guess 猜一猜
disposable income 可支配收入
brag 吹牛

peddler 小贩
critical of 对…持批评意见

thanks to 由于，亏了
affordable 买得起的

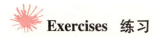 **Exercises** 练习

Answer these questions.

1. What do Chinese tourists like to do?
2. How do American tourists spend their holidays?
3. Why do Chinese tourists like to buy souvenirs?

Translate these sentences into Chinese.

1. You see lots of Chinese tourists almost everywhere.
2. Chinese people now have more disposable income.
3. Europeans didn't like American tourists because they behaved differently. ·
4. Chinese tourists prefer shopping and taking pictures of the well-known scenic spots.
5. You can imagine how crowded it must be.
6. American and Japanese tourists came through similar experience themselves.
7. I wonder why Chinese tourists like shopping rather than enjoying a relaxed holiday.
8. Chinese people like to share the joy of overseas travel with friends.
9. They need to find the right souvenirs at affordable prices.
10. The photographs give people the opportunity to brag.

Complete this paragraph with suitable words.

__1__ , this is something new. Thanks __2__ your economic reforms, Chinese people now have more __3__ income. It's like the Americans in the 19th __4__ or, the Japanese during the 1970's. As __5__ as people have more money to spend, they like to go __6__ overseas. When American tourists __7__ came to Europe, the Europeans didn't __8__ like them because, they behaved differently.

 Answers 答案

Translate these sentences into Chinese.

1. 几乎所有地方都能看到许多中国游客。
2. 中国人现在有了更多的可支配收入。
3. 那时，欧洲人不喜欢美国游客，因为他们的举止不能入乡随俗。
4. 中国游客喜欢购物以及在旅游景点照相留影。
5. 你可以想像的出来当时有多么乱。
6. 美国和日本游客当年也是这样过来的。
7. 我不知道为什么中国游客喜欢购物而不是轻松度假。
8. 中国游客喜欢与朋友分享海外旅游的喜悦。
9. 他们既要找到合适的礼物，价格还要便宜。
10. 照片成了人们炫耀的依据。

Complete this paragraph with suitable words.

1. Obviously   2. to   3. disposable   4. century   5. soon   6. sightseeing   7. first   8. quite

37. The Reputation of Dogs

狗的名声

Dialogue

A: Many Westerners don't understand why Chinese people eat dogs. After some of them have studied Chinese, they realized that the word "dog" is used in many **derogatory** expressions. Some of those expressions are "a running dog," "stinky dog droppings," or "like a dog who bites on the strength of its master's power." This last one describes a person who **takes advantage of** someone else's strength to **bully** others. Why do dogs have such a bad reputation in China?

B: My guess is that for hundreds of years in rural China, dogs have been used to guard houses. The more they bark **at the sight of** strangers, the more generous their owners are in rewarding them. That in turn makes the dogs even more aggressive. In the old days, a scholar visiting a village would knock on the door of a farmer's house, hoping to be greeted with hospitality. Often, **to his dismay**, he would be greeted by a barking dog that would sometimes bite him. The scholar would be scared and run back home and, out of anger and frustration, coin phrases to curse dogs.

A: That's a very imaginative story! However, it seems that people have begun to like dogs in recent years.

B: You're right. As people are becoming more and more affluent, the role of the dog has changed from a sentinel to a favorite pet. Nowadays, a lot of people are breeding dogs as pets and for sale. Many others still dislike dogs because dogs have invaded the already very crowded human space. Chinese cities are **densely populated** and a lot of people live in **pigeonholes** in high-rise apartment buildings. Usually, over 100 households share a couple of elevators or the same flight of stairs. Imagine, the elevator door opening and a dog running out and barking at you. Would you still consider dogs lovely if you had to face that every day? To look after the dogs properly, the owners have to walk their dogs everyday and, they end up leaving dog droppings all over the place. In this case, "stinky dog droppings" become a reality and not just a curse. You can step on them any time if you aren't careful. That's why more and more people feel offended by dogs. Unfortunately, some dog owners don't seem to care about all these problems.

A： I heard that some people are so frustrated that they put poison on public lawns to kill the poor dogs. Recently more than 50,000 dogs were **rounded up** and killed in a county in Yunnan Province. In Beijing, more than 70,000 people were bitten by dogs during 2006. Reports of rabies throughout the country have increased sharply.

B： It's unfortunate that dogs become responsible for the bad behavior of their owners. In fact, none of the derogative expressions related to dogs actually apply to the dogs. They really refer to people. In this sense, dogs have a chance to finally get back at the humans.

对 话

A： 许多西方人对中国人吃狗肉很不理解。学了中文以后，发现"狗"这个字被用于许多贬义词汇："走狗"、"臭狗屎"、"狗仗人势"等等，为什么狗的名声在中国这么坏？

B： 我猜大概是因为在数百年前的乡土中国，狗是用来看家护院的，见到陌生人越是狂吠主人就越给予褒奖，狗们就更具攻击性。读书人想到农家看一看，就敲响了农户的门，期待农人以礼相待，令他沮丧的是，迎接他的是一条狂叫的狗，然后又扑过来撕咬。读书人惊恐地回到家中，愤怒之下，就造出了那些贬损狗的词汇。

A： 一个很有想像力的故事。但是这些年，中国人好像开始喜欢狗了。

B： 对，我们的生活越发富裕，城市里的狗从看家变身为宠物，现在许多人都养狗，或作宠物或作买卖。同时讨厌狗的人也随之增多。原因在于狗侵犯了人们本来就拥挤的生活空间。中国城市的人口密度大、空间小，多数市民住在空间不大的高楼里，上百户的人共用一两部电梯或一道楼梯。想像一下，电梯门打开后，一条狗突然跑出来冲你狂叫的情形。如果天天如此，你还会觉得狗可爱吗？狗主人们为了照顾好自己的狗每天都要出去遛狗，可是他们却任由自己的狗到处排泄。这种情形之下，"臭狗屎"不再是咒骂，而成为现实，不小心就会踩到。这就是越来越多的人讨厌狗的原因。不幸的是，一些狗主人似乎并没有意识到这些问题。

A： 我听说有些人一怒之下在小区的草地上下毒杀那些可怜的狗。在云南省的一个县曾经扑杀了5万只狗。2006年仅北京就有7万人被狗咬伤，全国患狂犬病的人数急剧上升。

B： 不幸的是，狗主人的过失全部由狗承担了。事实上，那些贬损狗的词汇，从来都不是用来骂狗而是用来指人的不良行为的。对可怜的狗来说，这也算扯平了。

Rabies Is on the Rise 狂犬病例激增

Rabies is on the rise in China, where only 3 percent of dogs are vaccinated against the disease, which attacks the nervous system. The disease nearly always kills humans after the development of symptoms, though it can be warded off by a series of injections.

Rabies killed 318 people nationwide in September, according to the News Agency (New China News Agency). There were 2,651 reported deaths from the disease in 2004, the last full year for which data are available. In Beijing, 69,000 people sought treatment for rabies last year, according to state news media.

狂犬病在中国有所增加，只有3%的狗注射了狂犬病疫苗，这对并不严密的防范体系是一个打击。虽然它可能被一系列的预防药物所避免，但是在出现症状后，狂犬病几乎总是致命的。

据中国新闻社报道，今年9月，中国有318人死于狂犬病。2004年，有2651例死于狂犬病的报道，这是有关狂犬病伤人的最近的全年统计数字。据中国的媒体报道，去年北京有6.9万人因狂犬病就医。

The New Regulations on Dogs 养狗新规定

The limit on dogs in the capital was announced by the Beijing police and the city agencies for agriculture and commerce, the News Agency said. Abandoning dogs will be an offense under the new regulations. Dog owners will also be forbidden from taking their dogs to public places like markets, shops, parks, exhibition halls, amusement parks, railway waiting rooms and sightseeing areas. In a county in Yunnan Province, where three people had died of rabies, the authorities killed 50,000 dogs, many of them beaten to death in front of their owners.

Unlike in the West, where dogs have long been cherished as companions or helpmates, dogs have rarely had an easy time in China. Dog meat is eaten throughout the country, revered as a tonic in winter and a restorer of virility in men.

中国新闻社报道，北京市公安局以及农业和商务部门发布了限制养狗的规定。这一新的法规将导致遗弃狗的大幅增加。狗的主人被禁止带狗进入公共场所，如超市、商店、公园、展览馆、博物馆、火车站候车室以及旅游景点等。在云南省的一个县，有3人死于狂犬病，当地政府就杀掉了50 000只狗，许多是当着狗主人的面打死的。

在西方，狗长久以来作为人的伙伴和助手而受到珍视，与此不同，狗在中国一直处于不利的地位。中国都有吃狗肉的习惯，它被作为冬季的滋补品和男人的壮阳品。

---

derogatory 侮辱的，污蔑的	take advantage of 利用，占…便宜	bully 欺负
at the sight of 一看见就	to his dismay 令他沮丧的是	round up 包围
densely populated 人口密度高	pigeonhole 鸽子窝，小房间	

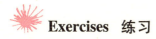 **Exercises 练习**

Answer these questions.

1. Why do dogs have a bad reputation in China?
2. Why are some people against raising dogs in the cities?
3. Why are some dogs poisoned to death?

Translate these sentences into Chinese.

1. Many Westerners don't understand why Chinese people eat dogs.
2. The word "dog" is used in many derogatory expressions.
3. To his dismay, he would be greeted by a barking dog.
4. Nowadays, a lot of people are raising dogs.
5. Dogs have invaded the already very crowded human space.
6. Dog owners have to walk their dogs in crowded areas.
7. Some people are so frustrated that they kill the poor dogs.
8. Over 50,000 dogs were recently rounded up and killed.
9. Reports of rabies have increased sharply throughout the country.
10. It's unfortunate that dogs become responsible for the bad behavior of their owners.

Complete this paragraph with suitable words.

In the __1__ days, a scholar visiting a village would __2__ on the door of a farmer's house, hoping to be __3__ with hospitality. Often, to his __4__, he would be greeted by a __5__ dog that would, sometimes, __6__ him. The scholar would be __7__ and run back home and, out of anger and frustration, he would __8__ phrases to curse dogs.

 Answers 答案

Translate these sentences into Chinese.

1. 许多西方人对中国人吃狗肉很不理解。
2. "狗"这个字被用于许多贬义词汇。
3. 令他沮丧的是，迎接他的是一条狂叫的狗。
4. 现在许多人都养狗。
5. 狗侵犯了人们本来就拥挤的生活空间。
6. 狗主人们在人多的地方遛狗。
7. 有些人一怒之下杀了那些可怜的狗。
8. 最近，5万多只狗被扑杀。
9. 全国狂犬病的人数急剧上升。
10. 不幸的是，狗主人的过失全部由狗承担了。

Complete this paragraph with suitable words.

1. old   2. knock   3. greeted   4. dismay   5. barking   6. bite   7. scared   8. coin

38. TOEFL or No TOEFL?

考不考托福?

Dialogue

A： Chinese students are good at taking exams and TOEFL has never been a problem for them. It's **not uncommon** that many students scored as much as 670 in the paper-based TOEFL exams. After TOEFL introduced its new, computer-based test format, the highest score was once again achieved by a Beijing High School student.

B： Many Chinese people knew how to take examinations more than 1,000 years ago. At that time, exams were the best way to improve one's life. You'd be fooled if you think a high TOEFL score means the student can speak English equally as well. About 10 years ago, a student scored 650 in his TOEFL test and was admitted to a **fairly** well-known university in the United States. When someone greeted him at the airport and said, "How do you do?" he replied, "I do." This is a good example to show the kind of problems that exist in such examinations.

A： I heard that the University Entrance examination in China is very difficult. Are they any different from TOEFL?

B： These examinations are given in two categories, one for students of science and the other for arts students. **In order to** prepare for these exams, high school students are reorganized into arts and science classes two years **in advance**. Chinese, mathematics, English and politics are shared tests. Science students will take additional tests in physics and chemistry, while arts students will take history and geography. **In comparison**, TOEFL is only a language test. Nowadays, a lot of students are taking the TOEFL examination because they want to attend overseas Universities to avoid facing the more challenging University Entrance exams. Also, more people can afford the tuition at a foreign university.

A： In order to **cater to** the increasing need for the TOEFL test, many training centers have been established. The most well-known is probably the New Oriental.

B: Such training centers have even developed solutions to TOEFL questions. For example, if you are not sure of the correct answers of multiple choice questions, they recommend you **follow** the BDCA pattern. That method allowed people to do fairly well in the exams.

A: Once TOEFL found out about the practice, they decided to introduce a new test format, by **putting more emphasis on** language proficiency.

B: Ironically, the best scorers of this new format are still Chinese students and training centers are once again trying to **figure out** solutions.

对 话

A: 中国学生善于应付各类考试，托福考试从来不在话下。旧式托福考试，不少人能达到670分。托福改为机考后，得到高分的竟然是北京的一名高中生。

B: 一千多年前，许多人就知道怎么考试了，当时，考试是人们改变命运的最佳途径。如果你认为托福高分者的英文水平一定很好，那就错了。大概10年前，一个学生托福成绩考到650分，被美国一所不错的大学录取。当到机场迎接这位学生的人问候他："How do you do?"这位学生回答："I do."这个例子说明了应试教育中存在的问题。

A: 我听说中国的高考很难，它与托福有什么区别吗？

B: 高考分文理两科。提前两年学生就被分进文科班和理科班。高考的统考科目是语文、数学、外语和政治，理科考生要加试物理和化学，文科考生要加试历史和地理。托福只不过是语言测试而已。这几年，不少高中生开始参加托福考试，以避开艰苦的高考，此外，更多人付得起国外大学的学费了。

A: 为了迎合日益增长的托福考试的需求，中国有专门培训托福考试技能的机构，最有名的就是新东方。

B: 这些培训中心甚至总结出托福答题技巧，比如，在多项选择题中，你如果不能确定正确答案，就按BDCA的顺序选择，这个办法使得人们可以考得很好。

A: 美方发现了这些问题，于是决定改用新的方式考托福，新方式更强调实际英文水平。

B: 滑稽的是，新托福初现，就被中国的学生拔了头筹而且已经有培训机构开始解读新托福的奥秘了。

Background Reading 背景阅读

IELTS Grew in Shanghai 雅思在上海

An explosion in the number of students sitting the English language test required for entry into overseas universities has forced organizers to expand exam capacity. Between May and July, International English Language Testing System (IELTS) examinees in Shanghai grew by around 70 percent over the same period last year, according to the British Consulate General in Shanghai.

Increased competition for jobs is one reason so many university graduates are looking to continue their studies abroad. Last year, around 100,000 people sat the exam on the Chinese mainland, with around 10,000 taking the exam in Shanghai between May and July. This year that figure has risen to around 17,000.

According to Ewan Davies, vice-consul of the British Consulate, there are currently around 60,000 Chinese students in Britain, of whom 53,000 are in higher education. "We can expect to see more and more Chinese students going to Britain and that will further feed the demand for IELTS. So we will continue to make it more convenient for people who want to take the exam," said Davies.

为进入海外大学读书而参加英语测试的学生人数激增，使得这类考试的组织者们不得不增加测试的次数。据英国驻上海总领事馆称，在今年的 5 月和 7 月间上海举办的雅思考试的参加者比去年同期增长了约 70%。

不断增长的就业竞争压力，是许多大学毕业生选择到海外继续读书的原因之一。去年，中国大约有 10 万人参加了雅思考试，其中 5 月和 7 月间的考试中，上海考生达到 10 000 人。今年，这个数字将增加到 17 000 人左右。

据英国驻上海总领馆副领事伊万·戴维斯说，目前有大约 6 万名中国学生在英国留学，其中有 53 000 人接受高等教育。"我们期望看到越来越多的中国学生到英国留学，也将满足由此而引起的对雅思考试日益增长的需要。所以我们将继续使这一考试对参加者们更加方便。"戴维斯说。

---

not uncommon 不足为奇	fairly 相对，非常	in order to 为了
in advance 提前	in comparison 相比之下	cater to 满足，迎合
follow 仿效，追随	put more emphasis on 更强调	figure out 琢磨

 **Exercises** 练习

Answer these questions.

1. Why do many Chinese people do well in exams?
2. How do Chinese students prepare for University Entrance exams?
3. Why are many students taking TOEFL exams nowadays?

Translate these sentences into Chinese.

1. Chinese students are good at taking exams.
2. TOEFL has never been a problem for Chinese students.
3. Many people knew how to take examinations more than 1 000 years ago.
4. You'd be fooled if you think a high scoring student can speak English equally as well.
5. Chinese University Entrance examinations are very difficult.
6. Students are reorganized into arts and science classes two years in advance.
7. Also more people can afford the tuition at a foreign University.
8. Such training centers have even developed solutions to TOEFL questions.
9. This method allows people to do fairly well in the exams.
10. The new test format puts more emphasis on language proficiency.

Complete this paragraph with suitable words.

Chinese students are good __1__ taking exams. TOEFL has never been a __2__ for Chinese students. It is not __3__ that many of them scored as __4__ as 670 in the paper-based TOEFL exams. After TOEFL __5__ its new computer-based test format, the highest score was, __6__ again, achieved by a Beijing High School student. Many Chinese people knew __7__ to take examinations more than 1, 000 years ago. Exams were the best way to __8__ one's life at that time.

 Answers 答案

Translate these sentences into Chinese.

1. 中国学生善于应付各类考试。
2. 托福考试对于中国学生来说从来不在话下。
3. 一千多年前，许多人就知道怎么考试了。
4. 如果你认为高分者的英文水平一定很好，那就错了。
5. 中国的高考很难。
6. 提前两年学生就被分进文科班和理科班。
7. 此外，更多人付得起国外大学的学费了。
8. 这些培训中心甚至总结出托福答题技巧。
9. 这个办法使得人们可以考得很好。
10. 新的考试方式更强调实际英文水平。

Complete this paragraph with suitable words.

1. at 2. problem 3. uncommon 4. much 5. introduced 6. once 7. how 8. improve

39. Blogging Fever

博客热

Dialogue

A： Have you ever heard of Xu Jinglei? She is a movie star and her blogs are very popular.

B： Yes. Her blogs received 10 million hits in less than four months.

A： Actually, her blogs are boring. People like her because she is **candid** and doesn't have the **pretentiousness** that is typical of many other actresses. People are tired of the entertainers who rely on seductive and absurd content to **attract eyeballs**. I much prefer another blogger. Her name is Hong Huang, a woman in her 40's. She does not have the pretty looks of a movie star but she is extremely intelligent. She studied in the US when she was only 12, so there is a strong Western influence in her articles. Although she talks a lot about herself, she is able to **reflect** on some of the social issues, which give her blogs a broader view. She is knowledgeable, unpretentious and has a sense of humor and her articles are always short and **to-the-point**, which makes them very easy to read on the computer screen.

B： But, she doesn't receive as many hits as Xu Jinglei. Is it because she's not as pretty?

A： That definitely is a reason. Another reason is that she is not a movie star. People who read Hong Huang tend to be more reasonable, thoughtful and mature.

B： Are more and more movie stars running their own blogs as a result of Xu's success?

A： Yes. Many of them have launched their own blogs. They are eager to tell people they can do more things than just being a movie star. In fact, many ordinary people are publishing blogs too. Maybe, this is because there aren't many other channels for people to express themselves. Originally, blogs were just an additional source of information beside the **mainstream media**. Now it has become a platform for people to show their personalities.

B： Some Shanghai people are writing blogs in English.

A： Yes. The Shanghai Blogger is probably the most popular. It attracts over a million hits a month. It has very thorough information about the scenic spots, local custom, dining, wining, and transportation in Shanghai. According to the bloggers, writing in English has allowed them to think in different dimensions.

B： The Shanghai Blogger sounds like an interesting place. I'll **check it out**. It could be an additional source of income.

对话

A： 你听说过徐静蕾吗？她是个女演员，她的博客被大家追捧。

B： 听说了。据说她的博客在不到 4 个月内点击率达到了 1 000 万次。

A： 其实，她的博客没有太大意思，我猜人们喜欢她是因为她率真，没有女演员的矫情。在她之前一些女性用情色、荒谬的博客吸引眼球，现在大家对这种不健康的表达厌烦了。我更喜欢另一个叫洪晃的人写的博客。她差不多 40 岁，长相平平，但智慧似乎高于一般人。她在 12 岁的时候到美国学习，所以她的博客有很强的西方文化的痕迹。她的博客也是讲述自己的一些经历，她能够反思社会上的一些问题，因此具有更宽的视角。她有学识、不矫情，而且有幽默感。她写的文章短小，不兜圈子，这样在电脑屏幕上读起来很容易。

B： 但是，为什么她没有徐静蕾那样高的点击率？难道因为她长相平平吗？

A： 这肯定是原因之一。另外也因为她不是电影明星。所以看洪晃博客的人应该是一些更理性、更智慧、更成熟的人。

B： 是不是有更多的演员开自己的博客，因为徐给了她们一个在网上成功的榜样？

A： 你说对了。不少演员开了博客，她们想表明他们除了作演员还能做其他更多的事情。事实上，不少普通人也开博客。这也许是因为人们没有太多表达自己的渠道。起初，博客只是除了主流媒体之外的另一个信息来源。现在它成为展示个性的平台。

B： 上海的一些人用英文写博客。

A： 对。"上海博客"最有名，每个月有超过百万的点击量。那里有一些关于上海的景点、风俗、餐饮、交通等非常详细的信息。据那些写英文博客的人说，用英文写作使他们可以从另一个角度思考。

B： 看来这是一个对我有用的平台，听上去是个有趣的地方。我要去试一试。这可能成为另一个收入来源。

New Sociable Habits 社交新风尚

As the Internet evolves—with its webcams, iPods, Instant Messaging, broadband, wi-fi and weblogs—its image as a relationship-wrecker is changing. Now a sociable habit is emerging among the Netorati: couple-surfing. Coined by bloggers responding to a column on the online version of "Wired", couple-surfing describes "netaholics" or "infomaniacs" who surf alongside each other—doing together what used to be seen as a solitary activity.

随着因特网的演变——网络视频、iPod、即时信息、宽带、无线上网和博客的出现，网络作为关系破坏者的形象也在改变。现在网络精英们当中又兴起了一种社交风尚：双人网络冲浪。作为博客们回应"连线"网上的一篇专栏文章而杜撰出来的新词，"双人网络冲浪"指"网络瘾君子"或者"信息迷"把过去视为单人活动的上网变成了两人并肩进行的活动。

Net: the Medium, Not the Root of Problems 网络：问题的媒介而不是根源

The Net is a boon for people who are verbally shy, and provides a great way to resolve disputes about facts, say some fans. Some couples play online games together, and computing seems to be a zone where men can be manly. But in the same way as real-life interests may diverge, couples who do not share what one blogger called "common geekdom" can find surfing divisive.

Relate, Britain's largest relationship counseling body, says about one in 10 couples who seek its help cite some sort of computer-related problem, and the trend is on the rise. "Increasingly, people are saying that time spent on the computer—not necessarily chat rooms or sexy or suggestive sites—is an issue," said Denise Knowles, a Relate counselor. But Knowles points out that the Net itself is often the medium, not the root, of problems.

一些网迷们说，对于那些不善言辞的人来说，网络是个好东西，而且为解决有关是非曲直的争论提供了一个很好的途径。一些伴侣共同玩网络在线游戏，而且男人玩电脑会显得更有男人味。但是就像在真实生活中兴趣爱好会有不同一样，如果两人不是一位博客所称的"同一极客族"，他们可能发现网络冲浪也会造成不和。

"关联"家庭关系顾问公司是英国最大的人际关系咨询机构。这家公司称，每10对向这家公司寻求帮助的伴侣中就有一对说是电脑引发的问题，而且这一趋势正在上升。该公司的咨询师丹尼斯·诺尔斯说："越来越多的人认为，将大把的时间花在电脑上（未必是进聊天室或浏览色情网站）是个问题。"但是诺尔斯指出，在很多时候，网络只是问题产生的媒介而不是根源。

candid 率真，坦诚	pretentiousness 矫揉造作	attract eyeballs 吸引眼球
reflect 反省，思考	to-the-point 一语中的，直截了当	mainstream media 主流媒体
check it out 看一看，试一试		

 **Exercises** 练习

Answer these questions.
1. What do you think of Xu Jinglei's blogs?
2. What do you think of Hong Huang?
3. Why is the Shanghai Blogger useful?

Translate these sentences into Chinese.
1. Her blogs received 10 million hits in less than four months.
2. I guess people like her because she is candid.
3. She is knowledgeable, unpretentious and has a sense of humor.
4. She is able to reflect on some of the social issues.
5. This makes it very easy to read on a computer screen.
6. There aren't many other channels for people to express themselves.
7. Originally blogs were just an additional source of information.
8. It has some very thorough information about Shanghai.
9. Writing in English has allowed them to think in different dimensions.
10. It could be an additional source of income.

Complete this paragraph with suitable words.
Although she talks a lot __1__ herself, she is able to go __2__ that. She reflects __3__ some of the social issues, which gives her blogs a __4__ view. She is knowledgeable, unpretentious and has a __5__ of humor, something that is not very common for a Chinese person. Above __6__, she understands blogging well, i. e., it is web-based, so her articles are, __7__, short, concise and to-the-point. This __8__ it very easy to read on a computer screen.

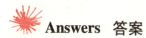 **Answers** 答案

Translate these sentences into Chinese.
1. 她的博客在不到 4 个月内点击率达到了 1 000 万次。
2. 我猜人们喜欢她是因为她率真。
3. 她有学识、不张扬，而且具有幽默感。
4. 她能够反思社会上的一些问题。
5. 这样在电脑屏幕上读起来很容易。
6. 人们没有太多表达自己的渠道。
7. 起初，博客只是另一个信息来源。
8. 那里有一些关于上海的非常详细的信息。
9. 用英文写作使他们可以从另一个角度思考。
10. 这可能成为另一个收入来源。

Complete this paragraph with suitable words.
1. about 2. beyond 3. on 4. broader 5. sense 6. all 7. always 8. makes

40. The Appeal of Crazy Stones

《疯狂的石头》的魅力

Dialogue

A： Although the movie *Crazy Stones* cost 3 million yuan to make, it achieved a **box office** return of 30 million yuan. That's **incredible**. By comparison, any United States movie that costs less than 10 million dollars is considered a small production.

B： Not only that, *Crazy Stones* was also very well received. To be honest, it is not a fine movie and doesn't have an intriguing **story line**. The movie is about a piece of rare jade in an art factory. Both Chinese and international gangs want to take possession of the jade. **Ironically**, all the gang members died one after the other. Only the head of the factory security survived. He is a very confused person and foolishly gives the jade to his wife as an ordinary gift. The film, and its storyline, is preposterous.

A： I've seen some Chinese movies. Some of them are either drama about politics in the Imperial Court or martial arts, both of which, I think, are trying to attract foreigners. Other films are stories about perfect people conveying some strong moral and educational messages. *Crazy Stones* isn't like any of them. It doesn't use any **celebrities**, costs little to make, and involves no major promotional effort. It does have a strong sense of humor and maybe people are tired of the other genres.

B： Some critics say, *Crazy Stones* appeals to its viewers only for its comedy because it doesn't have a memorable story line or any depth. They also say that the only reason for its success is the lack of variety on Chinese screens.

A： That, in other words, implies that there aren't many good movies made in China.

B： I think this is only part of the reason. Another reason is people's attitude towards the life portrayed in this movie. Chinese people believe that if something belongs to a person, they don't have to put up a fight in order to have it, and vice versa. The gangs in the movie are **desperate** to steal something that doesn't belong to them, so they **end up** losing their own lives. By contrast, the head of security is an honest man who isn't envious or criminally minded. He is never swayed by temptation, be it a big prize offered by Coca Cola or any other valuable item. He has spent almost his entire life guarding the jade and ends up having the jade without knowing it.

A： This is very much in line with the Chinese belief of "divine rewards for virtuous deeds."

B： Also, the movie tells a simple story with a strong sense of humor and uses an ending which appeals to the viewer's aspirations for a happy life. It has successfully combined both psychological and moral elements of life.

A： You are right. I know many foreigners who like this movie a lot. Although it talks about the life of the Chinese, we can find echoes of Guy Ritchie's *Lock, Stock and Two Smoking Barrels* in the black humor of the movie and its story line.

对 话

A： 电影《疯狂的石头》投资 300 万人民币，票房却高达 3 000 万元。真令人难以置信。在美国，投资少于 1 000 万美元的电影都被认为是小制作。

B： 不仅如此，这部电影还得到了好评。其实这是一部并不精制的电影，剧情也不复杂，是关于一个工艺品厂的一块稀世翡翠的故事。国际和国内的盗贼们都想得到这块翡翠。具有讽刺意味的是，所有盗贼都先后死掉，只有工厂保卫科长活下来。他是一个糊里糊涂的人，错把宝贝当作一般的礼物送给老婆。一部情节荒诞的电影。

A： 我看过一些中国电影，有些是关于宫廷政治或武侠的，我想它们是想吸引外国人。另一些电影是关于完美的人物，传达出强烈的道德和教育意识。《疯狂的石头》跟它们都不一样。它没有明星，没有大投入，也没有大规模的市场推广。它有强烈的幽默感，也许人们厌烦了其它艺术风格。

B： 一些影评人认为，这部电影用喜剧效果取悦观众，没有令人难忘的情节，也缺乏深度。它成功的唯一原因是中国电影种类的贫乏。

A： 或者说，中国出品的好影片太少了。

B： 我觉得这只是一方面。另一个原因是这部电影中所体现的中国人的处世态度。中国人信奉属于自己的东西，不争也终归是自己的，反之，争也无用。片中盗贼们拼命偷窃不属于自己的东西，他们最终落得死路一条。相反，保卫科长没有妄想和邪念，是个诚实的人，他面对任何诱惑也从不动心，像可口可乐大奖或其他值钱的东西等。他恪尽职守地看管翡翠，结果却是他不明不白地得到了这块翡翠。

A： 这符合中国人"善有善报"的信念。

B： 而且，这部电影用幽默讲述乏味的生活，结局使人们对生活充满信心，它成功地将心理和道德的因素融合在一起。

A： 你说的有道理。我知道许多外国人也喜欢这部电影。虽然它讲的是中国人的生活，但是从剧情和黑色幽默中，我们看到了盖伊·里奇《两杆大烟枪》的影子。

Chinese Movie Industry 中国的电影产业

Motion pictures were introduced to China in 1896, but it was almost a decade before the first local attempt at filmmaking with *Conquering Jun Mountain* (1905). But the Chinese film industry didn't officially begin until 1913 when Zheng Zhenqui and Zhang Shichuan shot the first Chinese movie *The Difficult Couple* (1913). China's first "talkie" was *The Songstress*, *Red Peony* (1931) played by the then "film queen" Butterfly Hu (Hu Die in Chinese). In the 1940s, filmmaking was in a chaotic state and some profiteers seized the chance to shoot pornographic and cheap horror movies. However there were still some wonderful films being made, such as *Spring River Lows Eastward* (1947) by Cai Chusheng and Zheng Junli, *Crow and Sparrow* (1949) by Chen Baichen and Zheng Junli and *Light of Million Hopes* (1948) by Shen Fu. In the 17 years between the establishment of the PRC and the Cultural Revolution, 603 feature films were produced, including the first wide-screen film in 1960. The film industry was severely restricted and no film was shot in the period 1966-1972. In the 1980s, filmmakers again began to probe the boundaries of their art. In 1984, *One and Eight* made mainly by the graduates of the Beijing Film Academy, and Chen Kaige's *Yellow Earth* (1984) introduced the public to the fifth generation of filmmakers, including Wu Ziniu, Tian Zhuangzhuang and He Ping. Zhang Yimou first won an international prize with *Red Sorghum* (1987). In the 1990s, the domestic film industry prospered, coinciding with a government decision to allow the showing of foreign movies from 1995.

1896 年电影进入中国，但是在差不多 10 年后才有了第一部中国电影《定军山》。而直到 1913 年中国正式的电影工业才出现，当时郑振秋和张石川拍摄了中国第一部真正意义上的电影《患难夫妻》。中国第一部有声电影是《歌女红牡丹》（1931），由当时的"电影皇后"胡蝶出演。20 世纪 40 年代，电影制作处于一种无序状态，一些奸商借机拍摄色情电影和粗劣的恐怖电影。然而这一时期也出现了一些优秀的影片，比如由蔡楚生和郑君里拍摄的《一江春水向东流》（1947），由陈白尘和郑君里拍摄的《乌鸦与麻雀》（1949），由沈浮拍摄的《万家灯火》（1948）。中华人民共和国建国到文化大革命的 17 年间，拍摄了 603 部电影，包括 1960 年拍摄的第一部宽银幕电影。1966 到 1972 年，中国电影工业的发展受到了极大的制约，这期间没有一部电影问世。到了 20 世纪 80 年代，电影工作者们又一次打破艺术的禁锢。1984 年，主要由北京电影学院的毕业生们创作了《一个和八个》、陈凯歌的《黄土地》将第五代导演群体推向公众。这些人包括：吴子牛、田壮壮、何平等。张艺谋第一次凭借《红高粱》（1987）获得国际电影奖。20 世纪 90 年代，国产电影工业蓬勃发展，与此同时，1995 年，政府开放外国影片在中国的上映。

---

box office　票房	incredible　不可思议	story line　故事情节
ironically　具有讽刺意义的是	celebrity　明星	desperate　绝望的，拼命的
end up　最后以…		

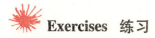 **Exercises** 练习

Answer these questions.

1. What is "Crazy Stones" about?
2. Why was "Crazy Stones" successful?
3. What happened to the head of security?

Translate these sentences into Chinese.

1. Any movie that costs less than 10 million dollars is considered a small production.
2. It is not a fine movie and does not have an intriguing story line.
3. The movie is about a piece of rare jade in an art factory.
4. He is a very confused person.
5. Maybe people are tired of the other genres.
6. "Crazy Stones" is not like any of them.
7. They end up losing their own lives.
8. The head of security is not envious or criminally minded.
9. He is never swayed by temptations.
10. He ends up having the jade without knowing it.

Complete this paragraph with suitable words.

On the __1__, the head of security is an __2__ man who isn't envious or criminally minded. He is never swayed __3__ temptation, be it a big prize __4__ by Coca Cola or any other valuable item. He has spent almost his __5__ life guarding the jade and __6__ up having the jade __7__ knowing it. This is, very much, in line with the Chinese belief of "divine rewards for virtuous deeds." The movie tells a __8__ story with a strong sense of humor and uses an ending which appeals to the viewer's aspirations for a happy life.

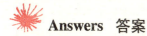 **Answers** 答案

Translate these sentences into Chinese.

1. 投资少于 1 000 万美元的电影都被认为是小制作。
2. 这是一部并不精制的电影，剧情也不复杂。
3. 这部电影是关于一个工艺品厂里的一块稀世翡翠。
4. 他是一个糊里糊涂的人。
5. 也许人们厌烦了其它艺术风格。
6. 《疯狂的石头》跟它们都不一样。
7. 他们最终落得死路一条。
8. 那个保卫科长没有任何的妄想和邪念。
9. 他面对任何诱惑也从不动心。
10. 结果却是他不明不白地得到了这块翡翠。

Complete this paragraph with suitable words.

1. contrary   2. honest   3. by   4. offered   5. entire   6. ends   7. without   8. simple

41. The Film Makers' Responsibility

电影人的责任

Dialogue

A： Recent research shows that there is a new pollutant in Los Angeles. The source of the pollution comes from emissions during film making, either car exhaust, generator emissions or the fireworks used for **special effects**. The research shows that every year the film industry produces 140,000 tons of pollutants. What is the situation with Chinese film industry?

B： In addition to pollution, another concern facing China's film industry is its negative impact on the **general public**. Many male characters in the movies are heavy smokers. They do not always wear seat belt while driving and they often use a mobile phone while **at the wheel**. The situation with female characters is not much better. In some scenes involving a beautiful environment, they may **tear up** documents in anger and throw the pieces into a lake. Even worse, they make a lot of noise in public places. Some parents are worried about these rowdy actions and the negative impact on their children.

A： I have indeed seen such scenes in Chinese movies and on TV. The situation is better in Japanese and Korean films. Most of the key characters in their films tend to be **well behaved**. Maybe their film directors are more worried about the social effect of their movies. I understand that the Chinese government has recently published a set of guidelines for Chinese tourists going overseas. One of the guidelines is not to make a lot of noise in public places. Chinese film makers could learn from this good example.

B： Talking about pollution caused by Hollywood, it **reminds** me of some news reports about how the environment was damaged during film making at home. One of the reports was about damage done to plants in the picturesque Shangri-la area. Another report was about damage to some rock carvings that were several hundreds of years

162

old. There was a lot of criticism about the damage.

A: Film makers shouldn't just worry about box office ticket sales and their profit. They should also have some social responsibilities and show respect for the environment.

B: Some Chinese film makers have done a good job in that respect. They have produced films to **raise** people's **awareness** of the environment and animal rights, as well as living conditions of human-beings.

A: A person may have a lot of money but that does not mean they are cultured. Likewise, a person may have fame, but that doesn't mean they can ignore their social responsibilities. There are already instances in the Chinese film industry to prove this.

对 话

A: 一项新的研究显示，洛杉矶出现了一种新的污染，它源自拍摄电影时使用的车辆和发电机以及烟火爆炸的特效所排放的废气。研究结果表明，电影行业每年排放14万吨污染物。中国的影视剧制作行业是什么情况呢？

B: 除了对环境的污染，在中国影视剧制作中，令人担忧的是给公众带来的负面影响。一些影视剧中的男性角色不停地吸烟，驾车时常常不系安全带，开车时使用手机。女性角色也好不到那去。她们很可能在一片美景中，愤怒地撕碎某些材料，然后把纸屑扔到脚下的湖水中。更有甚者，电影或电视剧中的角色们在公共场所大声说笑，弄出非常大的噪音。父母们担心这样的不良行为会给孩子们带来负面影响。

A: 我的确在一些中国的影视剧中看到过这些景象。这一点，日剧和韩剧做得比较好。他们的影视剧中的正面角色大多行为得体。也许导演考虑到了作品的社会影响。最近，中国政府颁布中国公民到海外旅游应遵守的行为规范，其中有一条是不要在公共场所高声喧哗。中国的影视制作者们可以从榜样那儿学点儿什么。

B: 说到好莱坞对自然环境的污染，让我想起几条中国电影制作破坏环境的新闻：一个是在拍戏时毁掉了香格里拉风景区中的植被；还有一个剧组毁掉了一幅有数百年历史的摩崖石刻。这引起了强烈批评。

A: 影视剧制作者不仅要关注票房和利润，更要对社会有责任感，对大自然有敬畏之心。

B: 一些中国导演做到了这点。他们制作影片，提高人们对环境、动物保护和普通人的生存状态的关注。

A: 有钱不等于有教养，有名声也不意味着可以逃避自己的社会责任感。中国的影视剧行业中已经有很多先例证明了这一点。

Violent TV Face Ban 暴力电视剧面临禁令

Guangdong Province is gearing up to tackle juvenile crime by banning violent television programmes from local airwaves and prohibiting schools from dismissing students. Juvenile crime has been on the rise in the provincial capital of Guangzhou in recent years.

The Guangdong Provincial People's Congress is currently in the process of passing the new rules, known as the Guangdong Provincial Regulations on Preventing Juvenile Delinquents, which are expected to combat the trend. The congress is currently reviewing the third draft of the new regulations and expects to pass them before the end of this year. The regulations would prohibit local television stations from broadcasting foreign cartoons between 5 pm and 8 pm. They will also ban films and TV series that feature violent or horrifying content. Residents of Guangzhou have welcomed the new regulations.

Courts there passed sentences on 514 juvenile offenders in 1998. That number grew to 935 in 2001, 1,584 in 2004 and 1,233 in the first nine months of 2005. The cases have involved crimes like robbery, theft, assault, rape, fighting and public disturbances.

Programmes about triads and other underworld organizations, many of them made in Taiwan, Hong Kong and Macao special administrative regions and foreign countries, have been the particular focus of criticism.

广东省正在加紧解决青少年犯罪问题，他们采取的方式是禁止当地电视播放有暴力内容的电视节目并禁止学校开除学生。近年来，在广东省首府广州市的少年犯罪有所增长。

广东省人大正在准备通过一项法规，即《广东省关于预防青少年犯罪条例》，期望以此遏制青少年犯罪的势头。广东省人大正在评议新条例的第三稿，预计在今年年底前通过。这一条例将禁止当地电视台在晚上5点到8点期间播放境外动画片。也将禁播那些有暴力倾向或恐怖内容的电影和电视剧。广州市民对这一条例表示欢迎。

1998年，广东省法院判决了514名青少年罪犯。这个数字在2001年增加到935人，2004年为1 584人，到了2005年前9个月已达到1 233人。他们涉及的案件多为抢劫、盗窃、伤害、强奸、斗殴和扰乱公共秩序等。

与黑帮和其他黑社会组织有关的电视节目，多数由台湾、香港和澳门特别行政区和外国制作，已经引起了批评。

---

special effects 特技	general public 公众	seat belt 安全带
at the wheel 开车	tear up 撕碎	well behaved 规矩
remind 使…想起，提醒	raise awareness 提高认识	

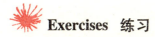 **Exercises** 练习

Answer these questions.

1. Where does the new pollution come from?
2. What do male characters in the movie like to do?
3. Are Japanese and Korean directors more concerned about the social effect?

Translate these sentences into Chinese.

1. Recent research shows that there is a new pollutant in Los Angeles.
2. Every year, the film industry produces 140,000 tons of pollutants.
3. The concern facing China's film industry is its negative impact on the general public.
4. They do not always wear seat belt while driving.
5. The situation with female characters is not any better.
6. Parents are worried about the negative impact of these rowdy actions on their children.
7. Most of the key characters in their films tend to be well behaved.
8. The government has published some guidelines for Chinese tourists going overseas.
9. They have produced films to raise people's awareness of the environment.
10. A person may have fame but that doesn't mean they can avoid their social responsibilities.

Complete this paragraph with suitable words.

Many male characters are __1__ smokers. They do not always __2__ seat belt while driving. They use a mobile phone while __3__ the wheel. The situation with female characters is not __4__ better. Here are some __5__ scenes. In a beautiful environment, they may angrily tear __6__ some documents and then throw the pieces into the lake. Even worse, they make a lot of __7__ in public places. Some parents are worried __8__ the negative impact of these rowdy actions on their children.

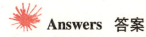 **Answers** 答案

Translate these sentences into Chinese.

1. 一项新的研究显示，洛杉矶出现了一种新的污染。
2. 电影行业每年排放 14 万吨污染物。
3. 在中国影视剧制作中，令人担忧的是给公众带来的负面影响。
4. 他们驾车时常常不系安全带。
5. 女性角色也好不到那去。
6. 父母们担心这样的不良行为会给孩子们带来负面影响。
7. 他们的影视剧中的正面角色大多行为得体。
8. 政府发布了一个关于中国公民到海外旅游时应遵守的行为规范。
9. 他们制作电影，提高人们对环境的关注。
10. 有人可能很有名声，但这不等于他可以逃避自己的社会责任感。

Complete this paragraph with suitable words.

1. heavy 2. wear 3. at 4. any 5. typical 6. up 7. noise 8. about

42. The Crazy TV Box

电视：疯狂的盒子

Dialogue

A： Television appeared in China some 20 years ago. People have since been captivated by this magic box and, in return, this box has turned them into idiots.

B： Americans were turned into idiots much earlier than you were. Television became popular in the US in the 1960s. Over 80% of the households had TV sets then. **Rather than** doing their own reading, many people **switched to** TV for information. Consequently, people's opinions were **swayed** by what they saw on TV. President Kennedy was the first President to benefit from TV campaigning. His **charisma** helped him defeat Richard Nixon.

A： Television does not turn people into idiots any more, it **drives** them **crazy**. By copying US and European TV shows, many Chinese TV stations have introduced their own versions of contest programs. The programs focus on various skills of the participants or their desire to chase wealth and fame. Many young people are crazy about these programs. The most well-known was a singing contest called Super Girls. It was the Chinese version of American Idol with the winners becoming instant **household names**.

B： It's not just the viewers. Editors and producers have also gone crazy. Take some of the **TV anchors** for example. In order to attract viewers, the broadcaster of a weather channel in Russia **stripped** herself on screen. Although we haven't seen any naked Chinese anchor women yet, they are equally crazy. Typically, Chinese anchor women like to yell or imitate Hong Kong and Taiwan accents. It's as if they have lost their senses or the feeling of decency.

A： An extreme example of a crazy TV anchor is a **soccer commentator**. He is now remembered for his hysterical yelling during last year's World Cup match between Italy and Australia.

B： As a result many Italians have become his fans because of his compliments to the Italian team.

A： The only people who seem to remain sober are the news anchors on CCTV. They look so restrained and unemotional. There is no eye contact between them and they always seem so eager to collect the manuscripts at the end of each show. I don't understand why they look so dull.

B： They are certainly not crazy. They are boring.

A： TV used to be called a low-IQ box. It should be called a Pandora's Box because there are a lot of bad things pouring out of it these days.

对 话

A： 二十多年前，电视出现在中国人的生活中，从此人们被这个神奇的盒子吸引了，然后，人们被这盒子变成了傻子。

B： 美国人比你们先变成傻子，因为早在 20 世纪 60 年代电视在美国就已普及。那时，80% 多的人家有了电视。人们不再通过阅读而是转向电视获得信息。结果，电视左右着大众的观念。20 世纪 60 年代，肯尼迪正是拜电视所赐赢得了总统竞选，他的魅力帮助他打败了尼克松。

A： 如今，电视不再将人变成傻子，而是使人变得疯狂。中国的电视节目模仿欧美，推出了形形色色的竞赛节目。这些节目的焦点集中在各种技能的竞争，以及对财富和名声的追逐上。许多年轻人对这样的节目发狂。最出名的就是被称为《超级女声》的歌唱比赛。它是中国版的《美国偶像》，胜出者立即成为家喻户晓的人物。

B： 不仅看电视的人疯狂了，电视节目的编辑和制作人也发了疯。那些主持人就是最好的例证。俄罗斯一家电视台的天气预报节目的女主播在镜头前开脱。虽然我们还不曾看到裸体出镜的中国主持人，但有些人的作为也差不多是疯狂的。最典型的诸如：女主持人的高声尖叫，或模仿港台腔，颇有些失去理智和尊严的感觉。

A： 主持人变得疯狂的极端例子是一位足球评论员。人们至今记得他在去年世界杯足球赛意大利对澳大利亚队的比赛时疯狂的叫喊。

B： 结果不少意大利人由此成为他的"粉丝"，因为他对意大利队的褒扬。

A： 唯一保持清醒的可能是中央台的新闻主播们。他们依然中规中矩。每次新闻结束时，总是忙于收拾手边的资料，两个人谁也不看对方一眼。我不明白他们为什么如此呆板。

B： 他们没有疯狂，但有点儿乏味。

A： 电视曾被人称作弱智盒子，现在也许该叫潘朵拉的盒子了，因为一打开它，很多不健康的东西就跑出来了。

Background Reading 背景阅读

The Invention of Color Television 彩色电视的发明

Born in Budapest on December 2, 1906, Peter Carl Goldmark was one of that generation of brilliant Hungarian scientists which included Edward Teller, John von Neumann, and Eugene Paul Wigner. But while they dedicated their talents to the technology of death, he became a leader in the communications revolution. They gave America the Bomb. He gave it the long-playing record, color television, and the promise of a whole new world of sight and sound.

Hired by Pye Radio, Ltd., in Cambridge, he built a mechanical TV transmitter. Although it worked, the Pye studios seemed indifferent to its possibilities, and after two years he left Cambridge with savings of $250 and boarded a boat for New York. There he applied for American citizenship and a job at RCA. To the subsequent chagrin of David Sarnoff, Sarnoff's underlings at NBC turned the slight Hungarian scientist away. CBS then hired him.

The next thing Peter's new superiors knew, he was glimpsed atop the Chrysler Building putting up a television antenna. Four relatively fallow years followed. Then, while visiting Canada in the spring of 1940, he happened to drop in at a theater showing the Technicolor Gone With the Wind. Stunned by the beauty of the color, he said later, he came away with "an inferiority feeling about television in black and white." He developed color television in just three months.

彼得·卡尔·戈德马克于 1906 年 12 月 2 日出生于布达佩斯。他和爱德华·特勒、约翰·冯·纽曼和尤金·波乐·威格纳等人属于同一代杰出的匈牙利科学家。但在那几个人把自己的才能用于杀人技术时，他却成为通讯革命中的领先人物。那几位给美国造出了原子弹，而他却为美国发明了慢转密纹唱片和彩色电视机，并展现出一个在声色两方面都完全崭新的世界前景。

他受雇于剑桥的派氏无线电有限公司，制作了一部机械的电视播放机。这部机器虽然能够使用，可是公司的播音部门却并不关心它的发展。两年后，彼得带着 250 美元的积蓄，离开剑桥，搭船来到纽约。在这里，他申请加入美国国籍，并向美国无线电公司求职。后来使戴维·萨尔诺夫大为苦恼的是，他的全国广播公司的下属竟没有雇用这位干瘦的匈牙利科学家。结果哥伦比亚广播公司雇用了他。

不久，彼得的新上司就了解到他已在克莱斯勒大厦的屋顶上安装了电视天线。接着过了 4 个相对清闲的年头。1940 年春，他去加拿大时，偶然走进影院，那儿正放映彩色影片《飘》。那绚丽的色彩使他看呆了，事后他说，他在离开那家影院时，想着"黑白电视，感到一种自卑"。仅仅过了 3 个月，他就发明了彩色电视机。

---

rather than 相反地，与其说	switch to 转为	sway 左右
charisma 魅力	drive... crazy 让…发疯	household name 家喻户晓的名字
TV anchor 电视主持人	strip 脱衣服	soccer commentator 足球解说

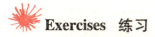 **Exercises 练习**

Answer these questions.

1. How did people get information after television appeared?
2. How crazy are some Chinese TV anchor women?
3. Why are CCTV news anchors boring?

Translate these sentences into Chinese.

1. People have since been captivated by this magic box.
2. Over 80% of the households had TV sets then.
3. Consequently, people's opinions were swayed by what they saw on TV.
4. His charisma helped him defeat Richard Nixon.
5. Many young people are crazy about these programs.
6. The broadcaster of a weather channel in Russia stripped herself on screen.
7. They have lost their senses or the feeling of decency.
8. He is now remembered for his crazy yelling during last year's World Cup.
9. There is no eye contact between them.
10. They are so eager to collect the manuscripts at the end of each show.

Complete this paragraph with suitable words.

Americans were ___1___ into idiots ___2___ earlier than you were. Television became popular in the United States ___3___ the 1960s. Over 80% of the ___4___ had TV sets then. Rather than doing their ___5___ reading, many people switched ___6___ TV for information. Consequently, people's opinions were ___7___ by what they saw on TV. President Kennedy was the first president to ___8___ from TV campaigning. His charisma helped him defeat Richard Nixon.

 **Answers 答案**

Translate these sentences into Chinese.

1. 从此人们被这个神奇的盒子吸引住了。
2. 那时，80％的人家拥有了电视。
3. 结果，电视左右着大众的观念。
4. 他的魅力帮助他打败了尼克松。
5. 许多年轻人对这样的节目发狂。
6. 俄罗斯一家电视台的天气预报节目的女主播在镜头前开脱。
7. 她们失去了理智和廉耻。
8. 人们仍然记得他在去年世界杯足球赛时疯狂的叫喊。
9. 两个人谁也不看对方一眼。
10. 每次节目结束时他们总是忙于收拾手边的资料。

Complete this paragraph with suitable words.

1. turned 2. much 3. in 4. households 5. own 6. to 7. swayed 8. benefit

43. English as a Door Opener

英语，敲门砖

Dialogue

A: Many people still remember Zhang Ziyi's poor English at an Oscar ceremony several years ago. It has become a permanent **embarrassment** to her.

B: People such as Joan Chen who went to Hollywood many years earlier had to speak good English **in the first place**. It is a different story today. Hollywood is **eager to** break into the Chinese market with its 1.3 billion people. Therefore, **English proficiency** has become a secondary consideration when selecting a Chinese actor. Gong Li's English was very bad when she made her **debut** in *Chinese Box*, but she was given a subsequent role in *Miami Vice*. As many as eight people were hired to help her speak English with a Cuban accent. Hollywood wanted to get into the Chinese market by having Gong Li in the movie.

A: Jet Li had to go through **a crash course** in English after he was selected by Hollywood. "You have to learn English if you want to have a role in Hollywood movies," he said.

B: It seems Hollywood's criterion is the person's appeal rather than their English proficiency.

A: Talking about appeal, I think Hollywood is wrong in **assuming** that its movies can only find their way into China by engaging certain actresses.

B: You are right. **No matter** how fluent they are in English, it is almost impossible for Gong Li and Zhang Ziyi to be as famous in the United States as Tom Cruise and Julia Roberts are in Asia. Only when China can produce movies, not just one or two but a lot, that appeal to American theater-goers, can Chinese movie stars become popular over there.

A: Unfortunately, many Chinese performers believe that English is very important for them to get a foothold in Hollywood. I am currently teaching English to a Chinese actor and I've heard many other performers have hired foreigners to teach them English.

B： That's correct. Zhang Ziyi, for example, is spending a lot of time learning English. Her English was much better at last year's Oscar award ceremony. Now she even speaks a few English words when doing promotions for her movies. Obviously she is very proud of her progress.

A： Every young artist has a dream to speak English as good as an American. Hollywood is a dream factory. These young artists are hoping to realize their dreams in Hollywood some day. Naturally English has become a **door opener** to this dream factory.

对 话

A： 许多人还记得几年前章子怡在奥斯卡颁奖礼上讲得结结巴巴的英文。这是她挥之不去的一个心结。

B： 早些年进入好莱坞的影星大多英文不错，比如陈冲。今天的情形就不一样了。好莱坞急于打开拥有 13 亿人的中国市场，因此，在选择中国演员时，英语已经成了次要标准。巩俐拍英文影片《中国盒子》时英文并不好，但是电影《迈阿密风云》中，还是请她饰演了一个配角。据说制片方聘用了 8 人之多以帮助她说一口带有古巴口音的英语。好莱坞是想借她打开中国市场。

A： 李连杰被好莱坞看中后开始恶补英文。李连杰说："你想拍好莱坞电影，就必须学习英语。"

B： 看起来，好莱坞的标准第一是名气，第二才是英语。

A： 说到名气，好莱坞以为某些女演员是它们进入中国市场的唯一途径，我认为这有些偏差。

B： 你说的对。既便英语很好，但巩俐或章子怡这样的演员想要像汤姆·克鲁斯或朱莉亚·罗伯茨在亚洲那样知名一般地在美国家喻户晓，几乎是不可能的。只有中国人拍出大量美国人喜欢的电影，中国影星在美国流行才有可能。

A： 但是，不少中国演员都认为英文是最重要的。我正在为一位中国的男演员做英语教练，据我所知，不少演员都请外国人教英文。

B： 一点儿不错。比如章子怡就在学英文上很下功夫。去年的奥斯卡颁奖礼上，她的英文好了许多。现在，甚至在中国做推广时，她也要说出几个英文词。显然，她对自己英文的进步感到骄傲。

A： 几乎每一个年轻的演员都有一个梦：说一口比美国人还棒的英文。好莱坞是个梦工厂，年轻的演员们渴望有一天在那里梦想成真。很自然，英文成了进入这个梦工厂的敲门砖。

The Rush Hour of Jackie Chan 成龙的尖峰时刻

As Asia's favorite action hero, Jackie Chan has finally conquered Hollywood. *Rush Hour*, Chan's new made-in-America blockbuster, rocketed to the top of the charts on its opening weekend in the United States, winning an unexpected cross-over audience. In three days, the box-office tally was $33 million—the highest weekend gross ever for New Line Cinema. Now in its sixth week in American theatres, the film, directed by Brett Ratner, has so far taken in more than $117 million.

Chan had already scored when such films as *Rumble in the Bronx* and *First Strike* were released in mainstream theatres in the U. S. , and not just in Chinatown and specialty video stores. Now Rush Hour has turned Jackie Chan into a household name the way *Enter the Dragon* made a legend of Bruce Lee.

Long-time Jackie Chan fans may find his antics too familiar and the film's slick editing relying more on camera tricks than real stunts. After all, Chan is almost 44 years old and Hollywood insurance codes prohibit actors from performing some of the outrageous stunts for which Hong Kong films are famous. Still, Chan has always been considered one of the most popular and respected stars in the Chinese film world. Given the typical typecasting of Asians as hookers or triads, Jackie Chan's relaunch as an action hero in the West is a resounding triumph.

作为亚洲颇受欢迎的动作巨星，成龙终于征服了好莱坞。他新近在美国摄制的巨片《尖峰时刻》首映周内即飚升至排行榜首，出人意料地赢得了大批非亚裔观众。仅仅三天，票房就达到3 300万美元——这是新线影院最高的周收入。这部由布雷特·兰特纳执导的影片，目前在美国本土影院的第 6 周收入已超过 1. 17 亿美元。

早在美国主流影院放映的如《布朗克斯区的喧嚣》和《第一次罢工》时成龙就已在主流影院获得了成功，而不仅仅是在唐人街和特色录影带商店。而今《尖峰时刻》就如同当年李小龙的《猛龙过江》所创造的神话那样，使得成龙成为家喻户晓的名字。

成龙迷们会发现，他的滑稽噱头多已较为眼熟，且许多抢眼镜头多是靠摄影技术而非真实的绝技。毕竟，成龙快 44 岁了，另外，在香港电影中一些引以为荣的危险绝技在好莱坞的保险条例中是不允许做的。尽管如此，成龙一直被认为是中国电影界最受欢迎和尊重的明星之一。与亚洲人常一成不变的扮演小偷或"天地会"会众的角色相比，成龙在西方影坛重树了动作片的英雄形象的确是一大成功。

---

embarrassment 窘迫	in the first place 首先	eager to 急于
English proficiency 英语水平	debut 首次出现	a crash course 恶补，速成班
assume 以为，假设	no matter 不管怎样	door opener 敲门砖

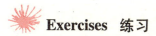 **Exercises 练习**

Answer these questions.
1. Why has English proficiency become a secondary consideration for Hollywood?
2. How did Jet Li learn his English?
3. Why are many Chinese performers learning English?

Translate these sentences into Chinese.
1. It has become a permanent embarrassment to her.
2. It is a different story today.
3. Hollywood is eager to break into the Chinese market.
4. English proficiency has become a secondary consideration.
5. As many as eight people were hired to help her.
6. Jet Li went through a crash course in English after he was selected by Hollywood.
7. Hollywood's criterion is the person's appeal rather than their English proficiency.
8. China can produce movies that appeal to American theater-goers.
9. Many Chinese performers believe that English is most important.
10. Naturally English has become a door opener to this dream factory.

Complete this paragraph with suitable words.
Zhang Ziyi is ___1___ a lot of time learning English. Her English was ___2___ better at last year's Oscar award ceremony. Now, she ___3___ speaks a few English words when ___4___ promotions for her movies. Obviously, she is very ___5___ of her progress. Every young artist has a dream to speak English as ___6___ as an American. Hollywood is a ___7___ factory. These young artists are hoping to realize their dreams in Hollywood ___8___ day. Naturally, English has become a door opener to this dream factory.

 **Answers 答案**

Translate these sentences into Chinese.
1. 这是她挥之不去的一个心结。
2. 今天的情形就不一样了。
3. 好莱坞急需打开中国市场。
4. 英语水平已经成为次要标准。
5. 聘用了 8 人之多帮助她。
6. 李连杰被好莱坞看中后开始恶补英文。
7. 好莱坞的标准第一是名气，第二才是英语。
8. 中国可以拍出美国人喜欢的电影。
9. 不少中国演员都认为英文是最重要的。
10. 很自然，英文成了进入这个梦工厂的敲门砖。

Complete this paragraph with suitable words.
1. spending 2. much 3. even 4. doing 5. proud 6. good 7. dream 8. some

44. When English Meets Chinese

当英语与汉语相遇

Dialogue

A： The Beijing government is **making an effort** to rectify all incorrect English signs in public areas. For example, the sign at an airport **emergency exit** says, "No entry to peace time" when what it really means to say is simply, "No entry unless authorized". Other examples are, "To take notice of safe. The slippery are very crafty" instead of "Slippery road. **Mind your steps**." Or on a restaurant menu "Corrugated iron beef" for "Beef fried on iron pan", and "Government abuse chicken" for "Spicy chicken".

B： In old Shanghai, people referred to such English expressions as "pidgin English", because "pidgin" was a mispronunciation of "business" in the Shanghai dialect. As English is becoming more and more popular, Chinese-styled expressions have become unavoidable. "People mountain, people sea," is a typical example of the mistranslated Chinese **set phrase**, "crowds of people". Some of these Chinese-styled expressions, such as "long time no see" or "Gung Ho" have been accepted into the English language. The latter is **a reference to** China's industrial cooperative movement. It has even acquired a new interpretation of being enthusiastic about something.

A： Mistakes also exist in some translations from English into Chinese. For example, **rather than** following the established translation for Jesus Christ, someone used a set of totally different but phonetically close Chinese characters, and caused a lot of confusion. **The same is true** with the Chinese translation of "fuzzy logic".

B： At its current rapid pace of development, China has created a lot of new expressions, many of which are almost impossible to translate. Not long ago, President Hu Jintao published eight points of moral advice for doing good and avoiding evil. The *Beijing Review* gave it a short title by translating it as "Eight Honors, Eight Disgraces".

A： When English meets Chinese, it is like two strangers coming together. It takes time to get to know each other. There are a lot of examples of how English is very appropriately translated into Chinese. The "beat generation" is one of them. It used to be translated to reflect the meaning only. The new translation is able to combine both meaning and pronunciation. According to a 2005 survey of the most commonly used words, Chinglish or Chinese English was ranked in fourth place. Chinglish reminds people of the expression "pidgin English" but it doesn't have any sarcastic implications. Rather, it **refers to** Chinese people who speak fluent English, which is likely to become the most commonly-spoken foreign language in China.

对 话

A： 北京市政府正在着手治理公共指示牌上那些翻译错误的英文。比如，在机场的紧急出口上标有"平时禁止入内"的牌子，英文却是 No entry on peacetime（和平时期禁止入内）。再比如，有一块警告路人注意路滑的牌子写成 To Take Notice of Safe; The Slippery are Very Crafty 翻成中文就是："要注意保险箱；那些滑是非常狡猾的。"在餐馆里，菜单上把"铁板牛肉"翻译成 Corrugated iron beef（有皱纹的牛肉），"宫保鸡"写成 Government abuse chicken（政府虐待鸡）。

B： 在旧上海，这种中国式的英文被称作"洋泾浜英语"，因为"洋泾浜"是旧上海方言对 business 的讹读。英语流行，中式英文难以避免。比如 people mountain, people sea（人山人海）之类。但一些中国式的英文由于使用多了，也被接受。比如旧时的 Long time no see（好久不见）和 Gung Ho，后者特指中国的工业合作运动。它的含义已变为"热心的"、"狂热的"的意思。

A： 英文译成中文也有不少失误。有人凭一套完全似是而非的音译法来进行翻译，"杰塞斯·克赖斯特"竟然是对"耶稣基督"的中译。还有 fuzzy logic（模糊逻辑），被译作"弗晰逻辑"。

B： 中国的迅速发展，也产生了许多新词汇，翻译起来是件难事。比如胡锦涛主席不久前提出的"八荣八耻"，《北京周报》就译成 Eight Honors，Eight Disgraces。

A： 当英语与汉语相遇，就像人们的相识一样，双方需要时间相互了解。英文译成中文也有许多优秀范例，比如 beat generation 原来只是意译，后来改译为"疲子一代"，专家认为新的译法音义兼顾。据 2005 年度常用词汇盘点结果，第四名是 chinglish（中式英语）。它或许让人想到"洋泾浜英语"，但这次上榜并无此意，而是指中国"英文通"渐增，英语大有成为中国"第二普通话"之势。

Background Reading 背景阅读

Chinese Hot in American 美国的汉语热

Mandarin Chinese, the official language of the People's Republic of China, is suddenly hot in American schools. With China poised to become the world's leading economy sometime this century, public and private schools are scrambling to add Mandarin to their roster of foreign languages or expand Chinese programs already in place. By some estimates, as many as 50,000 children nationwide are taking Mandarin in school.

The drive to develop Chinese-language programs has not been without its bumps. A shortage of trained, credentialed teachers has made it difficult for some schools to join the race. (With some exceptions, public schools require teachers to be credentialed, while private schools do not.) When schools do get teachers, they often recruit them straight from China— a recipe for a cacophonous culture clash.

Robert Liu, who taught in China before coming to Venice High School, remembers his first two years in an American classroom with the benefit of hindsight. It was not an easy adjustment, he said. In China, "respect is the No. 1 thing. Students respect their teachers," he said. Liu found a different paradigm here, where respect must be earned and teachers spend much of their time maintaining order.

"You have to quiet them down and find different activities to attract them or they will lose attention," he said.

中国的官方语言普通话在美国的学校中突然热起来。由于中国经济在本世纪的领先地位，公立和私立学校纷纷在外语教学中加入汉语，或将汉语教学项目扩展。据估计，在美国的学校中，有5万名孩子在学习汉语。

推动发展汉语项目不是没有遇到困难。由于缺乏受过训练、持有证书的教师，一些学校很难加入汉语教学的竞争。（有些公立学校会要求教师持有证书，而私立学校的要求就不严格。）当学校聘用教师时，它们通常直接从中国将他们招来，这种方式为文化冲突埋下了隐患。

罗伯特·刘在来到美国一所高中工作之前曾在中国任教。他回忆起在美国教学最初两年的情景时说，适应这里的情况并不容易。他说，在中国"尊敬是第一位的事情，学生们尊敬他们的老师"。刘发现美国有着不同的模式，教师必须从学生那里赢得尊敬，而且教师要将很多时间用于维持秩序。

他说："你不得不让他们安静下来，并找到不同的活动去吸引他们，否则他们就会走神。"

---

make an effort 努力	emergency exit 紧急出口	Mind your steps. 注意脚底下，看路
set phrase 俗语	a reference to 指，提到	rather than 非但
the same is true 相同	refer to 专指	

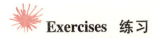 **Exercises 练习**

Answer these questions.

1. What is the Beijing government trying to do?
2. What does Gung Ho mean?
3. What is an example of good English translation into Chinese?

Translate these sentences into Chinese.

1. The government is making an effort to rectify all incorrect English signs in public areas.
2. In old Shanghai, people referred to such English expressions as "pidgin English".
3. "Pidgin" was a mispronunciation of "business" in the Shanghai dialect.
4. Chinese-styled expressions have become unavoidable.
5. The latter is a reference to China's industrial cooperative movement.
6. Mistakes also exist in some translations from English into Chinese.
7. At its current rapid pace of development China has created a lot of new expressions.
8. It takes time to get to know each other.
9. It used to be translated to only reflect the meaning.
10. The new translation is able to combine both meaning and pronunciation.

Complete this paragraph with suitable words.

At its current ___1___ pace of development, China has ___2___ a lot of new expressions, many of which are ___3___ impossible to translate. Not long ago, President Hu Jintao published eight points of ___4___ advice of doing good and avoiding evil. The *Being Review* gave it a short title by translating it ___5___ "Eight Honors, Eight Disgraces". When English ___7___ Chinese, it is like two strangers coming together. It ___8___ time to get to know each other.

 Answers 答案

Translate these sentences into Chinese.

1. 政府正在着手治理公共指示牌上那些翻译错误的英文。
2. 在旧上海，人们把这种中国化的不通英文称作"洋泾浜英语"。
3. Pidgin 是旧上海方言对 business 的讹读。
4. 中式英文难以避免。
5. 后者特指中国的工业合作运动。
6. 英文译成中文也有不少失误。
7. 中国的迅速发展，也产生了许多新词汇。
8. 双方需要时间相互了解。
9. 原来只是意译。
10. 新的译法音义兼顾。

Complete this paragraph with suitable words.

1. rapid 2. created 3. almost 4. moral 5. as 6. short 7. meets 8. takes

45. Chinese and Western Set Phrases

中国俗语和西方俗语

Dialogue

A: Whenever I try to use some Chinese set phrases, people seem surprised. They not only **marvel at** my language capability but also treat me as one of them. Set phrases help **close the gap** between the listeners and me. Usually people will offer to teach me more such phrases.

B: Set phrases can definitely reflect a person's life experience, as well as their attitude and **value propositions**. From such expressions you can see what people like and dislike.

A: In the West, health-related phrases are usually based on people's understanding of a healthy lifestyle. Benjamin Franklin, co-author of the Declaration of Independence, wrote a book in 1732, titled *Poor Richard's Almanac*. The book was on the **best-seller** list for 25 years. It contains a lot of wisdom in its memorable phrases. I think I can say with confidence that it reveals the secrets of America's **rise to success** in a little over 200 years. Those secrets are hard work, frugality, fairness and kindness. The phrases in *Poor Richard's Almanac* are very similar to what we have in Chinese. For example, in Chinese we say "Carrots and cabbages can ensure a peaceful life." In the *Almanac* a similar saying is "To lengthen your life, lessen your meals." While we say "In order to keep fit, **refrain from** over stuffing your stomach and don't wear excessively thick clothes," the *Almanac* translates this as "Eat few suppers, and you'll need few medicines."

B: Indeed, they all sound very similar.

A: There are also other phrases with moral implications. For instance, we say "Mind what you say." In the *Almanac*, it says "He that speaks much is much mistaken." Or the Chinese expression "Only the person who has come through hardships can stand out in a crowd. " That sounds very much the same as the *Almanac's* phrase "No man was glorious, who was not laborious. "

B： People share similar value propositions **regardless** of their background. This should help **mutual** understanding and communication and at the same time be good for social progress. In this regard, set phrases can even play the role of bridges between different cultures.

A： I think more vivid metaphors and stories should be introduced into our daily language. A phrase as "The sleeping fox catches no poultry. Up up！" is colorful and friendly.

对 话

A： 每当我用到一些中国的俗语时，人们都会表现出惊喜，这不仅是对我语言能力的惊讶，而且把我当成了他们中的一员。俗语有助于拉近我与谈话人之间的距离。通常他们会再教给我一些俗语。

B： 民间俗语是人类生活经验的浓缩，也是人类智慧的表达，它体现出人们的生活态度和价值标准。通过俗语，你可以了解人们推崇什么，贬斥什么。

A： 在西方，一些关于健康的俗语是基于人们对于健康生活方式的理解。本杰明·富兰克林是美国《独立宣言》的起草者之一，他在 1732 年写作了《理查·萨德斯历书》，它保持了 25 年的出版记录，集中了人类的生活经验和智慧。不夸张地说，它揭示了只有两百多年历史的美国迅速崛起的奥秘——勤勉、节俭、公正、善良。这本书所表达的价值观和生活态度与中国俗语有很多相似之处。比如中国俗语说："萝卜白菜保平安"，《历书》说："少吃肉，多长寿"。中国俗语说："要想身体健，七分饱三分寒"，《历书》说："不暴饮暴食，方可少打针吃药"。

B： 简直如出一辙。

A： 还有一些带有道德含义的俗语。中国人说："祸从口出。"《历书》说："话多误事。"中国俗语说："吃得苦中苦，方为人上人。"《历书》说："吃不了苦中苦，就作不了人上人。"

B： 看起来，尽管背景不同，人类有一些共同的价值观。这可以使人们相互理解和融通，使人类社会正常发展。俗语甚至还承担着沟通不同文化之间的桥梁作用。

A： 人们的日常用语中不妨多用形象的比喻。比如 "睡觉的狐狸找不到吃的。起来，起来"，听起来就亲近有趣。

Background Reading　背景阅读

Selected Phrases from Poor Richard's Almanac 《穷理查历书》选录

The discontented man finds no easy chair.
不满足的人难以找到舒适的椅子。

Nothing humbler than ambition, when it is about to climb.
最寒酸的是想高攀。

Love your neighbor, yet don't pull down your hedge.
爱你的邻居，但不要把篱笆拆掉。

A child thinks 20 shillings and 20 years can scarce ever be spent.
孩子以为 20 先令和 20 年永远花不完。

You may sometimes be much in the wrong, in owning your being in the right.
你有时犯大错，是因为你认为自己永远正确。

Where sense is wanting, everything is wanting.
什么都干不了，是因为什么都想去干。

Learning to the studious; riches to the careful; power to the bold; heaven to the virtuous.
学知识靠勤奋，致富靠谨慎，当官靠胆大，上天堂靠行善。

Diligence overcomes difficulties, sloth makes them.
勤者改造困难，懒人制造困难。

A long life may not be good enough, but a good life is long enough.
活得长不一定活得好，而活得好就能活得长。

Saying and doing, have quarreled and parted.
道不同，不相与谋。

Love your enemies, for they tell you your faults.
爱你的敌人吧，因为他们使你明白了自己的缺点。

Be civil to all; serviceable to many; familiar with few; friend to one; enemy to none.
尊重所有人，服务很多人，认识几个人，与一个人成为朋友，不与任何人为敌。

---

marvel at　惊叹	close the gap　拉进关系	value propositions　价值取向
best-seller　畅销书	rise to success　成功，崛起	refrain from　节制
regardless　不管，无论	mutual　相互	

 **Exercises 练习**

Answer these questions.

1. Why do some people like to use set phrases?
2. Who is Benjamin Franklin?
3. Why is "Poor Richard's Almanac" an important book?

Translate these sentences into Chinese.

1. Whenever I try to use some Chinese set phrases, people seem surprised.
2. They marvel at my language capability.
3. Set phrases help close the gap between the listeners and me.
4. From such expressions you can see what people like and dislike.
5. Benjamin Franklin is a co-author of the Declaration of Independence.
6. It contains a lot of memorable phrases.
7. Mind what you say.
8. People share similar value propositions regardless of their background.
9. Set phrases can even play the role of bridges between different cultures.
10. More vivid metaphors should be introduced into our daily language.

Complete this paragraph with suitable words.

Whenever I __1__ to use some Chinese set phrases, people __2__ surprised. They __3__ only __4__ at my language capability but also treat me as one of them. Set phrases help __5__ the gap between the listeners and me. Usually, people will offer to teach me more __6__ phrases. Set phrases can, definitely, __7__ a person's life experience, as well as their attitude and value propositions. From such expressions, you can see __8__ people like and dislike.

 Answers 答案

Translate these sentences into Chinese.

1. 每当我用到一些中国的俗语时，人们都会表现出惊喜。
2. 他们惊讶于我的语言能力。
3. 俗语可以拉进我与谈话人之间的距离。
4. 通过俗语你可以了解人们推崇什么，贬斥什么。
5. 本杰明·富兰克林是美国《独立宣言》的起草者之一。
6. 其中包含了许多给人留下深刻印象的警句。
7. 说话注意点儿。
8. 虽然背景不同，人类仍然有些共同的价值观。
9. 俗语甚至还承担着沟通不同文化之间的桥梁作用。
10. 人们的日常用语中不妨多用形象的比喻。

Complete this paragraph with suitable words.

1. try 2. seem 3. not 4. marvel 5. close 6. such 7. reflect 8. what

46. The Ideal Man

理想男人

Dialogue

A: A Chinese girl falls in love with a Frenchman who always buys her gifts. The girl feels **overwhelmed** with love. "A Chinese man would never buy me so many gifts," she said.

B: I've also heard that many Chinese girls like to have Western boyfriends. Men are good at making their girlfriends happy through buying them gifts. But you know what, when those girls really need help, Western men would usually tell them to "handle it themselves." Chinese girls are **disappointed** when their Western boyfriends are unwilling to spend a lot of money on them.

A: According to Chinese tradition, a woman marries for food and shelter. Although a Chinese man is not good at buying gifts for his wife, he feels obliged to support her for the rest of her life. Love becomes **secondary**. A Western man may be good at showering his girl friend with gifts but he usually has second thoughts when it comes to a meaningful relationship. That's why many Chinese girls feel it less advantageous to marry Western men. Western men, on the other hand, find Chinese girls too pragmatic and less independent.

B: I remember reading an article about a Chinese girl who married an American. The girl came all the way to Beijing to live with the man. She never asked him for money and neither did she rely on his **connections**. Instead she supported herself through an English training class and eventually found a nice job. When the man asked her to marry him, he told her "You are different from many Chinese girls. They are too dependent on men."

A: Chinese people believe that if two people fall in love, they should share happiness and hardship. Many Chinese women find it **unbelievable** that Western men would allow their girlfriends to **rough it** on their own. Sometimes I wonder if it is an excuse by

182

Western men to escape their responsibilities by talking about independence. One may get a lot of gifts by marrying a Western man but you will probably lose their life-long support, unless you are prepared to face all the challenges yourself. As for the girl who married the American, I just feel there are too many **uncertainties** for her, both physically and mentally.

B: The good news is Chinese men have learned to buy gifts for their girl friends. That's why roses cost a fortune on **Valentine's Day**.

A: You seem to suggest that Chinese men are preferable and more dependable.

对 话

A: 一个中国女孩交了个法国男朋友，他常送礼物给她。中国女孩为爱而倾倒。她说，"中国男人很少会给我买这么多礼物。"

B: 我也听说过中国女孩喜欢交外国男友。送礼物是洋男人的长项，但是到了女人需要实质性帮助时，洋男人通常用一句"我知道你能行"来打发。经济上的泾渭分明，让中国女孩感到失望。

A: 依据中国传统观念，嫁汉嫁汉，穿衣吃饭。虽然中国男人不善送礼物，却要承担女人一生的托付，爱情退居第二位。洋男人，擅长与女友分享小礼物，但进入实质性关系时，他通常不能一心一意。这就是许多中国女人觉得嫁这种男人不实惠的原因。而洋男人却觉得中国女人太实际，太依赖男人。

B: 我曾经读过一篇关于一个中国女孩的文章，讲她嫁给一个美国男人的故事。女孩子抛弃所有，到北京与这个男人住在一起。她不求男人在金钱上的帮助，也不靠他的人脉关系，她依靠自己的收入读完了英语培训课程，找到了体面的工作。当这个男人请求女孩嫁给他时，告诉她："你和那些中国女孩不同，他们都太想依靠男人。"

A: 中国人认为两个人相爱就应该有福同享，有难同当。洋男人看着女人独自打拼而不管不顾令中国女人感到不可思议。有时候我怀疑，强调女人独立这是不是洋男人为逃避责任而找的借口。无论如何，嫁这样的洋男人，得到的是小礼物，失去的却是终生依靠。除非你做好了独自面对所有难题的准备。像那位嫁给美国人的女孩，对她来讲，不论是心力还是体力，都有太多的不确定因素了。

B: 所幸的是，中国男人也开始为他们的女友买礼物了。这就是为什么情人节的鲜花卖出天价的原因。

A: 你似乎是说中国的男人比洋男人完美许多，也可靠许多。

Background Reading 背景阅读

The Wrong Place to Meet Mr. Right 佳偶难寻

As China's expatriate population grows, many foreign women looking for love are saying this is the wrong place to meet Mr. Right.

Many single expat women quickly find that most foreign dreamboats have already sailed, and their chemistry with local men rarely stirs the right mix for a love potion. The dating scene in Beijing is sad. A lot of expat women are single, but no foreign man is single. The reason there aren't many available foreign men is simple: there are a lot of Chinese women; they're available, and they have a lot to offer.

"Most Chinese guys are really shy. They work really long hours and don't come out to bars and parties, which is where you usually meet people." Josh Bernstein, 21, of Phoenix, Arizona, has organized an informal singles group and has seen first-hand the difficulties faced by Western women interested in Chinese men. He said, on the singles party he hosted a week ago, while the foreign men ignored the Western girls, the Chinese men struck up conversation with them. But in the end, it was only talk. "Chinese guys seem to be too shy or too worried about saving face to make a move. They're afraid of making a mistake because of cultural differences. A lot of Chinese guys don't know about foreign girls and don't know how to approach them."

随着在中国的外国人数不断增长，许多寻求爱情的洋女人说这里是寻找"合适先生"的不合适之地。

许多单身的洋女人很快发现大多外国的理想爱人已经是别人的了，而这些洋女人与中国本土男人很难产生情感上的化学反应。北京的约会场景很惨。许多洋女人都是单身，但是没有洋男人是单身的。没有许多可以恋爱的洋男人之原因很简单：这里有很多中国女人，她们是恋爱对象，而且她们还会对洋男人主动投怀送抱。

"许多中国男人很害羞。他们确实是长时间地投入工作，不去酒吧或聚会上消遣，而在那些场合通常才能遇到其他的人。" 21 岁，来自美国亚利桑那州凤凰城的约什·伯恩斯坦说。他曾经组织了一个非正式的单身小组，亲眼看到西方女性很难对中国男人产生兴趣。他说，在一星期前的一次单身人士的聚会上，当洋男人忽略了洋女人时，中国男人会主动与她们搭话。但是最终也只是谈话而已。"中国男人似乎太害羞或者太在乎自己的面子。他们担心由于文化差异而出错。许多中国男人不了解洋女人，也不知道该如何接近她们。"

---

overwhelmed 淹没，不知所措	disappointed 失望	secondary 第二位，不重要
connection 关系	unbelievable 不可思议	rough it 吃苦，艰辛度日
uncertainty 不稳定因素	Valentine's Day 情人节	

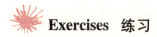 **Exercises** 练习

Answer these questions.

1. What are Western men good at?
2. What does a Chinese man feel obliged to do for his wife?
3. Are Western men ready to spend a lot of money on their girl friends?

Translate these sentences into Chinese.

1. The girl feels overwhelmed with love.
2. Men are good at buying gifts for their girlfriends.
3. A woman marries for food and shelter.
4. I remember reading an article about a Chinese girl.
5. She does not rely on his connections.
6. She supported herself through an English training class.
7. They should share happiness and hardship.
8. There are too many uncertainties for her, both physically and mentally.
9. Western men would allow their girl friends to rough it on their own.
10. The good news is that Chinese men are buying gifts for their girl friends.

Complete this paragraph with suitable words.

According to Chinese ___1___ , a woman marries ___2___ food and shelter. Although a Chinese man is not ___3___ at buying gifts for his wife, he feels ___4___ to support her for the ___5___ of her life. Love becomes ___6___ . Although a Western man may be good at ___7___ his girl friend with gifts, he usually has ___8___ thoughts when it comes to a meaningful relationship.

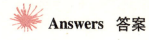 **Answers** 答案

Translate these sentences into Chinese.

1. 女孩感到充满了幸福。
2. 男人擅长为他们的女朋友买礼物。
3. 嫁汉嫁汉，穿衣吃饭。
4. 我曾经读过一篇关于一个中国女孩的文章。
5. 她不依靠他的人脉关系。
6. 她依靠自已的收入读完了英语培训课程。
7. 他们应该有福同享，有难同当。
8. 对她来讲，不论是心力还是体力，都有太多的不确定因素了。
9. 西方男人甚至会看着自己的女朋友独自打拼。
10. 所幸的是，中国男人也开始为他们的女友买礼物了。

Complete this paragraph with suitable words.

1. tradition　2. for　3. good　4. obliged　5. rest　6. secondary　7. showering　8. second

47. The Monkey King vs. Harry Potter

孙悟空 PK 哈利·波特

Dialogue

A: I read in the press that some people are thinking of making Sun Wu Kong, the Monkey King, an international star, just like Harry Potter. Their argument is that the Monkey King is a lot more talented and capable than Harry and could be **a big hit** for audiences outside China.

B: In China, the Monkey King is **a household name**. Everybody knows he uses a magical golden stick as a weapon and can be transformed into 72 alter egos.

A: But many young people seem to like Harry Potter better. Harry is real and **shares** a lot of things **in common** with them. For example, he has conflicts with his teachers and classmates and he has his own best friends. The Monkey King, on the other hand, is born out of a stone. He doesn't feel happy like an ordinary person, nor get angry like them. He doesn't **interact** with other people either. He does not have the familiarity which people find in Harry.

B: That's an interesting **observation**. Western characters like Superman, Spiderman and Batman, all have the qualities of an ordinary person. Even Tarzan has a sweetheart and friends. Those characters are very brave and always ready to help. In comparison, the Monkey King is **a lone ranger**. His only job is to protect his master, a saint. Although he rebels against the authority, the character lacks the worldly conflict between good and evil. As a result, he seems less approachable than Harry.

A: Many students told me that they like Harry because he has a girlfriend. The same is true of Superman and Spiderman. The girls are the source of their courage. The Monkey King doesn't have love. Of the four characters in the novel *Pilgrimage to the West*, only Zhu Ba Jie has some interest in women but as a consequence he is always scolded and scorned. Most female characters in this novel are evil incarnations, being portrayed as temptations for the saint and his disciples. In traditional Chinese culture women used to be considered a source of evil.

B: So it seems that an intimate understanding of a worldly life and the righteousness of the superhero are the deciding factors in the popularity of these characters.

A: It certainly makes it easier for people to **identify** themselves **with** those super characters. A monkey born out of a stone doesn't seem to **resonate** with the vibes of modern society.

对 话

A: 我在报上看到，有人计划把孙悟空打造成一个国际明星，因为孙悟空的本领比哈利·波特大得多，在世界范围内一定能更火。

B: 在中国，孙悟空是个家喻户晓的名字。谁都知道他手中的金箍棒和七十二变本领。

A: 但是许多年轻人似乎更喜欢哈利·波特。哈利·波特是个活生生的人，他有一般孩子的特点。比如他也和老师、同学发生冲突，有自己最好的朋友。孙悟空则是从石头中诞生的，缺乏常人的喜怒哀乐和人际交往。他没有人们在哈利·波特身上发现的相似性。

B: 那倒是一个有趣的看法。西方的超人、蜘蛛侠、蝙蝠侠等形象都具有普通人的特征。既便是人猿泰山，也有他的爱人和朋友。他们非常勇敢，并且随时准备出手相助。相比较而言，孙悟空是一个孤胆英雄。他身负着护卫圣人取经的职责，虽然他也反叛权威，但是缺少了俗世常有的善恶冲突。孙悟空的形象与哈利·波特比，少了亲近感。

A: 许多学生告诉我，他们喜欢哈利·波特，因为他有女朋友。超人和蜘蛛侠的故事也如此。这些女性给予英雄们力量。但孙悟空没有爱情。《西游记》中的师徒四人，只有猪八戒对女人有兴趣，却总是被其他人嘲弄或斥责。这部小说中的女性多数是妖怪，是用来诱惑圣人和他的徒弟们的。她们是中国古人观念中的祸水。

B: 看来，决定一个超级英雄能否被更广泛接受的主要因素，是他们易于亲近的特性和崇高的品行。

A: 超级英雄因为与人类的相似而易于被接受，石头缝里生出来的猴子似乎很难与人产生共鸣。

Spider Man 蜘蛛侠

Who am I, you ask? Are you sure you want to know? You say you want hear the story of my life. That story is not for the faint of heart.

If somebody said that my story was a happy little tale, if somebody told you I was just your average, ordinary guy without a care in the world... then somebody lied.

Mine is the story of a boy whose parents died when he was four years old. It's the tale of a scared, lonely, and confused child grasping the hand of a social worker as if it meant his very life, then releasing that grasp to go live with an aunt and uncle he hardly knew.

It's the story of a lonely childhood spent with books and chemistry sets, rather than other kids, as best friends.

Yes, mine is a tale of pain and sorrow, loss and grief, longing and heartache, anger and betrayal. And that just covers the high-school years.

My story, like so many worth telling, is also about a boy and a girl. About true feelings kept bottled up for years, about a lonely, shy boy desperate to tell the girl how he felt, yet so terrified of rejection, that he kept his those feelings hidden until he felt he might explode.

The boy? I'm sure you've guessed. The boy is me.

Who am I? Well, you did ask. I go by the name... Spider Man!

你问我是谁？你确定你想了解我吗？你说你想听听我的故事。我的故事可不适合心灵脆弱者。

如果有谁说我的故事只是不足挂齿的小经历，如果有谁告诉你，我只是一个像你们一样平凡而普通的不为世人所关注的人……那么，这些人错了。

这个故事是关于一个男孩的，他4岁时，父母双亡。那无异于一场恐惧而孤寂的风暴来袭，这个充满迷茫的小男孩，依靠着社会工作人员以求生存，后来，他脱离了他们，与他并不熟悉的叔叔婶婶一起生活。

这个故事是关于男孩孤独的童年，他与书和化学实验为伴，而不是那些要好的小伙伴们。

是的，这是我的故事，充满着痛苦和悲伤，失落和不幸，渴望和伤心，愤怒和背叛。这些情绪笼罩着整个高中时期。

我的故事就像所有值得一说的故事一样，也是关于一个男孩和一个女孩的。有关多年沉在心底的真实情感，有关一个孤独、羞怯的男孩无法对女孩言说他的感受，遭受拒绝的苦痛，他一直隐藏着这种情感，直到他有机会流露。

这个男孩是谁？我想你一定猜到了，就是我。

我是谁？你会这样问。我就是——蜘蛛侠！

---

a big hit 轰动	a household name 家喻户晓的名字	share... in common 与…有共同之处
interact 互动	observation 看法	a lone ranger 孤胆英雄
identify with 与…相似		resonate 共鸣

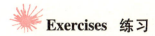 **Exercises** 练习

Answer these questions.
1. What does Harry Potter have in common with many young people?
2. Do you think the Monkey King will be an international hit?
3. Why can many people identify themselves with super heroes?

Translate these sentences into Chinese.
1. Some people are thinking of making the Money King an international star.
2. In China the Monkey King is a household name.
3. But many young people seem to like Harry Potter better.
4. That's an interesting observation.
5. Western superman characters all have the qualities of an ordinary person.
6. The Monkey King is a lone ranger.
7. They are very brave and always ready to help.
8. The Monkey King seems to be less approachable than Harry.
9. Most female characters in this novel are evil incarnations.
10. A monkey born out of a stone doesn't seem to resonate with the vibes of modern society.

Complete this paragraph with suitable words.
Many people __1__ to like Harry Potter better. Harry is real and __2__ a lot of things in __3__ with them. For example, he has conflicts __4__ his teachers and classmates, and has his own friends. The Monkey King, on the __5__ hand, is born __6__ of a stone. He doesn't feel happy like an ordinary person __7__ get angry like them and, he doesn't __8__ with other people, either.

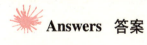 **Answers** 答案

Translate these sentences into Chinese.
1. 有人计划把孙悟空打造成一个国际明星。
2. 在中国，孙悟空是个家喻户晓的名字。
3. 但是许多年轻人似乎更喜欢哈利·波特。
4. 那倒是一个有趣的看法。
5. 西方的超人形象都具有一些普通人的特点。
6. 孙悟空是一个孤胆英雄。
7. 他们非常勇敢，并且随时准备出手相助。
8. 比起哈利·波特，孙悟空似乎不太容易接近。
9. 这本小说里的大部分女子都是邪恶的化身。
10. 石头缝里生出来的猴子似乎很难与人产生共鸣。

Complete this paragraph with suitable words.
1. seem 2. shares 3. common 4. with 5. other 6. out 7. nor 8. interact

48. New Year Movies

贺岁片

Dialogue

A： *The Chronicles of Narnia* was a huge success in the United States and won several Oscar awards last year. As a New Year movie it certainly was a big hit.

B： In China *The Banquet* and *Curse of the Golden Flower* were both major movie productions. Being released at the end of the year, these movies were called New Year movies. Do you agree with this classification?

A： They are New Year movies **as far as** their release timing is concerned but certainly not **in terms of** content. *The Chronicles of Narnia* is a fairy tale about good and evil and has **a happy ending**. It emphasizes the mainstream value concept of good defeating evil. Such ideals should be the basis of New Year movies. The 1996 comedy *Jingle All the Way* talks about a man who is a **workaholic** and ignores his wife and family. He has to **go through** various experiences on Christmas Eve to buy some superman toys for his children. Eventually he succeeds and the movie has a happy ending.

B： What about *The Banquet*? It stars very famous actors.

A： *The Banquet* follows the same **story line** as Shakespeare's Hamlet but is about politics in the Imperial Court. The movie is embroiled in an atmosphere of adultery, incest and infidelity. Consequently, it is quite inappropriate as a New Year movie. *The Chronicles of Narnia* is an opportunity for a family gathering because its story appeals to every member of the family. This is not the case with a movie about bloody court in-fighting and adultery. It could be embarrassing for all the family members to see such a movie. Popular culture must follow accepted mainstream values.

B： It is also very expensive to see New Year movies in China. They can cost a lot, especially when the whole family goes together.

A： The Chinese people do not have any problems with the ticket price because people tend to be **spendthrifts** during holidays. In fact, some people may not buy the less expensive tickets because it might be viewed as a lack of **festive spirit**. The producers of New Year movies understand people's spending habits and have no problem asking for a high price. Although *The Banquet* and *Curse of the Golden Flower*, are New Year movies, I don't think they are suitable for the holidays. They are too gloomy and **depressing**.

B： Some people suggest that *The Banquet* is a comedy because it imitates Hamlet in a funny way. A well-known comedian plays the role of the Emperor, which makes the movie even funnier.

对 话

A： 《纳尼亚传奇》在美国赢得了高票房，也获得了去年奥斯卡的多项大奖。作为贺岁片，其收获颇丰。

B： 《夜宴》和《满城尽带黄金甲》都是去年中国的大制作电影，因为在年底放映，有人称它们是贺岁片。你同意这个分类吗？

A： 从上映时间上看算得上贺岁片，从电影的内容看，则不算。《纳尼亚传奇》是有关善恶的童话故事，并以大团圆结局，它强调正义战胜邪恶的主流价值观。这也应该是贺岁片的价值取向。1996年的美国贺岁片《圣诞老豆》讲述的是一个平时忙于工作，忽略妻子和家庭的男人，在圣诞前夜，他经历了种种磨难，为孩子买超人玩具。最终，他成功了，影片以大团圆结局。

B： 那么《夜宴》呢？里面可是明星荟萃啊！

A： 《夜宴》是以莎士比亚的《哈姆雷特》为故事蓝本，讲述宫廷中的政治斗争。充满着相互猜疑、乱伦和背叛的阴森气氛。用来贺岁实在不妥。《纳尼亚传奇》的故事情节适合一家老少同坐一处观看，而一部充满了血腥的宫廷争斗和乱伦的电影则不然。父母和儿女一起观看，会陷入尴尬中。大众文化一定要符合主流的价值取向。

B： 另外，中国贺岁大片的票价太贵，全家人观看就是一大笔开销。

A： 对中国人来说票价不是问题，因为过节时人们容易大手大脚地花钱。事实上，有些人可能不买低价票，因为他们觉得这样缺少节日的气氛。贺岁片的制作者十分了解人们的花钱习惯，了解高票价不成问题。从这一点上说，《夜宴》和《满城尽带黄金甲》是贺岁片。但是这两部戏都笼罩着悲哀阴郁的气氛，不适合在年节时观看。

B： 不过有人提议《夜宴》可以当成喜剧片看。因为它是对莎士比亚《哈姆雷特》的恶搞。一位著名的喜剧演员出演片中的皇帝，也使这部电影更搞笑。

Background Reading 背景阅读

The Story and It's Meaning 故事及其隐喻

Peter, Susan, Edmund and Lucy were four children who came to a magical country called Narnia by chance. The White Witch promised Edmund she would make him King if he brought his brother and sisters to danger. Edmund tried to, but learned that the Witch was lying to him. The great lion Aslan, the true ruler of Narnia finally showed up and wanted to save Edmund from the White Witch. But the White Witch knew the "Deep Magic" —that a traitor must die for being so bad. At a special secret meeting, the Witch and her wicked helpers killed Aslan on a Stone Table. But the Witch didn't know the "Deeper Magic" from before the beginning of time, which was that if a person who had done nothing wrong was willing to take the punishment for someone who had done wrong, the Stone Table would be broken. Finally, Aslan was resurrected and the four children became the kings of Narnia.

The story is based on the event of the Resurrection in the New Testament. The four children are people like you and I. Yes, Edmund was very bad. But we all are bad too. And the bad has to be punished. Aslan is Jesus Christ. Jesus paid the punishment for all of our sin, BUT HE CAME ALIVE! Jesus forgives us and promises that we will go to heaven when we die, but life still will have problems. But, just like Susan could call for help with her special horn, we can pray and ask God for help. The 4 thrones in Narnia show that God makes us all kings and Queens after we join His family. This life often has many battles—but God has a perfect plan that we will finally see one day!

彼得、苏珊、埃德蒙和露西兄妹4人无意中来到一个魔幻的国度纳尼亚。白女巫许诺埃德蒙，如果他将其他兄妹带入险境，他将成为国王。埃德蒙按照她的话做了，但发现女巫骗了他。纳尼亚真正的领袖、伟大的狮子阿斯兰最终出现，并想救下埃德蒙。女巫利用了"背叛者必须去死"的神秘魔法。于是，在一个特殊的秘密仪式中，女巫和她的同伙们在石台上杀死了巨狮。但是女巫并不知道这个神秘魔法还有一条规定，即一个并没有做坏事的人如果愿意替作恶的人受罚，石台就会裂开以保全替代者的生命。最终，阿斯兰获得新生，4个孩子当上了纳尼亚的国王。

这部电影取材于《圣经新约》中耶稣复活的故事。4个孩子是指你我这样的凡人。当然，埃德蒙是个坏孩子，我们大家也都各有劣迹。做了错事就要受惩罚。巨狮阿斯兰就是耶稣基督。耶稣为所有人的罪过被罚，但他却复活了！耶稣宽恕我们的过错并许诺我们死后升入天堂，但我们的生活仍然麻烦不断。但就像苏珊可以用她特别的号角来呼唤上帝的帮助一样，人们也能够祈祷并请求上帝的帮助。城堡中的4个王座象征了上帝帮助众人加入他的大家庭。人的一生遭际纷乱，但上帝自有一个完美的计划，终有一天人们能够看到。

as far as 就…来说	in terms of 从…来讲	a happy ending 大团圆结局
workaholic 工作狂	go through 经历	story line 故事主线
spendthrift 大手大脚	festive spirit 节日气氛	depressing 令人抑郁的

192

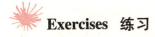 **Exercises** 练习

Answer these questions.

1. Why are some movies called New Year movies?
2. What is "The Chronicles of Narnia" about?
3. Why isn't "The Banquet" suitable for the New Year?

Translate these sentences into Chinese.

1. It won several Oscar awards last year.
2. "The Banquet" and "Curse of the Golden Flower" were released at the end of the year.
3. They are New Year movies as far as the release timing is concerned.
4. "The Chronicles of Narnia" is a fairy tale with a happy ending.
5. The man is a workaholic and ignores his wife and family.
6. He has to go through various experiences.
7. Its story appeals to every member of the family.
8. This is not the case with a movie about bloody court in-fight.
9. People tend to be spendthrifts during holidays.
10. The producers of New Year movies understand people's spending habits.

Complete this paragraph with suitable words.

The Chinese people do not ___1___ any problems ___2___ the ticket price. People tend to be spendthrifts ___3___ holidays. In fact, people may not ___4___ less expensive tickets, which could be ___5___ as ___6___ a festive spirit. The producers of New Year movies, understand people's ___7___ habits and have no problem ___8___ for a high price. Although "The Banquet" is a New Year movie, I don't think it is suitable for the holidays.

 Answers 答案

Translate these sentences into Chinese.

1. 它获得了去年奥斯卡的多项大奖。
2. 《夜宴》和《满城尽带黄金甲》都是年底首映的。
3. 从上映时间上看算得上贺岁片。
4. 《纳尼亚传奇》是个童话故事，并以大团圆结局。
5. 这个人平时忙于工作，忽略了妻子和家庭。
6. 他经历了各种磨练。
7. 它的故事情节适合一家老少同坐一处观看。
8. 而一部充满了血腥的宫廷争斗的电影则不然。
9. 过节时人们容易大手大脚地花钱。
10. 贺岁片的制作者十分了解人们的花钱习惯。

Complete this paragraph with suitable words.

1. have 2. with 3. during 4. appreciate 5. viewed 6. lacking 7. spending 8. asking

49. Globalization of Sports

体育运动的全球化

Dialogue

A： Have you heard of hula hoops?

B： Of course. It was very popular in China during the 1990s. Nearly everyone played with the plastic ring. Doctors **recommended** it as a good tool for **keeping fit**. Various contests were held on TV. Someone even tried to **apply for** a Guinness world record. The demand for hula hoops was so high that they were **out of stock** for quite some time.

A： Did you know that hula hoops were also very popular in the United States?

B： No, I didn't.

A： It was in March 1958. One company began making plastic hula hoops that sold for 93 cents each. That's when the big ring got its name, Hula Hoop. By September that year, over 2 million hula hoops were sold, **reaping** a profit of over $300,000. By the year end, if all copycats were also counted, tens of millions of hula hoops were sold. In Japan, hospitals were crowded with people who had hurt themselves while playing with hula hoops. Even Japan's Prime Minister received a hula hoop as his 62nd birthday present. When a group of Belgian scientists went on an exploration trip to the Antarctic, they took 20 hula hoops with them. In Johannesburg, local charity organizations made a donation of hula hoops to the poor. In Warsaw, a newspaper article called on the government to immediately start producing hula hoops or Poland would **lag** far **behind** the other countries.

B： It sounds like a globalization of hula hoops. What happened afterwards?

A： By summer 1959 many cities had deserted hula hoops all over the place.

B： More than 30 years later, thanks to its open door policy, the waves of hula hoops

194

finally reached China.

A: Sports globalization started **way ahead of** economic globalization. If the origin of soccer were traced to a similar sport during the Song Dynasty, as some Chinese have suggested, then it's much earlier than hula hoops. It also has a much longer lasting effect.

B: Over a century ago, shepherds in Scotland started a game called golf. Now golfing has become a sport exclusively for the wealthy in China. That's an even more convincing example to illustrate the magnitude of globalization.

对 话

A: 你知道呼拉圈吗？

B: 当然知道。20 世纪 90 年代时它一度风靡中国。几乎每个人都玩起这种塑料圈圈。医生称它有强身健体的功效。电视台举办各种呼拉圈比赛，还搞过申请吉尼斯世界纪录的事。对呼拉圈的需求如此之大，以至于一段时间内呼拉圈脱销。

A: 你知道呼拉圈在美国也曾经这样火过吗？

B: 不太清楚。

A: 一家公司从 1958 年 3 月开始生产这种塑料圈，每只售价美元 9 角 3 分。这家公司给这种玩具定名为呼拉圈。到了 9 月份，公司一共售出 200 万个呼拉圈，获利三十多万美元。到了年末，若把国内外的仿制品都算在内，这个东西的总销量约有几千万个。在日本，医院里挤满了因玩呼拉圈而受伤的病人。当时的日本首相的 62 岁寿辰礼物中竟有一个呼拉圈。一支比利时的探险队出发去南极时，也带了 20 个呼拉圈。在约翰内斯堡，当地的慈善机构向穷人捐赠一批呼拉圈。在华沙，一家报纸发表文章督促政府立即生产呼拉圈，否则波兰就会远远落后于别人。

B: 好一派呼拉圈全球化的景象。结果如何呢？

A: 到了 1959 年夏天，在一些城市里，被丢弃的呼拉圈到处都是。

B: 三十多年后，拜中国改革开放之赐，这一波全球化的热潮终于影响到中国。

A: 体育全球化要远远早于经济全球化。如果真像中国人所说，足球发源于中国宋朝人玩的一种球的话，它流传于世的时间比呼拉圈早得多，持续的时间也长久得多。

B: 一个世纪前，苏格兰牧羊人开始了今天称为高尔夫的游戏，现在高尔夫在中国成为一项贵族运动。高尔夫运动的传播是全球化的例证。

Background Reading 背景阅读

Expensive Social Ladder 昂贵的等级阶梯

Golf is being used increasingly by Chinese property developers to lend a cachet of Western sophistication to their properties. China's last emperor Pu Yi learned the game from his English tutor in the 1920s but it wasn't until the 1980s that economic planners began to see the game as a chance to attract foreign investment to China. The first golf course built in post-revolutionary China was designed by golfing icon Arnold Palmer and opened in southern Guandong Province in 1984. More than 4. 5 billion euros have been spent on China's courses since then, according to international consultancy firm the Golf Research Group, making the country the fifth largest golfing nation in the world in terms of green space.

Young middle-class social status seeking professionals have caught on to coffee, horse riding, cocktails and now, golf. In a land where the average GDP per capita barely reaches 1,000 euros, it's an expensive way to climb the social ladder. Green fees at the Beijing Golf Country Club in Shunyi District hit 1,200 yuan (119 euros) at weekends, and the prestigious Silport Club in Shanghai charges 60,000 yuan (5,950 euros) for full membership. "Golf is a very popular sport in America and most professionals can afford it there. But in China, like in Japan and Korea, the price of playing is extremely high. It is just for the elite," says Zhang Shidong, a consultant at the Beijing office of Mercer, an international recruitment company.

越来越多的中国富人把高尔夫当作与其财富相称的西式生活的标志而趋之若鹜。20 世纪 20 年代，中国的末代皇帝溥仪从他的英文老师那里学会了这种运动，但是直到 20 世纪 80 年代，高尔夫运动才被认识到可以作为一种吸引外资的手段。改革开放之后，中国于 1984 年在广东省建起了第一个高尔夫球场，当时的设计者是高尔夫球星安诺庞马先生。国际咨询公司高尔夫研究会根据球场大小将中国排为第五高尔夫大国。根据他们的数据，从建立第一个球场开始，中国已经累计在高尔夫球场建设上面投资超过 45 亿欧元。

年轻的中产阶级喜欢喝咖啡、骑马、饮鸡尾酒，现在又爱上了高尔夫。在一个人均 GDP 总量刚刚达到 1 000 欧元的地方，要爬上这个社会阶梯是很昂贵的。在北京顺义区的北京乡村高尔夫俱乐部，周末的果岭费达到 1 200 元（相当于 119 欧元），在享有很高声望的上海旭宝高尔夫俱乐部，需要缴纳 60 000 元（相当于 5950 欧元）才能获得会员资格。国际人力资源公司美世咨询北京办事处的咨询顾问张世东说："在美国，高尔夫是一种非常流行的运动，大多数职业者都能参与。但是在中国，和日本和韩国一样，这种运动的价格极高，只有极少数人能够负担得起那么高昂的费用。"

---

recommend 推荐	keeping fit 健体	apply for 申请	out of stock 脱销
reap 收获	copycat 仿冒品	lag behind 落后	way ahead of 远远领先于

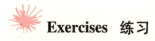

Answer these questions.

1. How popular was the hula hoop in China during the 1990s?
2. How popular was the hula hoop in the United States during late 1950s?
3. What did the Polish newspaper ask for?

Translate these sentences into Chinese.

1. Doctors recommended it as a good tool for keeping fit.
2. The demand was so high that they were out of stock for quite some time.
3. One company began making plastic hula hoops in March, 1958.
4. Over 2 million hula hoops were sold, reaping a huge profit.
5. Local charity organizations made a donation of hula hoops to the poor.
6. Poland would lag far behind others.
7. Deserted hula hoops were all over the place in many cities.
8. Sports globalization started way ahead of economic globalization.
9. It also has a much longer lasting effect.
10. Golf in China has become a sport exclusively for the wealthy.

Complete this paragraph with suitable words.

One company began __1__ plastic hula hoops, which were sold __2__ 93 cents each. That's when the big ring got its name, "hula hoop". By September, __3__ 2 million hula hoops were sold, reaping __4__ a profit of __5__ $300,000. By year end, if all copycats were also counted, tens of millions of hula hoops were sold. In Japan, hospitals were crowded __6__ people who had hurt themselves __7__ playing with hula hoops. Even Japan's Prime Minister received a hula hoop __8__ his 62nd birthday present.

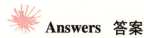 **Answers** 答案

Translate these sentences into Chinese.

1. 医生称它有强身健体的功效。
2. 需求量太大，以至于呼拉圈脱销了一段时间。
3. 一家公司从1958年3月开始生产塑料呼拉圈。
4. 一共售出两百多万个呼拉圈，获利高昂。
5. 当地的慈善机构向穷人捐了一批呼拉圈。
6. 波兰会远远落后于别人。
7. 在一些城市里，被丢弃的呼拉圈到处都是。
8. 体育全球化要远远早于经济全球化。
9. 持续的时间也长久得多。
10. 高尔夫在中国成为一项贵族运动。

Complete this paragraph with suitable words.

1. making 2. for 3. over 4. in 5. over 6. with 7. while 8. as

50. NBA：Popular or Privileged？

NBA：大众还是精英？

Dialogue

A： Last year, a group of us went to Miami for a vacation. The hotel receptionist suggested we should go and see a NBA game. I was surprised when she said it only cost $10 per person. When the Sacramento Kings, and Houston Rockets, came to China for **a pre-season game** in 2004, it cost well over 1,000 yuan for a ticket. That's about $120, and, even at that price; they were very difficult to buy.

B： NBA is part of American culture. There are different kinds of tickets to **cater to** different needs. The season tickets, and group tickets, are fairly inexpensive but, the VIP tickets do cost a lot of money.

A： I remember watching some Chinese businessmen discussing NBA's **marketing strategy** in China with an American NBA representative on TV last year. One of the businessmen displayed some expensive NBA souvenirs he had received, when visiting the US as an NBA guest. The TV host asked the audience if they were willing to pay for such expensive gifts and a couple of, 20-something, young men said they'd buy them anyway. Only one person said the souvenirs were too expensive and he would never buy them. The businessman explained that NBA was a costly sport and that's why the souvenirs were expensive. When asked about his opinions, the NBA representative replied that, NBA is a very popular sport. Various kinds of souvenirs are available, from a few dollars a piece to, over, one thousand dollars an item. Everyone can find something to meet their budget.

B： Using a **staggered** pricing strategy to attract different customers is a normal characteristic of a **market economy**.

A： It is different from a class-conscious society where people are segregated by social status, as was the case in medieval Europe, and ancient China. At that time art products were for the exclusive consumption of the privileged. Ordinary people were denied access to those things because they lacked power and money. Even today, some people in China still seem to be **under the influence** of this status mentality. Ironically, it is not the bureaucrats but, the so-called elites, who **hang on to** this idea. These people are well educated, have a successful career, and are very vocal in the public arena. They are interested in cultural events that are exclusively for the privileged and the wealthy. For example, tennis used to be a sport for the privileged and now, it is golf. **So much so that** some University Presidents **feel obliged to** play golf in order to become a member of the elite class.

B：I hope NBA is not going to be perceived as a sport exclusively for the privileged. The fact is, a lot of NBA star players come from the **ghettos** and, it's the popularity of NBA that has pushed them into stardom.

对　话

A：去年我们几个人到迈阿密玩，酒店服务生建议我们去看 NBA 的比赛。当她说票价 10 美元时，我有点儿吃惊，要知道 2004 在中国举行的国王队对火箭队的 NBA 季前赛的票价都要一千多元人民币，相当于 120 美元，而且还一票难求。

B：在美国，NBA 是大众文化的一部分，不同的票价满足不同的需求。这里有季票、家庭套票等各种相对便宜的票价，也有昂贵些的 VIP 票价。

A：记得在电视上看到过几位中国商人和负责 NBA 在中国推广的美国人讨论 NBA 的营销策略。一位中国商人展示了对方奉送的几样纪念品，介绍它们不菲的价格，他曾被 NBA 邀请作为 VIP 赴美观看比赛。主持人问现场的观众，是否会购买如此昂贵的纪念品。有两位 20 岁左右的年轻人表示无论如何也买。有一个小伙子说太贵，绝对不买。中方的商人说：NBA 是一种高档次的运动，所以纪念品很贵。美方的 NBA 代理谈了他的看法，他说：NBA 是一项大众运动。纪念品的价格是多种多样的，既有成百上千美元的东西，也有几元钱的，每个人都可以找到符合自己预算的纪念品。

B：用不同档位的价格，吸引不同层次消费者，这显然是商品经济社会特有的观念。

A：这不同于按照社会地位划分的等级制社会。就像欧洲中世纪和中国古代，那个时代的艺术品是为少数特权者享用的。普通人被拒于艺术品之外，因为他们没有权力和金钱。今天有些人似乎依然受到这种等级观念的影响。具有讽刺意味的是，划定等级的不再是官方，而是那些所谓的精英。他们受过良好教育，有良好的职业，丰裕的财富，还不乏话语权。他们只对针对富人的活动感兴趣。比如前些年网球就被定为贵族运动，这些年被高尔夫所代替，以至于一些高校的校长感觉必须会打高球才有可能成为精英。

B：希望 NBA 在中国不要被垄断为贵族的运动。其实，许多 NBA 球星都是从贫民窟成长起来的，并因这一运动的大众化才得以出人头地。

Background Reading 背景阅读

Equestrian Clubs in China 骑术俱乐部在中国

In the last century China has not distinguished itself as an equestrian nation. That, however, appears to be changing as the country's better-off begin to indulge in pursuits beloved of the Western middle classes such as golf, tennis, sailing and equestrian sports. While the majority of Chinese people may not have had any formal horse riding experience, a significant number are proving keen learners at a new wave of equestrian clubs that have opened in main Chinese city suburbs.

Fees are at the higher end of the worldwide scale. At an average 200 yuan per one-hour lesson, learning to ride in Beijing's suburbs is not for the average-earning local, say for instance a construction worker, who earns little more than 600 yuan per month. Similar lessons in German and French equestrian schools cost slightly less. And Claremorris Equestrian School in the west of Ireland, located in a region famed for its horse riding prowess, charges 15 euros, or 150 Yuan, per one-hour lesson. Chinese equestrian clubs are now schooling Chinese officials and stewards for equestrian events in the 2008 Beijing Olympic Games.

在上个世纪，骑术在中国并不盛行。不过近年来，中国的有钱人开始仿效西方人的一些喜好，比如高尔夫、网球、航行等，骑马也是其中之一。绝大多数中国人没有在马背上驰骋的经历，但是最近在中国一些主要城市周边兴起的骑术俱乐部浪潮，却正在吸引着越来越多的中国人加入到骑师的队伍中去。

在中国，加入骑术俱乐部的费用与其他国家相比显得有点儿高。平均一个小时 200 元的骑术课程，显然不是工薪阶层能够接受的。举例来说，一名建筑工人一个月挣的钱就是 600 元多一点儿，他怎么可能有钱去学骑术呢？事实上，就是在德国和法国，骑术课程的费用也没有这么高。在爱尔兰西部有个地区以马术闻名，那里有所 Claremorris 骑术学校，一个小时课程的费用也不过 15 欧元，相当于 150 元人民币。中国的骑术俱乐部负责培训与 2008 年北京奥运会马术比赛相关的官员和其他工作人员。

---

a pre-season game NBA 季前赛
staggered 分级的，渐进的
under the influence of 受…影响
so much so that 非常…以至于
ghettos （以黑人为主的）贫民区

cater to 提供，迎合
market economy 市场经济
hang on to 抓住不放
feel obliged to 感到不得不
marketing strategy 市场战略

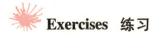 **Exercises** 练习

Answer these questions.

1. Do you agree that NBA is an expensive sport?
2. Do you think NBA will become a sport exclusive for the privileged only in China?
3. How does NBA set its ticket price?

Translate these sentences into Chinese.

1. A group of us went to Miami for a vacation last year.
2. There are different tickets to cater to different needs.
3. NBA is part of the American culture.
4. I remember watching some people discussing NBA's marketing strategy on TV.
5. A couple of 20-something young men said that they'd buy them anyway.
6. Everyone can find something.
7. Ordinary people were denied access to art products.
8. They are only interested in events that are exclusive for the wealthy.
9. Some university presidents feel obliged to play golf.
10. A lot of NBA star players come from the ghettos.

Complete this paragraph with suitable words.

NBA is ___1___ of the American culture. There are different ___2___ of tickets to ___3___ to different ___4___, such as ___5___ tickets and group tickets, which are ___6___ inexpensive. But there are ___7___ VIP tickets that ___8___ a lot of money.

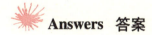 **Answers** 答案

Translate these sentences into Chinese.

1. 去年，我们几个人到迈阿密玩。
2. 不同的票满足不同的需求。
3. NBA 是美国文化的一部分。
4. 记得在电视上看到过几个人讨论 NBA 的营销策略。
5. 有两位 20 岁左右的年轻人表示无论如何也会买。
6. 每个人都能找到自己所需要的。
7. 普通人被拒艺术品之外。
8. 他们只对仅为富人准备的活动感兴趣。
9. 一些大学校长不得以也得打高尔夫。
10. 许多 NBA 球星都是从贫民窟成长起来的。

Complete this paragraph with suitable words.

1. part 2. kinds 3. cater 4. needs 5. season 6. fairly 7. also 8. cost

图书在版编目（CIP）数据

英语畅谈中国文化 50 主题：英汉对照/李霞著；
董玉国译．－北京：外文出版社，2007
（英语国际人）
ISBN 978-7-119-04742-3

Ⅰ．英… Ⅱ.①李…②董… Ⅲ.①英语－汉语－对照读物
②文化史－中国 Ⅳ. H319.4：G

中国版本图书馆 CIP 数据核字（2007）第 023636 号

英语国际人
英语畅谈中国文化 50 主题

作　　者　李　霞
翻　　译　董玉国

选题策划　蔡　箐
责任编辑　李　湲　王　欢
封面设计　红十月设计室
印刷监制　冯　浩

ⓒ外文出版社
出版发行　外文出版社
地　　址　中国北京西城区百万庄大街 24 号　　　邮政编码　　100037
网　　址　http：//www.flp.com.cn
电　　话　（010）68995964/68995883（编辑部）
　　　　　（010）68995844/68995852（发行部/门市邮购）
　　　　　（010）68320579/68996067（总编室）
电子信箱　info@flp.com.cn/sales@flp.com.cn
印　　制　北京外文印刷厂
经　　销　新华书店/外文书店
开　　本　小 16 开　　　　　　　　　　印　　张　13
印　　数　26001—46000 册　　　　　　字　　数　216 千字
装　　别　平
版　　次　2008 年第 1 版第 4 次印刷
书　　号　ISBN 978-7-119-04742-3
定　　价　25.00 元